MAX'S
Digital
SAT
Reading

Essential Guide and Drill
Second Edition

Max's SAT Prep Series:

- **Max's Digital SAT Reading: Essential Guide and Drill**
- **Max's Digital SAT Grammar: Essential Guide and Drill**
- **Max's Digital SAT Practice Test #1: Reading and Writing**
- **Max's Digital SAT Practice Test #2: Reading and Writing**

Max's Digital SAT Reading: Essential Guide and Drill

Copyright © 2023 Byung Seuk Kim
Cover and design © 2023 Boeun Min

ISBN: 979-8-9886526-5-6

INTRODUCTION

Welcome to *Max's Digital SAT Reading: Essential Guide and Drill*. Just like its companion volume on grammar, this guide is designed to empower you with the skills and confidence needed to excel on the SAT Reading section. Here, you'll find a carefully curated collection of strategies, step-by-step lessons, and intensive practice exercises—all crafted to help you approach the exam with poise and precision.

The first part of this book, the Essential Guide, offers a comprehensive overview of the reading skills you'll be expected to master on the SAT. You'll learn how to dissect passages methodically, interpret subtle textual cues, and navigate the complexities of tone, purpose, and evidence. Our explanations are clear, concise, and supported by illustrative examples, ensuring that students at all levels can build a strong foundation of reading comprehension strategies.

Once you've absorbed the core concepts, you'll move on to the Drill—a series of practice questions, drills, and full-length exercises designed to mimic the rigor and style of the actual SAT. Each practice set is accompanied by detailed answer explanations, allowing you to understand not just which answers are correct, but why they are correct and why others may be misleading. These insights will guide your progress, helping you sharpen your critical thinking and analytical reading skills with each completed exercise.

As with any skill, consistency and reflection are key. Use this guide to reinforce your understanding, revisit challenging concepts, and hone your timing and pacing. Think of it as your personal coach—helping you become more confident, more efficient, and ultimately more successful on test day.

Whether you're new to SAT Reading practice or aiming to refine your established strategies, *Max's Digital SAT Reading: Essential Guide and Drill* is here to support your journey. Together, we'll tackle the demanding passages, uncover hidden meanings, and transform complexity into clarity. By the end, you won't just be prepared—you'll be primed to achieve your best possible score and carry your refined reading abilities into your academic future and beyond.

Max (Byung Seuk) Kim

Seoul, Korea

Dec. 2024

Overview of SAT Reading and Writing

Digital SAT Structure

The Digital SAT has two modules, each consisting of 27 questions. The test is adaptive, meaning that if you perform well on the first module, you will receive a harder version for the second module. You have 32 minutes for each module.

Question Types

The questions in the Reading and Writing sections cover a range of topics, including Literature, History/social studies, Humanities, and Science. The first 14-16 questions are reading questions, and the remaining questions are writing questions.

Reading Section

Reading texts typically range from 40 to 120 words, and reading questions assess your ability to comprehend and analyze the text. Some questions may focus on facts and information, while others may test your understanding of the argument and its structure.

Question Types and Frequency

Specific question types appear with varying frequencies in the test, and some may not be included in every test. Here is a breakdown of the question types and their relative frequencies:

Question type	Frequency
1. Words in context	★ ★ ★ ★
2. Detail	★ ★ ★
3. Main Idea	★ ★
4. Main Purpose	★
5. Overall Structure	★
6. Function of a sentence	★ ★
7. Illustrating a claim	★
8. Cross-Text	☆ (One per test)
9. Supporting/Weakening a claim	★ ★ ★
10. Completing a text	★ ★ ★
11. Using infographics	★ ★ ★

How to Prepare for the Test

Take a Diagnostic Test

Start by downloading the Bluebook app from the College Board website and taking a diagnostic test. This will give you an idea of your baseline performance. The College Board has released only six official tests, so use them wisely for the most accurate score prediction.

Identify Weaknesses

After taking the diagnostic test, identify the types of questions or topics where you are weak. This self-assessment will help you focus on areas that need improvement.

Practice Thoroughly

Work on your weak points by practicing with study materials or prep books. Review and understand your mistakes and develop strategies to solve questions more efficiently.

Work on Timing

As your accuracy improves, shift your focus to timing. Don't allocate equal time to each question. Prioritize "words in context" and "writing" questions, which you should aim to solve more quickly.

Take Practice Tests

Once you are familiar with question types and strategies, take another official test provided by the College Board. If your score is around your target, continue practicing with the remaining official tests. If your score is still below your goal, consider reviewing the prep books you've already studied.

Table of Contents

CHAPTER 01

Vocab in Context

Hi! I'm Max

Let me explain
Two Types of Words in Context Questions

There are two types of vocabulary in context questions: Type 1, which involves filling in a missing word, and Type 2, which requires understanding a word's meaning in context. Let's explore example questions to learn how to approach and answer them.

Type 1. Vocabulary-in-Context

The more frequent of the two, this type of question asks you to select the most precise word or phrase to complete a sentence. These questions test your vocabulary knowledge and ability to select the most contextually appropriate word. The vocabulary level of the answer choices can vary greatly, from easy to difficult.

If you do not know more than two of four options, it's a clear sign that you need to enhance your vocabulary. If there's only one unfamiliar option, practice using the process of elimination to find the correct answer.

Example Question

The biologist Sarah Hartman conducted a study on honeybees and found that the insects' advanced communication system, known as the "waggle dance", was far more _____ than previously believed. This dance, performed by worker bees, provides detailed information about the direction and distance to food sources from the hive.

1 ☐ Mark for Review

Which choice completes the text with the most logical and precise word or phrase?

- (A) theatrical
- (B) sophisticated
- (C) confusing
- (D) time-consuming

Type 2: Comprehension-in-Context

This type of question demands a deeper understanding of context. Here, the meaning of the word isn't strictly its dictionary definition. Instead, the word's meaning is shaped by its context in the sentence or paragraph. These questions require you to identify words that logically fit within a certain context.

This passage is from J.D. Salinger's 1951 novel The Catcher in the Rye.
Almost every time somebody gives me a present, it ends up making me sad. She bought me the wrong kind of skates—I wanted racing skates and she bought hockey—but it made me sad anyway. It was harder to get off the ice that day, even, I felt so <u>empty</u>.

1 ◻ Mark for Review

As used in the text, what does the word "empty" most nearly mean?

(A) Hungry

(B) Devoid

(C) Unfulfilled

(D) Hollow

Sentence Completion

Mastering Vocabulary in Context Questions: An In-depth Exploration

Introduction

Simplifying vocabulary-in-context questions requires a clear and systematic approach. This comprehensive guide offers a solid framework to help you tackle these questions with ease, turning what may seem difficult into manageable tasks.

Dissecting Words in Context Questions

Detect the Direct Signal

Identify the "direct signal" — the word or phrase that offers an immediate clue to the word in question. Spotting this signal is pivotal, as it guides you toward the intended meaning.

Recognize the Context Flow Indicator

The "context flow indicator" can be a demonstrative pronoun(this, these, that, or those), transitional phrase, or punctuation mark that gives insights into the nature of the word required in the sentence. It suggests whether the answer should be an antonym, synonym, or a term of stronger or weaker intensity.

Know the logic of the text

Some questions are designed to test your logical thinking rather than relying on direct or obvious clues. In these cases, the correct answer can be inferred through reasoning based on the overall meaning of the sentence.

Max's Note

By fully comprehending the text and practicing these strategies, you'll enhance your ability to decipher challenging vocabulary and improve your overall reading comprehension.

Example Question

John often donates his blood to save other people's lives. This _____ behavior inspired many of his classmates to do the same.

1 ◻ Mark for Review

Which choice completes the text with the most logical and precise word or phrase?

(A) thoughtless

(B) altruistic

(C) proactive

(D) illicit

Explanation

In this instance, the direct signal is *John often donates his blood to save other people's lives*, and the context flow indicator is *This*. Consequently, the missing term should mirror the direct signal. The appropriate response is *altruistic*.

Example Question

John is not well-educated, but Mike is _____.

2 ◻ Mark for Review

Which choice completes the text with the most logical and precise word or phrase?

(A) erudite

(B) renowned

(C) loquacious

(D) unintelligent

Explanation

In this case, the direct signal is *not well-educated*, and the context flow indicator is *but*, which necessitates an antonym of the direct signal. The correct response, therefore, should be a term synonymous with *well-educated*. The answer is *erudite*.

A colon (:) commonly serves as the punctuation for the direct signal, as it clarifies or expands upon the preceding statement.

Example Question

John and Yoshi are somewhat _____ in their action: they say they care for the Earth, but they do not recycle.

3 🔖 Mark for Review

Which choice completes the text with the most logical and precise word or phrase?

(A) sarcastic

(B) demanding

(C) hypocritical

(D) formal

Explanation

In this question, the direct signal is *they say they care for the Earth, but they do not recycle,* and the colon (:) operates as the context flow indicator. Given that the colon expands on the preceding clause, the missing term should be synonymous with the direct signal. The correct response is *hypocritical*.

Example Question

The newly designed safety protocols for the manufacturing plant are intended to minimize accidents and protect workers. These measures can _____ employees' fears about potential hazards, allowing them to focus on productivity and efficiency.

4 🔖 Mark for Review

Which choice completes the text with the most logical and precise word or phrase?

(A) exacerbate

(B) alleviate

(C) overlook

(D) intensify

Explanation

In this question, rather than relying on a direct signal or context flow indicator, you are being tested solely on logic. The sentence implies that the safety protocols are designed to reduce fears. Therefore, the word that best fits is *alleviate* (which means to lessen or relieve), making it the most logical choice.

Sentence Completion Problem Set

The biologist Sarah Hartman conducted a study on honeybees and found that the insects' advanced communication system, known as the "waggle dance", was far more _____ than previously believed. This dance, performed by worker bees, provides detailed information about the direction and distance to food sources from the hive.

1 ☐ Mark for Review

Which choice completes the text with the most logical and precise word or phrase?

(A) theatrical

(B) sophisticated

(C) confusing

(D) time-consuming

Due to the _____ pace of technological advancement, CEO of the tech company ZetaSphere, Mark Rogers, believes that businesses must adapt quickly or risk becoming irrelevant. He emphasized the need for a culture of continuous learning and innovation to stay competitive in the market.

2 ☐ Mark for Review

Which choice completes the text with the most logical and precise word or phrase?

(A) stagnant

(B) haphazard

(C) breakneck

(D) trivial

The historical fiction novel *Sands of Time* by acclaimed author John G. Walker _____ between two time periods – Ancient Rome and present day, offering readers a unique and intriguing perspective on the social and political dynamics of both eras.

3 3 ☐ Mark for Review

Which choice completes the text with the most logical and precise word or phrase?

(A) fluctuates

(B) oscillates

(C) stagnates

(D) dives

When introduced to new environments, invasive species often thrive because they lack natural _____ that would otherwise keep their populations in check. This can lead to ecological imbalances in their new habitats.

4 ☐ Mark for Review

Which choice completes the text with the most logical and precise word or phrase?

(A) allies

(B) predators

(C) habitats

(D) nutrients

As a prolific writer, Jane often found herself immersed in her stories for hours, losing track of time. Her ability to _____ herself so deeply into her work was a testament to her passion and talent.

5 ☐ Mark for Review

Which choice completes the text with the most logical and precise word or phrase?

(A) entrust

(B) envelop

(C) enclose

(D) ensnare

While many find the desert to be a barren and lifeless place, it is actually teeming with specialized flora and fauna that have adapted to its harsh conditions. Its ecosystem, although appearing simple at first glance, is incredibly _____ in its functionality and resilience.

6 ☐ Mark for Review

Which choice completes the text with the most logical and precise word or phrase?

(A) fragile

(B) complex

(C) static

(D) mundane

Marine biologist Dr. Emily Warren discovered a species of deep-sea fish with luminescent properties. Its ability to produce light in the dark abyssal depths of the ocean is an essential adaptation to its environment, helping the fish both in attracting prey and _____ potential predators with its sudden glow.

Which choice completes the text with the most logical and precise word or phrase?

(A) luring

(B) startling

(C) entertaining

(D) guiding

The massive sculptures of the Easter Island, known as Moai, have long fascinated historians and archaeologists. These statues are not just monumental in size but also in cultural significance. However, the methods by which the Rapa Nui people transported these massive structures to their final locations remain largely _____.

Which choice completes the text with the most logical and precise word or phrase?

(A) celebrated

(B) mundane

(C) insignificant

(D) enigmatic

In the dense rainforests of Borneo, bioluminescent fungi captivate the attention of anyone lucky enough to witness them. They emit a gentle green glow during the night-time, a phenomenon that many believe is a strategy for _____ insects for pollination or spore distribution.

9 🔖 Mark for Review

Which choice completes the text with the most logical and precise word or phrase?

- (A) repelling
- (B) captivating
- (C) camouflaging
- (D) overpowering

After years of meticulous research, Dr. Claire Montgomery has released her findings on the impact of urbanization on bird migration patterns. Her conclusions, while thorough, have been met with some _____ from fellow ornithologists, who believe that certain external factors were not adequately considered.

10 🔖 Mark for Review

Which choice completes the text with the most logical and precise word or phrase?

- (A) applause
- (B) skepticism
- (C) indifference
- (D) enthusiasm

With the advent of global communication platforms, linguistic barriers are no longer as insurmountable as they once were. Nonetheless, a deep understanding of cultural _____ remains essential for effective international collaboration.

11 ⬚ Mark for Review

Which choice completes the text with the most logical and precise word or phrase?

(A) anomalies

(B) nuances

(C) trivialities

(D) monotony

The ancient city of Petra, carved into the rose-red cliffs of modern-day Jordan, was once a thriving trading hub. However, as trade routes shifted and the city's water sources dwindled, it was gradually _____ until it was only rediscovered by the Western world in the early 19th century.

12 ⬚ Mark for Review

Which choice completes the text with the most logical and precise word or phrase?

(A) fortified

(B) abandoned

(C) expanded

(D) prohibited

While many view the art of dance as purely a form of entertainment, for some, it represents a powerful _____ of self-expression and cultural identity. This perspective is especially evident in traditional dances, where the movements often tell a story or convey a message that has been passed down through generations.

Which choice completes the text with the most logical and precise word or phrase?

(A) genre

(B) medium

(C) spectacle

(D) pastime

Despite its fragile appearance, spider silk exhibits a remarkable combination of strength and elasticity, making it a subject of interest for material scientists. In fact, weight-for-weight, it can be stronger than steel, leading many to see it as a potential _____ for certain industrial applications.

Which choice completes the text with the most logical and precise word or phrase?

(A) anomaly

(B) detriment

(C) substitute

(D) hindrance

The extensive research done on the planet Mars has yielded evidence that suggests the planet might have once been _____ water. Such findings open the possibility of life having existed on the red planet in the distant past.

15 ◫ Mark for Review

Which choice completes the text with the most logical and precise word or phrase?

(A) inundated with

(B) isolated from

(C) deprived of

(D) polarized by

In the field of sustainable architecture, bamboo has become a favorite material among builders due to its rapid growth and renewability. Yet, despite these benefits, many traditionalists _____ the use of bamboo, favoring more conventional materials like brick and concrete.

16 ◫ Mark for Review

Which choice completes the text with the most logical and precise word or phrase?

(A) endorse

(B) resist

(C) explore

(D) magnify

In the realm of classical music, Ludwig van Beethoven's symphonies are celebrated not only for their musical brilliance but also for their ability to evoke profound emotion. Many scholars believe that his compositions _____ the turbulence and passion of his personal life.

Which choice completes the text with the most logical and precise word or phrase?

(A) negate

(B) mirror

(C) dilute

(D) abandon

For centuries, the deep-sea remained one of Earth's last unexplored frontiers. With advancements in technology, marine biologists are now able to venture into these depths, revealing a world that seems almost _____ in its strangeness and diversity.

Which choice completes the text with the most logical and precise word or phrase?

(A) terrestrial

(B) ordinary

(C) alien

(D) transparent

Interlibrary loan services allow members to borrow a book from one branch of the library and return it to any other branch within the network. This flexibility, however, can lead to challenges in book distribution and reader demand across the library's branches. Dr. Emily Thompson utilizes digital cataloging and literary trends analysis to determine when popular titles might _____ in certain branches, leaving other locations with a limited selection of sought-after books.

Which choice completes the text with the most logical and precise word or phrase?

(A) cluster

(B) vanish

(C) replicate

(D) decrease

Great!
You can check your answers and explainations on page 172.

Type 2 Meaning in Context

Step 1: Read the Context Carefully

Focus on the sentences around the highlighted word. Pay attention to how the word fits into the overall meaning of the passage.

Step 2: Paraphrase the Sentence

Try to rephrase the sentence in your own words, replacing the highlighted word with a term or phrase that makes sense.

Step 3: Eliminate Wrong Answers

Cross out any options that are clearly unrelated to the meaning of the sentence. Look out for answers that are correct in other contexts but do not fit this specific usage.

Step 4: Select the Best Answer

Choose the option that most closely matches the meaning of the word based on its role in the passage.

Tips for Success

Consider the Tone and Style of the Passage
Some words take on meanings that align with the mood or tone of the text. For example, "suddenly" in a dramatic moment might mean "abruptly."

Beware of Overthinking
Stick to what the text suggests. Avoid making assumptions beyond the information provided.

Look for Clues
Words or phrases near the highlighted term often provide clues. For example, synonyms, descriptions, or even the structure of the sentence can guide you to the correct answer.

Example Question

This passage is from J.D. Salinger's 1951 novel *The Catcher in the Rye*.

Almost every time somebody gives me a present, it ends up making me sad. She bought me the wrong kind of skates—I wanted racing skates and she bought hockey—but it made me sad anyway. It was harder to get off the ice that day, even, I felt so underline empty.

As used in the text, what does the word "empty" most nearly mean?

(A) Hungry

(B) Devoid

(C) Unfulfilled

(D) Hollow

STEP 1 ▶ Read the Context Carefully

The passage discusses the narrator's sadness about receiving the wrong gift and the emotional impact it had on them.

The word "empty" appears in the sentence:

"It was harder to get off the ice that day, even, I felt so empty."

Here, "empty" seems to describe an emotional state related to feeling sad and unfulfilled.

STEP 2 ▶ Paraphrase the Sentence

The narrator felt emotionally drained or lacking something, likely due to disappointment. We might paraphrase "I felt so empty" as "I felt unfulfilled or emotionally hollow."

STEP 3 ▶ Eliminate Wrong Answers

A) Hungry: While "empty" can mean physically hungry in some contexts, this does not fit the emotional tone of the passage.

B) Devoid: "Devoid" means lacking entirely, which is too literal for the emotional context of the passage.

C) Unfulfilled: This aligns well with the emotional state of the narrator, who feels disappointed and lacking fulfillment.

D) Hollow: While "hollow" can describe an emotional state, it suggests a more detached or numb feeling, which doesn't perfectly fit the sadness described here.

STEP 4 ▶ Select the Best Answer

The word that best fits the emotional tone and context of the passage is **C) Unfulfilled**.

Meaning in Context Problem Set

Let's practice matching questions to get used to how a word conveys different meanings according to the context. Select the correct meaning of the word in its context.

1> The following text is from Herman Melville's 1851 novel *Moby Dick*.

The captain "simply" pointed towards the horizon, where a faint line suggested land. There was no grand gesture, no long speech, just a single extended finger, a silent indication of their destination after months at sea.

A
only

2> The following text is from Mark Twain's 1884 novel *The Adventures of Huckleberry Finn*.

After all the noise and commotion of the day, Huck retreated to his corner and "simply" read his book. He didn't participate in any of the wild games or fervent discussions of the other boys, he just wanted a moment of calm and quiet.

B
purely

3> The following text is from Henry David Thoreau's 1854 work *Walden*.

In the midst of his solitude, Thoreau did not keep his thoughts to himself. Instead, he "simply" shared his reflections with the reader, inviting them into his solitary world, full of wonder and contemplation about the natural surroundings.

C
quietly

4> The following text is from Emily Bronte's 1847 novel *Wuthering Heights*.

Her feelings for him were complex, interwoven with a history of joy, sorrow, and regret. But in this moment, she "simply" loved him, without conditions or reservations. Nothing else mattered but this raw emotion, this profound connection between their hearts.

D
openly

1> This passage is from Lewis Carroll's 1865 novel *Alice's Adventures in Wonderland*.

As Alice fell down the rabbit hole, she found herself "puzzling over" the peculiar nature of her journey. Would she ever stop falling? And if she did, where would she land? These questions buzzed in her head, each more curious and confusing than the last.

2> The following text is from Mary Shelley's 1818 novel *Frankenstein*.

Dr. Frankenstein was constantly "puzzling over" his creation. The creature was unlike anything the world had ever seen, a testament to human ingenuity and a terrifying glimpse into the unknown. His awe was mixed with a sense of dread, creating an unsettling mixture of emotions.

3> The following text is from Bram Stoker's 1897 novel *Dracula*.

After his encounter with the Count, Jonathan Harker found himself "puzzling over" the strange events of the night. The eerie atmosphere, the Count's peculiar behavior, everything seemed off, as if he had stumbled into a realm where normal rules did not apply.

4> The following text is from Charles Dickens's 1861 novel *Great Expectations*.

Despite his efforts to put it out of his mind, Pip found himself "puzzling over" the strange encounter with the escaped convict. The man's words, his desperate plea for help, stirred a sense of unease in Pip that he couldn't shake off.

A
dazed by

B
worrying about

C
marveling at

D
wondering about

1> The following text is from Jules Verne's 1870 novel *Twenty Thousand Leagues Under the Sea.*

In the engine room of the Nautilus, the complex machinery was held together by various "connections". These were crucial in maintaining the functioning of the submarine, each link ensuring the smooth transfer of power and control.

A
physical link

2> The following text is from Alexander Graham Bell's 1876 notes on the creation of the telephone.

The advent of the telephone revolutionized how people communicated. It established a "connection" that allowed voices to travel across vast distances, turning a global community into neighbors, able to converse across the miles.

B
means of communi-cation

3> The following text is from Emily Bronte's 1847 novel *Wuthering Heights.*

Despite their differences and the turmoil that surrounded their lives, Catherine and Heathcliff shared a deep "connection". It transcended the ordinary, a bond forged by shared experiences and intense emotions that bound them together.

C
influential person

4> The following text is from Alexandre Dumas's 1844 novel *The Count of Monte Cristo.*

In his quest for revenge, Edmond Dantès used every "connection" he had. Among these was the influential Count of Morcerf, a man of considerable power and reach who could open doors that would otherwise remain closed.

D
recognized relationship

1> The following text is from Arthur Conan Doyle's 1892 collection *The Adventures of Sherlock Holmes.*

Sherlock prided himself on his "sound" reasoning. His deductions were not hasty guesses, but the result of careful observation and logical analysis. Each conclusion was based on verifiable facts, making them hard to refute.

2> The following text is from Louisa May Alcott's 1868 novel *Little Women.*

I am not afraid of storms, for I am learning how to sail my ship,' said Amy, with a brave, hopeful smile. Her "sound" attitude in the face of challenges inspired her sisters, who admired her courage and determination to persevere.

3> The following text is from Charles Dickens's 1859 novel *A Tale of Two Cities.*

Mr. Lorry's handling of the Tellson's Bank was "sound". Every decision he made was based on careful consideration of the facts. His comprehensive approach ensured that the bank's operations ran smoothly and efficiently.

4> The following text is from Charles Dickens's 1843 novel *A Christmas Carol.*

Despite the constant turbulence in their relationship, Elizabeth Bennet's regard for Mr. Darcy remained "sound". It was not swayed by rumors or misunderstandings, but remained steady, rooted in her understanding of his character.

A
thorough

B
positive

C
accurate

D
firm

This passage is from Harper Lee's 1960 novel *To Kill a Mockingbird*.

"Atticus said to Jem one day, 'I'd rather you shot at tin cans in the back yard, but I know you'll go after birds. Shoot all the blue jays you want, if you can hit 'em, but remember it's a <u>sin</u> to kill a mockingbird.' That was the only time I ever heard Atticus say it was a sin to do something."

1 🔖 Mark for Review

As used in the text, what does the word "sin" most nearly mean?

(A) Mistake

(B) Crime

(C) Disobedience

(D) Immorality

This passage is from Mark Twain's 1884 novel *The Adventures of Huckleberry Finn*.

"Jim said that bees won't sting idiots, but I didn't believe that, because I tried them lots of times myself and they wouldn't sting me. I had heard about some of these things before, but not all of them. Jim knew all kinds of <u>signs</u>. He said he knowed most everything."

2 🔖 Mark for Review

As used in the text, what does the word "signs" most nearly mean?

(A) Warnings

(B) Symbols

(C) Directions

(D) Omens

This passage is from Lewis Carroll's 1865 novel *Alice's Adventures in Wonderland.*

"Would you tell me, please, which way I ought to go from here?" "That <u>depends</u> a good deal on where you want to get to," said the Cat. "I don't much care where—" said Alice. "Then it doesn't matter which way you go," said the Cat.

3 ☐ Mark for Review

As used in the text, what does the word "depends" most nearly mean?

(A) Hinges

(B) Relies

(C) Descends

(D) Pertains

This passage is from Jane Austen's 1813 novel *Pride and Prejudice.*

"Their visits to Mrs. Phillips were now <u>productive</u> of the most interesting intelligence. Every day added something to their knowledge of the officers' names and connections. Their lodgings were not long a secret, and at length they began to know the officers themselves."

4 ☐ Mark for Review

As used in the text, what does the word "productive" most nearly mean?

(A) Industrious

(B) Fertile

(C) Yielding

(D) Effective

This passage is from Emily Bronte's 1847 novel *Wuthering Heights*.

"I bestow my own attributes over liberally on him. Mr. Heathcliff may have entirely dissimilar reasons for keeping his hand out of the way when he meets a would-be-acquaintance, to those which <u>actuate</u> me. Let me hope my constitution is almost peculiar: my dear mother used to say I should never have a comfortable home."

5 🔖 Mark for Review

As used in the text, what does the word "actuate" most nearly mean?

(A) Perform

(B) Drive

(C) Begin

(D) Design

This passage is from Charles Dickens' 1859 novel *A Tale of Two Cities*.

"A wonderful fact to reflect upon, that every human creature is <u>constituted</u> to be that profound secret and mystery to every other. A solemn consideration, when I enter a great city by night, that every one of those darkly clustered houses encloses its own secret; that every room in every one of them encloses its own secret; that every beating heart in the hundreds of thousands of breasts there, is, in some of its imaginings, a secret to the heart nearest it!"

6 🔖 Mark for Review

As used in the text, what does the word "constituted" most nearly mean?

(A) Formed

(B) Authorized

(C) Composed

(D) Elected

In the tumultuous streets of Paris, every cobblestone seemed to echo with the <u>want</u> of justice. The hunger of the people, reflected in the desperation of their actions, had become an omnipresent reminder of the societal divides. In the heart of the city, the commoners faced a daily struggle for survival, their hollowed eyes a testament to the lack of even the most basic necessities of life: bread to feed the belly, a roof to shield from the harsh elements, and a peaceful night's sleep safe from the specter of crime and oppression.

7 ▢ Mark for Review

As used in the text, what does the word "want" most nearly mean?

- (A) Need
- (B) Absence
- (C) Ambition
- (D) Greed

The experience of phantom vibrations is widespread—it's the sensation that your phone is vibrating when it's not, say, when you're expecting an important call but it turns out to be a false alarm. This bizarre perception has made its way into our everyday lives due to our constant interactions with digital devices. Phantom vibrations can sometimes be a mere <u>curiosity</u>, but other times they might be indicative of our dependence on technology and its impact on our mental health.

8 ▢ Mark for Review

As used in the text, what does the word "curiosity" most nearly mean?

- (A) Concern
- (B) Question
- (C) Oddity
- (D) Wonder

During the orchestra performance, the conductor was very particular about the <u>exact</u> timing of each instrument. He had a keen ear and could discern if the violin was even slightly out of sync. The musicians knew that if they failed to follow the conductor's exact indications, it could disrupt the harmony of the entire piece.

9 🔖 Mark for Review

As used in the text, what does the word "exact" most nearly mean?

(A) Precise

(B) Rigorous

(C) Honest

(D) Distinct

In an attempt to maintain the integrity of the ancient forest, park authorities decided to limit human impact. They implemented a <u>control</u> on the number of tourists who could visit each day. In addition to this, they introduced rules about where visitors could walk and where they could set up camp.

10 🔖 Mark for Review

As used in the text, what does the word "control" most nearly mean?

(A) Regulating force

(B) Restrictive mechanism

(C) Comparative element

(D) Supervising factor

A professional athlete must maintain a strict routine to stay in peak condition. This routine often includes precise nutrition, regimented training, and a consistent sleep schedule. When an athlete adheres to such a routine, he or she is practically living the life of a monk, with little room for deviation.

11 Mark for Review

As used in the text, what does the word "practically" most nearly mean?

(A) Effectively

(B) Reasonably

(C) Cleverly

(D) Partially

The following text is from a speech delivered in July 2013 by Malala Yousafzai, "Address to the United Nations Youth Assembly."

"In many parts of the world, especially Pakistan and Afghanistan, terrorism, war, and conflict stop children from going to school. We are really tired of these wars. Women and children are suffering. In many parts of the world, students are going to school every day. It's their normal life. But in other parts of the world, we are starving for education... it's like a precious gift. It's like a diamond. The terrorists are trying to stop us, but the disposition towards change, towards equality, and towards freedom is stronger than ever."

12 Mark for Review

As used in the text, what does the word "disposition" most nearly mean?

(A) Habit

(B) Placement

(C) Settlement

(D) Attitude

The following text is adapted from Charles Dickens' *Oliver Twist*:

"Oliver was but a child. Great God! to send the rain on the just and unjust alike, to make the young form bend before its time, to seek out the innocent and helpless, that they might perish. What had poor Oliver done, which had brought him to this sad and lonely place, so far from home, surrounded by misery and <u>want</u>?"

13 🔖 Mark for Review

As used in the text, what does the word "want" most nearly mean?

(A) Need

(B) Absence

(C) Ambition

(D) Greed

From William Shakespeare's Romeo and Juliet:

LADY CAPULET: O, he is a lovely gentleman!
Romeo's a dishclout to him. An eagle, madam,
Hath not so green, so quick, so fair an eye
As Paris hath. Beshrew my very heart,
I think you are happy in this second match,
For it <u>excels</u> your first: or if it did not,
Your first is dead; or 'twere as good he were,
As living here and you no use of him.

14 🔖 Mark for Review

As used in the text, what does the word "excels" most nearly mean?

(A) Shines

(B) Surpasses

(C) Extinguishes

(D) Masters

The following text is adapted from Henrik Ibsen's play "Hedda Gabler".

HEDDA:
Well, we happened to pass here one evening; Tesman, poor fellow, was writhing in the agony of having to find conversation; so I took pity on the learned man—

BRACK:
[Smiles doubtfully.] You took pity? H'm—

HEDDA:
Yes, I really did. And so—to help him out of his torment—I happened to say, in <u>pure</u> thoughtlessness, that I should like to live in this villa.

As used in the text, what does the word "pure" most nearly mean?

(A) Clean

(B) Simple

(C) Complete

(D) Innocent

The following text is adapted from Molière's play "Tartuffe".

MARIANE: Who is it, father, you would have me say
Has won my heart, and I would like to have
Become my husband, by your choice?
ORGON: Tartuffe.
MARIANE: But, father, I protest it isn't true!
Why should you make me tell this dreadful lie?
ORGON: Because I mean to have it be the truth.
Let this suffice for you: I've <u>settled</u> it.

As used in the text, what does the word "settled" most nearly mean?

(A) Stabilized

(B) Paid

(C) Resolved

(D) Compromised

At the market, the vendor's stall was filled with <u>common</u> fruits and vegetables, things like apples, bananas, potatoes, and carrots. Amidst the ordinary, however, were some more exotic offerings that caught the eye of discerning shoppers.

17 🔖 Mark for Review

As used in the text, what does the word "common" most nearly mean?

- (A) Usual
- (B) Shared
- (C) Inferior
- (D) Widespread

The following text is adapted from George Bernard Shaw's play "Pygmalion."

HIGGINS: The moment I let you sit down in that chair and talk to me as if we were equals, you presume to give yourself airs. It's quite amusing, really. You might dress like a duchess, but you can't hide the truth. Your airs, your voice, your demeanor—they're all as <u>artificial</u> as your manners. You've put on a facade, but beneath it, you're the same flower girl I found in Covent Garden.

18 🔖 Mark for Review

As used in the text, what does the word "artificial" most nearly mean?

- (A) Exaggerated
- (B) Misleading
- (C) Forced
- (D) Fabricated

The following text is adapted from Anton Chekhov's play "The Cherry Orchard."

LYUBOV: We're at a crossroads, and the future of our beloved estate hangs in the balance. We must come to a decision, one way or another. If we can find the money, we'll keep the estate. If not, then we'll have to let it go. But before any of that, we must produce a plan. A solid, actionable plan that will guide our next steps and determine our family's future.

19 ⬚ Mark for Review

As used in the text, what does the word "produce" most nearly mean?

(A) Provoke

(B) Devise

(C) Fund

(D) Disclose

The following text is adapted from Oscar Wilde's play "The Importance of Being Earnest."

ALGERNON: "The very essence of romance is uncertainty. If ever I get married, I'll certainly try to forget the fact."

JACK: "I have no doubt about that, dear Algy. The Divorce Court was specially invented for people whose memories are so curiously constituted."

ALGERNON: "Oh! there is no use speculating on that subject. Divorces are made in Heaven."

20 ⬚ Mark for Review

As used in the text, what does the word "curiously" most nearly mean?

(A) Strangely

(B) Eagerly

(C) Suspiciously

(D) Frequently

CHAPTER 02
Detail Question

Objective: Identify specific information explicitly stated or clearly implied in the passage to answer questions about details, relationships, or factual information.

Step 1: Read the Main Instruction

o **Identify the Task:** Determine exactly what the question is asking. Look for keywords like "according to the text," "why," "how," or "what is one difference."

o **Highlight Keywords:** Highlight important terms or phrases in the question to focus your search in the passage.

Step 2: Understand the Context

o **Read Relevant Sections Thoroughly:** Don't rely solely on memory; revisit the passage to ensure accurate comprehension.

o **Pay Attention to Relationships:** Notice cause and effect, comparisons, contrasts, sequences, and examples that relate to the question.

Step 3: Locate Specific Information

o **Find the Exact Sentence(s):** Identify where in the passage the relevant information is presented.

o **Highlight or Note Key Sentences:** This helps in cross-referencing options later.

Step 4: Paraphrase When Necessary

    o **Match with the Text:** Ensure each option aligns with the passage.

    o **Eliminate Distractors:** Remove options that distort meaning, add unsupported information, or overgeneralize.

    o **Beware of Extreme Language:** Words like "always," "never," or "only" are rarely correct unless explicitly supported.

Step 5: Confirm Your Answer

Verify with the Passage: Double-check that your choice is the best-supported answer.

Example Question

Paleontologist Dr. Hyeon-Jin Min and her team have reported the discovery in a remote southern region of North Korea of a remarkably well-preserved stone sculpture from the Goguryeo Dynasty. Dr. Min and her colleagues have concluded that the sculpture represents a style of art previously unknown for this era in North Korea. The finding is significant given the previous lack of known artifacts from the Goguryeo Dynasty in southern regions of North Korea, which led many historians to assume that its territory was broader.

■ ☐ Mark for Review

What does the text most strongly suggest about the site discovered by the researchers?

(A) The sculpture represents a unique and previously unknown artistic style of the Goguryeo Dynasty.

(B) The discovery challenges previous assumptions about the cultural reach of the Goguryeo Dynasty in North Korea.

(C) The site may have been a significant cultural center in the southern regions of the Goguryeo Dynasty.

(D) It suggests that the geographical extent of the Goguryeo Dynasty's realm in North Korea was farther south than previously thought.

STEP 1 ► Read the Main Instruction
- **Identify the Task:** Determine what the text most strongly suggests about the site discovered
- **Highlight Keywords:** "site discovered"

STEP 2 ► Understand the Context

<u>Revisit Relevant Sections</u>
- The discovery is in a remote southern region of North Korea.
- There's a well-preserved stone sculpture from the Goguryeo Dynasty.
- There was a previous lack of known artifacts from this dynasty in southern North Korea.
- Historians assumed its territory was broader due to this lack.

<u>Pay Attention to Relationships</u>
- **Cause and Effect:** Lack of artifacts in the south led historians to assume a broader territory.
- **New Discovery's Impact:** Finding an artifact in the south challenges previous assumptions.

STEP 3 ► Locate Specific Information

<u>Key Sentences</u>
"The finding is significant given the previous lack of known artifacts from the Goguryeo Dynasty in southern regions of North Korea, which led many historians to assume that its territory was broader."

<u>Highlight Key Details</u>
- The site provides evidence that the Goguryeo Dynasty was present in the southern regions.
- This challenges the idea that the dynasty's territory was broader (i.e., extended beyond the south).

STEP 4 ► **Analyze and Compare Answer Choices**

Option A: *"The sculpture represents a unique and previously unknown artistic style of the Goguryeo Dynasty."*

- **Analysis:** While the passage mentions the sculpture's unique style, the question asks about the site, not just the sculpture.
- **Conclusion:** Not the best answer regarding the site.

Option B: *"The discovery challenges previous assumptions about the cultural reach of the Goguryeo Dynasty in North Korea."*

- **Analysis:** The passage focuses on territorial assumptions due to the lack of artifacts, not specifically on cultural reach.
- **Conclusion:** Partially correct but not the strongest match.

Option C: *"The site may have been a significant cultural center in the southern regions of the Goguryeo Dynasty."*

- **Analysis:** The passage does not provide evidence that the site was a significant cultural center.
- **Conclusion:** Not supported by the text.

Option D: *"It suggests that the geographical extent of the Goguryeo Dynasty's realm in North Korea was farther south than previously thought."*

- **Analysis:** - The discovery in the southern region contradicts previous assumptions based on the lack of artifacts.
    - Historians thought the territory was broader (perhaps more northern or extended beyond current findings) because there were no southern artifacts.
    - Finding an artifact in the south suggests the dynasty's realm extended farther south than previously believed.
- **Conclusion:** This option is strongly supported by the passage.

STEP 5 ► **Confirm Your Answer**

Verify with the Passage: Option D aligns closely with the passage's implication that the Goguryeo Dynasty's territory included southern regions, suggesting it was farther south than historians previously thought.

Detail Question Problem Set

Literary scholar Dr. Marianne Elston developed a computational model to analyze thematic patterns across 19th-century novels. Using text mining algorithms, her model identifies recurring words and phrases to detect themes like love, betrayal, and industrialization. To build her dataset, Dr. Elston sourced digitized texts from public archives and literary repositories. However, many of the texts were limited to well-preserved works from prominent authors, leaving less-known regional authors underrepresented. Despite this limitation, the model has proven effective in revealing trends in popular literary themes of the era.

1 🔖 Mark for Review

According to the passage, what is one potential drawback of Dr. Elston's method?

A	It relies on algorithms that might misinterpret themes in the texts.
B	It focuses on specific themes that are less relevant to modern readers.
C	It excludes works by lesser-known authors, potentially skewing the results.
D	It assumes that all 19th-century authors had similar thematic concerns.

The following text is adapted from Herman Melville's 1851 novel *Moby-Dick*.

Whenever I find myself growing grim about the mouth; whenever it is a damp, drizzly November in my soul; whenever I find myself involuntarily pausing before coffin warehouses, and bringing up the rear of every funeral I meet; and especially whenever my hypos get such an upper hand of me, that it requires a strong moral principle to prevent me from deliberately stepping into the street, and methodically knocking people's hats off—then, I account it high time to get to sea as soon as I can.

2 🔖 Mark for Review

According to the text, why does Ishmael go to sea?

A	Ishmael goes to sea for leisure and relaxation.
B	Ishmael goes to sea to attend funerals and coffin warehouses.
C	Ishmael goes to sea to escape the strong moral principles of society.
D	Ishmael goes to sea to alleviate his periods of melancholy and restlessness.

Covering more than five and a half million square kilometers, the Amazon Rainforest is the largest tropical rainforest in the world. It spans nine countries in South America and is home to an estimated 400 billion individual trees representing more than 16,000 species. However, this rich biodiversity is under threat due to extensive deforestation primarily driven by agriculture, livestock farming, and illegal logging. The Amazon Rainforest, often referred to as the "lungs of the Earth", plays a crucial role in the world's climate regulation and carbon cycle. Thus, its degradation has serious global implications.

3 ☐ Mark for Review

According to the text, what is the primary reason for the threat to the rich biodiversity of the Amazon Rainforest?

- (A) Shifts in climatic conditions and global temperature
- (B) Unforeseen calamities and uncontrolled blazes
- (C) Widespread clearing of forests propelled by human actions
- (D) Intrusive species and diseases caused by deforestation

The renowned poet Emily Dickinson is often celebrated for her extensive collection of poems, many of which were discovered after her death in 1886. During her lifetime, Dickinson maintained an intense correspondence with Thomas Wentworth Higginson, a literary critic, and editor. Their connection began in 1862 when Dickinson, seeking guidance, sent a letter to Higginson that included four of her poems. Higginson, intrigued by her unconventional style, responded and continued to mentor her through letters. Although the two met in person only twice, their written exchanges reveal a relationship that profoundly influenced Dickinson's approach to poetry.

4 ☐ Mark for Review

According to the text, how did Dickinson and Higginson initially communicate?

- (A) Dickinson and Higginson met during a literary workshop.
- (B) Dickinson sent Higginson a letter including some of her poems.
- (C) Dickinson and Higginson were introduced by a mutual friend.
- (D) Higginson read Dickinson's poems in a published anthology.

An article on urban planning discusses the role of public parks in city life. It states that parks are not just recreational spaces but also vital for the mental and physical health of city dwellers. They provide a natural oasis amidst the concrete jungle, offering a place for relaxation, exercise, and community gatherings. The article emphasizes that parks contribute to the well-being of residents by providing a connection to nature, which is often lacking in urban environments. Furthermore, they play a crucial role in environmental conservation within cities, offering habitats for local wildlife and contributing to air purification.

5 🔖 Mark for Review

According to the text, public parks in cities are similar to which of the following?

A libraries, as places that store valuable resources for public use.

B hospitals, as essential services that contribute to the health and well-being of the community.

C museums, as they preserve historical and cultural artifacts for public viewing.

D schools, as they provide educational opportunities for the community.

The following text is adapted from J.D. Salinger's 1951 novel *The Catcher in the Rye*.

I was trying to feel some kind of a good-by. I mean I've left schools and places I didn't even know I was leaving them. I hate that. I don't care if it's a sad good-by or a bad good-by, but when I leave a place I like to know I'm leaving it. If you don't, you feel even worse. It's like you're missing something important. You're just left with this empty feeling inside.

6 🔖 Mark for Review

According to the text, what is true about the narrator's feelings?

A He enjoys the thrill of leaving without notice.

B He feels a void when he doesn't acknowledge his departures.

C He always ensures he leaves places with a cheerful farewell.

D He believes good-byes are unnecessary formalities.

The International Space Station (ISS) is a space station, or a habitable artificial satellite, in low Earth orbit. Its first component was launched into orbit in 1998, and since then, the station has been continuously occupied since November 2000. The station is divided into two sections: the Russian Orbital Segment (ROS), operated by Russia, and the United States Orbital Segment (USOS), which is shared by many nations. Research conducted on the ISS often requires one or more of the unusual conditions present in low Earth orbit, such as low gravity or oxygen.

7 🔖 Mark for Review

According to the text, what is true about the International Space Station (ISS)?

(A) The ISS has been unoccupied since its launch in 1998.

(B) The ISS is located in high Earth orbit.

(C) The United States Orbital Segment (USOS) is operated by the United States.

(D) Research conducted on the ISS often requires conditions found in low Earth orbit.

The following text is adapted from Emily Bronte's *Wuthering Heights*.

He's more myself than I am. Whatever our souls are made of, his and mine are the same. If all else perished, and he remained, I should still continue to be; and if all else remained, and he were annihilated, the universe would turn to a mighty stranger. I cannot imagine a world without him. His presence is as essential to me as the air I breathe.

8 🔖 Mark for Review

According to the text, what is true about the speaker's feelings?

(A) She can easily envision a life without him.

(B) She feels a casual fondness for him.

(C) She believes their bond is deep and essential to her existence.

(D) She thinks he is just like everyone else in her life.

In a recent study on environmental conservation, it was found that public awareness campaigns significantly contribute to environmental protection. These campaigns educate the public about the importance of preserving natural resources and the detrimental effects of pollution. By increasing awareness, people are more likely to adopt environmentally friendly practices in their daily lives, such as recycling, conserving water, and reducing the use of plastic. Moreover, heightened public awareness often leads to increased pressure on governments and corporations to adopt sustainable practices and policies. The study concludes that these campaigns are vital in shaping a more environmentally conscious society, leading to a collective effort to protect our planet.

9 🔖 Mark for Review

According to the text, why are public awareness campaigns important for environmental conservation?

- (A) provide financial support for environmental research.

- (B) encourage individuals to adopt eco-friendly practices.

- (C) offer new technological solutions for environmental problems.

- (D) create job opportunities in the field of environmental science.

The Amazon Rainforest, also known as Amazonia, is the world's largest tropical rainforest, famous for its biodiversity. It covers most of the Amazon Basin in South America, spanning eight countries: Brazil, Bolivia, Peru, Ecuador, Colombia, Venezuela, Guyana, and Suriname, as well as French Guiana, a territory of France. The forest is so dense that sunlight can take as long as ten minutes to reach the ground from the canopy. The rainforest is currently under threat due to deforestation for agriculture and illegal logging.

10 🔖 Mark for Review

According to the text, what is true about the Amazon Rainforest?

- (A) The Amazon Rainforest only spans across one country.

- (B) Sunlight reaches the ground instantaneously in the Amazon Rainforest.

- (C) The Amazon Rainforest is currently under threat due to deforestation and illegal logging.

- (D) The Amazon Rainforest is not known for its biodiversity.

The following text is adapted from Charlotte Bronte's 1847 novel *Jane Eyre*.

I returned to my book—Bewick's History of British Birds: the letterpress thereof I cared little for, generally speaking; and yet there were certain introductory pages that, child as I was, I could not pass quite as a blank. They were those which treat of the haunts of sea-fowl; of 'the solitary rocks and promontories' by them only inhabited; of the coast of Norway, studded with isles from its southern extremity, the Lindeness, or Naze, to the North Cape—

11 ☐ Mark for Review

According to the text, what is true about Jane Eyre?

- (A) Jane was reading a novel about a family.
- (B) She was particularly interested in the parts about sea-fowl.
- (C) Jane found every page of the book engaging.
- (D) The book was about the coast of France.

Eight weather forecasting agencies each predicted the expected rainfall for three coastal towns. Two of the towns typically experience consistent rainfall patterns, and the predictions for current and future rainfall from each agency showed minimal variation. However, for the third town, which is prone to sudden weather changes, the rainfall predictions varied significantly across agencies.

12 ☐ Mark for Review

According to the text, what can be inferred about the rainfall predictions?

- (A) It is more challenging to predict rainfall accurately for coastal towns than for inland towns.
- (B) Rainfall forecasts are usually inaccurate for towns with regular weather patterns.
- (C) The rate of change in rainfall patterns for coastal towns with sudden weather changes is constant.
- (D) The agencies are likely to be equally reliable in predicting rainfall for towns with consistent weather patterns.

The following text is adapted from Leo Tolstoy's novel *War and Peace*.

Prince Andrew listened to the account of the opening of the Council of State, which he had so impatiently awaited and to which he had attached such importance, and was surprised that this event, now that it had taken place, did not affect him, and even seemed quite insignificant. He listened with quiet irony to Bitski's enthusiastic account of it. A very simple thought occurred to him: 'What does it matter to me or to Bitski what the Emperor was pleased to say at the Council? Nothing at all.'

13 ☐ Mark for Review

According to the text, how does Prince Andrew feel about the Council of State's opening?

(A) He finds it to be the most significant event of his life.

(B) He is indifferent and views it as insignificant.

(C) He is eagerly waiting for the next Council meeting.

(D) He is upset that he wasn't present at the Council.

The article on renewable energy emphasizes the significance of transitioning from fossil fuels to sustainable energy sources like solar and wind power. It argues that renewable energy is not just a means of power generation but a pathway to a sustainable future. By reducing reliance on non-renewable resources, countries can decrease their carbon footprint, combat climate change, and preserve the environment for future generations. The article suggests that investing in renewable energy is a proactive step towards ensuring a healthier planet and a more stable ecological balance.

14 ☐ Mark for Review

The text suggests that investing in renewable energy is similar to which of the following?

(A) saving money in a bank for future financial security.

(B) planting trees to contribute to a greener environment.

(C) educating children to prepare them for future challenges.

(D) building infrastructure to support economic growth.

The following text is adapted from Bram Stoker's 1897 novel *Dracula*. Van Helsing speaks to Dr. John Seward about the limitations of science and the mysteries of the unknown.

'You are a clever man, friend John; you reason well, and your wit is bold; but you are too prejudiced. You do not let your eyes see nor your ears hear, and that which is outside your daily life is not of account to you. Do you not think that there are things which you cannot understand, and yet which are; that some people see things that others cannot? But there are things old and new which must not be contemplate by men's eyes, because they know - or think they know - some things which other men have told them. Ah, it is the fault of our science that it wants to explain all; and if it explain not, then it says there is nothing to explain.'

15 ☐ Mark for Review

According to the text, what does the speaker believe about Dr. John Seward?

(A) They should always trust science to explain everything.

(B) They are too hasty in their judgments and quick to accept the unknown.

(C) They should not contemplate things they don't understand.

(D) They are too closed-minded to see beyond what they encounter in their daily life.

In the past, people primarily used traditional incandescent light bulbs in their homes. However, as awareness of energy conservation grew, governments began promoting the use of energy-efficient LED bulbs, claiming they would significantly reduce electricity consumption. Once LED bulbs became widely adopted, some consumers reported experiencing increased eye strain and discomfort.

16 ☐ Mark for Review

According to the text, what is true about LED bulbs?

(A) LED bulbs emit a different type of light that can cause eye strain compared to traditional incandescent bulbs.

(B) Traditional incandescent bulbs are no less energy-efficient than LED bulbs.

(C) The government's promotion of LED bulbs was based on misinformation about their energy-saving benefits.

(D) LED bulbs have no impact on eye comfort compared to traditional incandescent bulbs.

The following text is adapted from Oscar Wilde's *The Picture of Dorian Gray*. Dorian and Basil Hallward ascend the stairs of Dorian's home in the late evening.

He passed out of the room and began the ascent, Basil Hallward following close behind. They walked softly, as men do instinctively at night. The lamp cast fantastic shadows on the wall and staircase. A rising wind made some of the windows rattle. When they reached the top landing, Dorian took out the key and turned it in the lock.

17 ☐ Mark for Review

According to the text, what did the rising wind cause?

(A) The lamp to cast fantastic shadows.

(B) The men to walk more quietly.

(C) Some of the windows not to stay still.

(D) Dorian to take out the key.

In 2022, a group of scientists led by Dr. Maria Alverez embarked on a project to study the impact of climate change on marine biodiversity. They conducted research over a span of one year, monitoring the number of different species in a particular marine ecosystem and comparing the data with the records from the past decades. They found a significant reduction in the number of species, indicating a loss of biodiversity. Their findings suggested that warmer ocean temperatures and acidification due to climate change have negatively impacted marine life.

18 ☐ Mark for Review

According to the text, why is marine biodiversity declining?

(A) Because the marine ecosystem is naturally evolving over time.

(B) Because of the overfishing practices carried out by humans.

(C) Because marine animals are moving to different habitats.

(D) Because of rising ocean temperatures and acidification.

In 2025, Dr. Lisa Mitchell and her team made a groundbreaking discovery in the field of quantum computing. They developed a quantum computer with significantly greater processing power than any existing classical computer. This quantum computer used the principles of superposition and entanglement to process massive amounts of data simultaneously. The team's accomplishment was hailed as a giant leap forward for technology and has the potential to revolutionize fields like cryptography, machine learning, and drug discovery.

19 🔖 Mark for Review

According to the text, why is Dr. Mitchell's quantum computer significant?

A) It is the first quantum computer ever developed.

B) It is made larger than any existing classical computer to process significant abouts of data.

C) It boasts a substantially superior computational capacity compared to its classical counterparts.

D) It is primarily aimed at revolutionizing the field of cryptography, machine learning, and drug discovery.

In 2030, Astrophysicist Dr. Elena Rodriguez and her team made an extraordinary discovery. They detected signs of a potential exoplanet in the Proxima Centauri system, the closest star system to our own. This new planet, dubbed Proxima Centauri c, appears to be in the star's habitable zone, meaning it could have conditions suitable for life as we know it. The planet is approximately 1.5 times the size of Earth, and further observations and studies are being conducted to learn more about its atmosphere and potential for water.

20 🔖 Mark for Review

According to the text, why is the discovery of Proxima Centauri c significant?

A) It is the first exoplanet ever discovered.

B) It is the largest planet discovered in the Proxima Centauri system.

C) It is the closest planet to Earth.

D) It could potentially have conditions suitable for life.

In 2031, a group of archaeologists led by Dr. Matthew Hopkins discovered the remains of an ancient city buried beneath the sands of the Sahara desert. The well-preserved artifacts found at the site indicated that the city was once a thriving metropolis with a complex social structure and advanced architectural techniques. The archaeologists estimate that the city was at its peak around 2000 BC, making it one of the oldest known urban settlements in Africa.

According to the text, why is the discovery of the ancient city significant?

(A) The city was once the capital of a powerful African empire.

(B) The city was built with advanced architectural techniques that were not known to have existed in 2000 BC.

(C) The city was discovered in the Sahara desert, which is unusual for an urban settlement.

(D) The city is estimated to be one of the earliest known urban settlements in Africa.

CHAPTER 03

Main Idea

Objective: Identify the central point or primary message that the author intends to convey in the passage.

Step 1: Read the Passage Carefully

- o Focus on the overall content, not just isolated sentences.
- o Note the introduction and conclusion—they often contain the main idea.
- o Look for repeated themes or concepts emphasized throughout.

Step 2: Recognize Contrasts and Shifts

- o Look for contrast words like "however," "but," "yet," "nevertheless," which signal shifts in perspective.
- o Understand that the main idea may follow these shifts.

Step 3: Differentiate Main Ideas from Supporting Details

- o Identify the overarching point the author is making.
- o Don't confuse examples or evidence (supporting details) with the main idea.
- o Avoid focusing on minor details.

Step 4: Summarize the Passage

- o Condense the main idea into one or two sentences in your own words.
- o Use simple language to clarify the essence of the passage.

Step 5: Evaluate Answer Choices

    o Ensure each option aligns with the main idea you've identified.

    o Eliminate distractors that are too narrow, too broad, misrepresent the author's intent, or distort information.

    o Be cautious of extreme statements unless they are justified by the passage.

Step 6: Select and Confirm the Best Answer:

    o Choose the option that best reflects the main idea.

    o Double-check the passage if necessary to confirm your choice.

Example Question

The following text is adapted from Charles Dickens' 1843 novella "A Christmas Carol."

Foggier yet, and colder. Piercing, searching, biting cold. If the good Saint Dunstan had but nipped the Evil Spirit's nose with a touch of such weather as that, instead of using his familiar weapons, then indeed he would have roared to lusty purpose. The owner of one scant young nose, gnawed and mumbled by the hungry cold as bones are gnawed by dogs, stooped down at Scrooge's keyhole to regale him with a Christmas carol: but at the first sound of
"God bless you, merry gentleman!
  May nothing you dismay!"
Scrooge seized the ruler with such energy of action, that the singer fled in terror, leaving the keyhole to the fog and even more congenial frost.

☐ Mark for Review

Which choice best states the main idea of the text?

(A) The severe cold is unbearable for everyone in the city so the young man flees away after singing a Christmas carol.

(B) A young person tries to spread Christmas cheer through song despite the freezing weather, but Scrooge scares him away.

(C) The cold weather is compared to the effectiveness of Saint Dunstan's methods.

(D) The Christmas carol is about the festive celebration of the holiday season.

STEP 1 ▶ Read the Passage Thoroughly

The passage describes a freezing, foggy setting where a young person attempts to sing a Christmas carol at Scrooge's door but is scared away by Scrooge's hostile reaction.

STEP 2 ▶ Recognize Contrasts and Shifts

Contrast: Between the severe cold and the warmth of the young person's attempt to spread cheer.

Shift: From the caroler's hopeful singing to Scrooge's aggressive response.

STEP 3 ▶ Differentiate Main Ideas from Supporting Details

Main Idea: A young person tries to bring Christmas cheer despite the cold, but Scrooge frightens him away.

Supporting Details: Description of the cold weather, reference to Saint Dunstan, specific lines of the carol.

STEP 4 ▶ Summarize the Passage

Despite the biting cold, a young caroler attempts to spread Christmas cheer to Scrooge, who responds aggressively, causing the singer to flee.

STEP 5 ▶ Evaluate Answer Choices

A. Incorrect—Suggests the young man flees because of the cold, not Scrooge's actions.
B. Correct—Accurately reflects the main idea of the passage.
C. Incorrect—Focuses on the comparison to Saint Dunstan, a minor detail.
D. Incorrect—Emphasizes the content of the carol, not the main event.

STEP 6 ▶ Select and Confirm the Best Answer

Answer: B. A young person tries to spread Christmas cheer through song despite the freezing weather, but Scrooge scares him away.

Max's Note

Remember that the main idea is the overall message or point that the author is trying to convey through the text. It's not necessarily about specific details but rather the general theme or argument presented.

Main Idea Problem Set

Autonomous vehicles, or self-driving cars, hold immense potential to reshape our cities and our lives. Proponents argue that they could reduce the number of traffic accidents, alleviate congestion, and cut carbon emissions. Critics, however, worry about job losses in the transportation sector and unforeseen safety risks. As these vehicles become more prevalent, society will have to weigh the benefits against the potential drawbacks.

1 🔖 Mark for Review

Which choice best states the main idea of the text?

A) Autonomous vehicles are the future of transportation and will have many benefits.

B) Autonomous vehicles are controversial due to potential job losses and safety risks.

C) The impact of autonomous vehicles on society will depend on the balance between their potential benefits and drawbacks.

D) Critics believe autonomous vehicles pose more risks than benefits to society.

Scientists recently discovered a new species of bird in the Amazon rainforest. It is named 'The Flame Crest', due to its bright red crest which is visible from a distance. This bird is characterized by its loud, distinct call that echoes throughout the rainforest. Unfortunately, with deforestation rampant in the Amazon, the Flame Crest's habitat is under threat, which could lead to a swift decline in its numbers.

2 🔖 Mark for Review

Which choice best states the main idea of the text?

A) The Flame Crest is a newly discovered species in the Amazon rainforest that is under threat due to deforestation.

B) Scientists discovered the Flame Crest bird due to its distinctive loud vocalizations.

C) Deforestation in the Amazon rainforest is the primary reason for the decline in bird species.

D) The Flame Crest is the only bird in the Amazon rainforest with a bright red crest.

The city of Copenhagen, Denmark is known for its bicycle culture. Nearly half of its residents commute to work, school, or shopping by bike. The city has over 400 kilometers of bike lanes and prioritizes cycling infrastructure in its urban planning. This not only reduces congestion and pollution but also contributes to the physical health and well-being of its citizens.

3 🔖 Mark for Review

Which choice best states the main idea of the text?

(A) Copenhagen, Denmark is a city that highly values and promotes cycling as a primary mode of transport.

(B) Cycling in Copenhagen, Denmark is primarily for commuting to work or school.

(C) The citizens of Copenhagen, Denmark are exceptionally physically healthy due to cycling.

(D) The city of Copenhagen, Denmark has over 400 kilometers of bike lanes.

The following text is adapted from Jane Austen's 1813 novel *Pride and Prejudice*. Elizabeth Bennet, the novel's protagonist, is reflecting on Mr. Darcy's proposal.

Elizabeth felt how improbable it was that they should ever see each other again on such terms of cordiality as had marked their several meetings in Derbyshire; and as she threw a retrospective glance over the whole of their acquaintance, so full of contradictions and varieties, she sighed at the perverseness of those feelings which would now have promoted its continuance, and would formerly have rejoiced in its termination.

4 🔖 Mark for Review

Which choice best states the main idea of the text?

(A) Elizabeth Bennet is thrilled by Mr. Darcy's proposal and can't wait to see him again.

(B) Elizabeth Bennet is confused about her feelings toward Mr. Darcy and their complicated relationship.

(C) Elizabeth Bennet strongly regrets ever meeting Mr. Darcy.

(D) Elizabeth Bennet is indifferent to Mr. Darcy and his proposal.

The following text is adapted from Harper Lee's 1960 novel *To Kill a Mockingbird*. Scout, the narrator, describes the town of Maycomb.

Maycomb was an old town, but it was a tired old town when I first knew it. In rainy weather the streets turned to red slop...[s]omehow it was hotter then...bony mules hitched to Hoover carts flicked flies in the sweltering shade of the live oaks on the square. Men's stiff collars wilted by nine in the morning. Ladies bathed before noon, after their three-o'clock naps, and by nightfall were like soft teacakes with frostings of sweat and sweet talcum.

5 ☐ Mark for Review

Which choice best states the main idea of the text?

A) Maycomb is a bustling town full of activity throughout the day.

B) The people of Maycomb are unhappy due to the hot and uncomfortable weather.

C) Scout dislikes living in Maycomb due to its old age and hot weather.

D) The town of Maycomb is described as old and weary, with a hot and uncomfortable climate.

The following text is adapted from Ella Wheeler Wilcox's poem "Will."

There is no chance, no destiny, no fate,
Can circumvent or hinder or control
The firm resolve of a determined soul.
Gifts count for nothing; will alone is great;
All things give way before it, soon or late.
What obstacle can stay the mighty force
Of the sea-seeking river in its course,
Or cause the ascending orb of day to wait?

6 ☐ Mark for Review

Which choice best states the main idea of the text?

A) Destiny and fate are the primary drivers of one's life.

B) The power of will and determination can overcome any obstacle or challenge.

C) The natural world, like rivers and the sun, is unpredictable and uncontrollable.

D) Gifts and talents are the most important factors in achieving success.

The following text is adapted from Fyodor Dostoevsky's 1866 novel *Crime and Punishment*. Raskolnikov, a former student, grapples with his internal moral conflicts after committing a crime.

He wandered aimlessly. The sun was setting. A special form of misery had begun to oppress him of late. There was nothing poignant, nothing acute about it; but there was a feeling of permanence, of eternity about it. It brought a foretaste of hopeless years of this cold leaden misery, a foretaste of an eternity 'on a square yard of space.' The streets seemed to echo his desolation, with every corner whispering of his guilt. The weight of his conscience made even the fading light of the day seem oppressive.

7 ☐ Mark for Review

Which choice best states the main idea of the text?

(A) Raskolnikov was enjoying the beauty of the sunset.

(B) Raskolnikov felt a temporary sadness that he believed would pass soon.

(C) The weight of his actions led Raskolnikov to feel an enduring, inescapable misery.

(D) Raskolnikov was contemplating the vastness of the universe.

Quantum computing is a rapidly developing field that leverages the principles of quantum mechanics to process information. Unlike classical computers, which use bits as their smallest units of information, quantum computers use quantum bits, or "qubits." These qubits exist in a state of superposition, meaning they can be both 0 and 1 at the same time. This allows quantum computers to perform complex computations much more quickly than classical computers.

8 ☐ Mark for Review

Which choice best states the main idea of the text?

(A) The state of superposition is the main advantage of quantum computing.

(B) Quantum computing is a complex field that only experts can truly understand.

(C) Quantum computing, with its use of qubits, has the potential to perform computations faster than classical computers.

(D) Classical computers are becoming obsolete due to the development of quantum computing.

The following text is adapted from Lewis Carroll's 1865 novel *Alice's Adventures in Wonderland*. Alice, the protagonist, has just fallen down a rabbit hole.

Down, down, down. Would the fall never come to an end? 'I wonder how many miles I've fallen by this time?' she said aloud. 'I must be getting somewhere near the center of the earth. Let me see: that would be four thousand miles down, I think--' (for, you see, Alice had learned several things of this sort in her lessons in the schoolroom...)

9 🔖 Mark for Review

Which choice best states the main idea of the text?

A Alice is reflecting on her lessons from school while falling down a rabbit hole.

B Alice believes that she has fallen to the center of the earth.

C Alice is growing bored and frustrated with her seemingly endless fall.

D Alice is estimating the distance she has fallen down the rabbit hole.

The rapid development of Artificial Intelligence (AI) technologies has paved the way for significant improvements in various sectors, including healthcare, finance, transportation, and education. These systems can process vast amounts of data, identify patterns, and make predictions, enhancing decision-making and efficiency. However, the rise of AI also poses challenges and ethical considerations, such as job displacement, privacy concerns, and potential misuse.

10 🔖 Mark for Review

Which choice best states the main idea of the text?

A Artificial Intelligence has significantly improved several sectors but also presents ethical challenges and concerns.

B AI's ability to process vast amounts of data is transforming various sectors, despite the potential for job displacement.

C The most significant impact of AI has been in healthcare, finance, transportation, and education.

D The rapid development of AI technologies is causing significant concern about job displacement and privacy.

The following text is adapted from H. G. Wells's 1895 novella "The Time Machine." The Time Traveller, having ventured far into the future, observes the world and its inhabitants.

I looked about me to see if any traces of animal life remained. A certain indefinable apprehension still kept me in the saddle of the machine. But I saw nothing moving, in earth or sky or sea. The green slime on the rocks alone testified that life was not extinct. A shallow sandbank had appeared in the sea and the water had receded from the beach. The air was still and heavy, making each breath a labor. The silence was broken only by the soft murmur of the waves lapping against the shore.

Which choice best states the main idea of the text?

A. The Time Traveller was eager to explore the vibrant world around him.

B. Life seemed almost extinct, with only subtle signs indicating its presence.

C. The Time Traveller was surrounded by a variety of animals and plants.

D. The green slime on the rocks was harmful and dangerous.

Global warming is a critical issue that is having severe effects on our planet. The increase in the Earth's average temperature is causing melting ice caps, rising sea levels, and extreme weather events. These changes can have catastrophic impacts on human lives, wildlife habitats, and the global economy. Urgent action is needed to mitigate these effects, including reducing greenhouse gas emissions, protecting and restoring forests, and transitioning to renewable energy sources.

Which choice best states the main idea of the text?

A. Melting ice caps and rising sea levels are among the most concerning effects of global warming.

B. The impacts of global warming are severe, requiring immediate measures like reducing greenhouse gas emissions and transitioning to renewable energy.

C. Global warming is negatively affecting wildlife habitats, human lives, and the global economy.

D. The primary solution to global warming is transitioning to renewable energy sources.

The following text is a direct excerpt from Jules Verne's *Around the World in Eighty Days*.

He lived alone in his house in Saville Row, whither none penetrated. A single domestic sufficed to serve him. He breakfasted and dined at the club, at hours mathematically fixed, in the same room, at the same table, never taking his meals with other members, much less bringing a guest with him; and went home at exactly midnight, only to retire at once to bed.

13 ☐ Mark for Review

Which choice best states the main idea of the text?

A Phileas Fogg is a social individual who frequently invites guests to his home.

B Fogg is a creature of habit, living a life of strict routine and solitude.

C The club is a lively place where Fogg interacts with various members.

D Fogg's domestic life is chaotic and unpredictable.

The following text is adapted from Jules Verne's 1870 novel *Twenty Thousand Leagues Under the Sea*. Captain Nemo, the enigmatic commander of the submarine Nautilus, takes his guests on a journey beneath the oceans.

The sea is everything. It covers seven-tenths of the terrestrial globe. Its breath is pure and healthy. It is an immense desert where man is never lonely, for he feels life, pulsating around him on every side. The sea is only a receptacle for all the prodigious, supernatural things that exist inside it; it is only movement and love; it is the living infinite.

14 ☐ Mark for Review

Which choice best states the main idea of the text?

A Captain Nemo believes that the sea is a dangerous and unpredictable place.

B The sea, for Captain Nemo, represents a vast, living entity full of wonder.

C Humans should avoid the sea because of the supernatural entities that reside within.

D The terrestrial world is more fascinating than the underwater realm.

The following text is adapted from George Orwell's 1945 novel *Animal Farm*. The animals on the farm have revolted against their human owner and are trying to establish a new order.

All animals are equal, but some animals are more equal than others. The pigs, who were the brains of the revolution, began to take charge, making decisions for the betterment of the farm, they claimed. Yet, as days turned into weeks, it became clear that their leadership was not as altruistic as it once seemed.

15 ☐ Mark for Review

Which choice best states the main idea of the text?

(A) The pigs were the least intelligent animals on the farm.

(B) All the animals on the farm lived in harmony and equality.

(C) The pigs began to exert dominance and betray the ideals of the revolution.

(D) The revolution was a complete success with no negative consequences.

Plastic pollution is a serious environmental issue. Millions of tons of plastic waste are discarded each year, ending up in our oceans, rivers, and landscapes. This not only harms wildlife, but also poses significant risks to human health. Plastic waste can take hundreds of years to decompose, and even then, it breaks down into microplastics that continue to pollute the environment. Efforts are needed to reduce plastic consumption, improve waste management, and invest in eco-friendly alternatives.

16 ☐ Mark for Review

Which choice best states the main idea of the text?

(A) Plastic pollution is a grave environmental issue that requires efforts to reduce plastic consumption, improve waste management, and develop eco-friendly alternatives.

(B) The danger of plastic waste lies in its slow decomposition and its eventual breakdown into microplastics.

(C) The massive amounts of plastic waste discarded annually are severely damaging wildlife and human health.

(D) Efforts to combat plastic pollution must prioritize the development and investment in eco-friendly alternatives to plastic.

The following text is adapted from George Eliot's 1861 novel *Silas Marner*. Silas, a weaver in the village of Raveloe, has been living a life of solitude after a traumatic event in his past.

His life had reduced itself to the functions of weaving and hoarding, without any contemplation of an end towards which the functions tended. The same sort of process has perhaps been undergone by wiser men, when they have been cut off from faith and love—only, instead of a loom and a heap of guineas, they have had some erudite research, some ingenious project, or some well-knit theory.

17 ☐ Mark for Review

Which choice best states the main idea of the text?

A. Silas Marner's life was centered around academic pursuits.

B. Silas's life was devoid of purpose, focused only on repetitive tasks.

C. Wealth and possessions were the primary concerns for most men in Raveloe.

D. Silas often compared his life to that of wiser men.

During the Renaissance, artists and thinkers were inspired by classical art, science, and literature from ancient Greece and Rome. This revival not only influenced the art of the period but also introduced new techniques and perspectives. Painters like Leonardo da Vinci and Michelangelo adopted these methods, leading to some of the most iconic artworks in history.

18 ☐ Mark for Review

Which choice best states the main idea of the text?

A. Michelangelo and Leonardo da Vinci were the only significant artists of the Renaissance period.

B. The Renaissance was marked by the revival of classical influences, profoundly affecting the arts and sciences.

C. Artists during the Renaissance period strictly adhered to ancient techniques without introducing any new ones.

D. Ancient Greek and Roman literature had no influence on the Renaissance thinkers.

In ancient times, the Library of Alexandria in Egypt was a beacon of knowledge, housing thousands of scrolls containing the accumulated wisdom of antiquity. The library's exact fate remains a mystery, as records of its ultimate destruction are scarce. However, its legacy persists, symbolizing the value humans have long placed on collecting and preserving knowledge for future generations.

19 ⎗ Mark for Review

Which choice best states the main idea of the text?

- (A) The exact date of the destruction of the Library of Alexandria is unknown.
- (B) The Library of Alexandria was primarily known for its vast collection of scrolls.
- (C) The Library of Alexandria represents the enduring human desire to store and cherish knowledge.
- (D) Ancient records about the library are the primary sources of knowledge for modern historians.

Octopuses are renowned for their intelligence and adaptability. Their soft bodies allow them to squeeze through tiny spaces, change color to match their surroundings, and even use tools. While they have been observed opening jars to get food and camouflaging themselves from predators, their lifespan is surprisingly short, usually lasting only one to two years.

20 ⎗ Mark for Review

Which choice best states the main idea of the text?

- (A) Octopuses have a shorter lifespan compared to other intelligent creatures.
- (B) Octopuses are recognized for their ability to change color and open jars.
- (C) Despite their impressive intelligence and adaptability, octopuses live only a short time.
- (D) The soft bodies of octopuses are the primary reason for their adaptability.

The following text is adapted from Walt Whitman's poem *O Me! O Life!*

Oh me! Oh life! of the questions of these recurring,
Of the endless trains of the faithless, of cities filled with the foolish,
Of myself forever reproaching myself, (for who more foolish than I, and who more faithless?)
Of eyes that vainly crave the light, of the objects mean, of the struggle ever renewed,
Of the poor results of all, of the plodding and sordid crowds I see around me,
Of the empty and useless years of the rest, with the rest me intertwined,
The question, O me! so sad, recurring—What good amid these, O me, O life?

21 🔖 Mark for Review

Which choice best states the main idea of the text?

A) The poem celebrates the vibrant and bustling life in cities.

B) The speaker is content and satisfied with the life he observes around him.

C) The poem reflects on the challenges and disappointments of life.

D) The speaker is focused on the positive outcomes of life's struggles.

Throughout the 20th century, plastic emerged as a popular and versatile material, revolutionizing industries from packaging to automotive. Its durability and longevity made it particularly sought after. However, these same qualities contributed to a growing environmental crisis. Non-biodegradable plastic waste began accumulating in landfills and oceans, threatening marine life and the ecosystem.

22 🔖 Mark for Review

Which choice best states the main idea of the text?

A) Plastic has been the primary material for the automotive industry in the 20th century.

B) The durability of plastic has led to an environmental crisis due to its non-biodegradability.

C) Marine life is the only aspect of the ecosystem affected by plastic waste.

D) Industries have completely stopped using plastic due to its environmental impact.

The following text is adapted from E.M. Forster's 1908 novel *A Room with a View*. Lucy Honeychurch is on a journey in Italy, experiencing the beauty of the countryside.

She did not answer. From her feet the ground sloped sharply into view, and violets ran down in rivulets and streams and cataracts, irrigating the hillside with blue, eddying round the tree stems collecting into pools in the hollows, covering the grass with spots of azure foam.

23 ☐ Mark for Review

Which choice best states the main idea of the text?

(A) Lucy was overwhelmed by the beauty of the Italian landscape.

(B) The hillside was devoid of any vegetation or color.

(C) Lucy was searching for an answer amidst the beauty around her.

(D) The violets were the only plants growing on the hillside.

Robotic Process Automation (RPA) is a technology that uses software robots or 'bots' to automate routine tasks, which can free up human workers to focus on more complex and creative tasks. By mimicking human actions in carrying out tasks, RPA bots can drastically improve efficiency and accuracy. While RPA offers promising benefits, it also raises concerns about job displacement and data security.

24 ☐ Mark for Review

Which choice best states the main idea of the text?

(A) RPA is a promising technology that is likely to replace human workers in routine tasks.

(B) RPA is a technology that improves efficiency and accuracy but raises concerns about job displacement and data security.

(C) RPA bots mimic human actions and are primarily used to improve accuracy in tasks.

(D) Concerns about job displacement and data security are hindering the widespread adoption of RPA.

CHAPTER 04

Main Purpose

Objective: Determine the author's primary reason for writing the passage, focusing on the overarching goal or function the text serves.

Step 1: Read the Passage Carefully

o Grasp the main topic and focus on the introduction and conclusion, which often reveal the purpose.

Step 2: Identify the Author's Intent

o Purpose Categories: Decide if the author aims to inform, persuade, explain, describe, argue, or evaluate.

o Focus on Intent (Why): Understand why the author wrote the passage.

Step 3: Recognize Shifts and Contrasts

o Do Not Miss Contrast Words: Words like "however," "but," "nevertheless" can indicate the author's main purpose.

o Understand the Shift: The author's true purpose may be revealed after these words.

Step 4: Understand the Structure of the Passage

o Analyze How Ideas Are Organized: Look for patterns like problem-solution, cause-effect, or comparison-contrast.

Step 5: Evaluate Each Answer Choice Carefully

o Relevance to the Entire Passage: Ensure the choice reflects the main purpose of the whole text.

o Avoid Distractors: Eliminate options that are too narrow, too broad, or not aligned with the author's intent.

Step 6: Select the Best Answer

o Match with Your Understanding: Choose the option that best aligns with the author's main purpose.

o Double-Check Against the Passage: Confirm that your choice is supported by the text.

Example Question

Artificial intelligence (AI) holds tremendous promise, but also potential risks that need societal attention. As AI sophistication increases, it's impacting significant areas: employment eligibility, credit scoring, healthcare, and even legal sentencing. Yet, these systems can be opaque, leading to concerns about fairness, bias, and accountability. AI's impact on privacy and data security is also profound, due to potential data misuse. As we advance in AI, it's crucial to continually assess and mitigate these risks.

☐ Mark for Review

Which choice best states the main purpose of the text?

(A) To call attention to the risks of AI

(B) To argue that AI technology should be banned

(C) To illustrate the benefits of using AI

(D) To discuss the data security features of AI

STEP 1 ► Read the Passage Carefully:
- Content Summary:
  - Introduction: Artificial intelligence (AI) offers significant promise but also poses potential risks requiring societal attention.
  - Impact Areas: AI is affecting critical sectors like employment eligibility, credit scoring, healthcare, and legal sentencing.
  - Concerns: These AI systems can be opaque, leading to issues of fairness, bias, and accountability.
  - Privacy and Data Security: AI significantly impacts privacy due to potential data misuse.
  - Conclusion: As AI advances, it's crucial to assess and mitigate these risks continuously.

STEP 2 ► Identify the Author's Intent:
- Primary Purpose: To highlight the potential risks associated with AI and emphasize the need for ongoing assessment and mitigation of these risks as AI technology progresses.
- Focus: Drawing attention to the societal concerns and dangers posed by AI, despite its promise.

STEP 3 ► Recognize Contrasts and Shifts:
- Contrast Word: "But" in the first sentence indicates a shift from discussing AI's promise to its risks.
- Understanding the Shift: While acknowledging AI's benefits, the author emphasizes the significant risks that need attention.

STEP 4 ▶ Understand the Structure of the Passage

1. Acknowledgment of AI's Promise: Recognizes the tremendous potential of AI.
2. Introduction of Risks: Presents the potential risks that accompany AI's advancement.
3. Specific Concerns:
   - Opaqueness of AI systems.
   - Issues of fairness, bias, and accountability.
   - Impact on privacy and data security due to data misuse.
4. Call to Action: Stresses the importance of assessing and mitigating these risks as AI continues to develop.

STEP 5 ▶ Choose the Best Answer:

Option A: To call attention to the risks of AI
- Analysis:
  - Accurate Representation: Aligns with the primary focus of the passage.
  - Reflects Author's Intent: Highlights the need for societal attention to AI's risks.

Option B: To argue that AI technology should be banned
- Analysis:
  - Too Extreme: The passage does not advocate for banning AI.
  - Contradicts Introduction: The author acknowledges AI's tremendous promise.

Option C: To illustrate the benefits of using AI
- Analysis:
  - Opposite Focus: While the promise of AI is mentioned, the passage centers on risks, not benefits.
  - Does Not Match Main Purpose: The main emphasis is on potential dangers, not advantages.

Option D: To discuss the data security features of AI
- Analysis:
  - Too Narrow: Data security is one of several risks mentioned.
  - Does Not Encompass Entire Passage: The passage addresses multiple concerns beyond just data security.

STEP 6 ▶ Select the Best Answer:

Best Choice: Option A

Justification: It precisely captures the main purpose of the text—to highlight the risks associated with AI and emphasize the need for societal attention and mitigation efforts.

Main Purpose Problem Set

With the advent of 3D printing in recent years, anyone can now make tangible objects from digital models. A CAD application is used to build the design at first, or a pre-made design file is downloaded. This file is read by the 3D printer, which then adds more material in layers until the print is finished. The materials utilized can vary, although thermoplastics are frequently used in home printers whereas metal alloys or ceramics may be used in commercial printers. The final product could be anything, including useful mechanical components or aesthetic artifacts.

1 ☐ Mark for Review

Which choice best states the main purpose of the text?

(A) To highlight the aesthetic artifacts that can be produced through 3D printing.

(B) To emphasize the importance of CAD applications in the 3D printing industry.

(C) To differentiate between the materials used in home and commercial 3D printers.

(D) To provide an overview of the 3D printing process.

Research into avian communication has produced some fascinating findings, particularly with regard to crows. Several studies have specifically analyzed note patterns in crow calls, aiming to discern their functions. These investigations have revealed that crows use specific patterns to signal danger, identify food sources, and even communicate individual identity. Notably, these patterns vary across different crow populations, implying a degree of regional "dialect" within this species.

2 ☐ Mark for Review

Which choice best states the main purpose of the text?

(A) To describe studies that identified the function of particular note patterns in crow calls

(B) To summarize that crows are the most intelligent bird species

(C) To account for a discrepancy between the results of several studies that analyzed note patterns

(D) To compare crow communication patterns with those of other birds

Slavery is a desecration of the basic principles that America stands for and is an institution that has marred the history of our country. It undercuts the libertarian and just values that our forefathers battled for. The rights to life, liberty, and the pursuit of happiness should not be denied to anyone, regardless of where they were born. We must categorically repudiate this institution as a distortion of our national values in order to protect our moral compass, our confidence in mankind, and the principles of our democracy.

3 ☐ Mark for Review

Which choice best states the main purpose of the text?

A. To argue that the founding fathers were against slavery

B. To convince the audience that slavery opposes American values

C. To discuss the history of slavery in America

D. To debate the effects of slavery on modern society

Stem cells are unique cells with the potential to develop into many different cell types in the body. They serve as a sort of internal repair system, dividing without limit to replenish other cells. Stem cell research has been a topic of much debate and excitement, primarily because of its potential in regenerative medicine and therapeutic interventions. While the promise of using stem cells to treat diseases like Parkinson's and diabetes is immense, ethical concerns, particularly regarding embryonic stem cells, have led to controversies and regulations.

4 ☐ Mark for Review

Which choice best states the main purpose of the text?

A. To explain the biological functions and characteristics of stem cells in detail.

B. To discuss the ethical dilemmas and regulatory challenges surrounding stem cell research.

C. To provide an overview of stem cell research, its potential, and associated controversies.

D. To analyze the future prospects of regenerative medicine in healthcare.

The following text is adapted from Mark Twain's 1884 novel *The Adventures of Huckleberry Finn*. In this passage, Huck reflects on the river at night:

It's lovely to live on a raft. We had the sky up there, all speckled with stars, and we used to lay on our backs and look up at them, and discuss about whether they was made or only just happened. Jim he allowed they was made, but I allowed they happened; I judged it would have took too long to make so many. Sometimes the river would quiet down, and we could hear the sounds from the shore, making everything feel close and safe.

5 ☐ Mark for Review

Which choice best states the main purpose of the text?

A. To convey the sense of wonder Huck feels while gazing at the stars.

B. To highlight a disagreement between Huck and Jim about the origin of stars.

C. To describe the peaceful nature of life on the raft and the intimacy of the river at night.

D. To express Huck's skepticism about the creation of the universe.

In 1517, Martin Luther, a German monk and theologian, penned the "95 Theses," a list of grievances against the Catholic Church's practices, particularly the sale of indulgences. By nailing his theses to the door of the Wittenberg Castle Church, Luther unintentionally sparked the Protestant Reformation, leading to significant religious, cultural, and political changes in Europe. This act, symbolic in its defiance, marked the beginning of a schism that reshaped the religious map of the continent.

6 ☐ Mark for Review

Which choice best states the main purpose of the text?

A. To discuss the architectural significance of the Wittenberg Castle Church.

B. To emphasize the impact of Luther's 95 Theses on European religious dynamics.

C. To outline the entirety of the Protestant Reformation.

D. To analyze the economic implications of the sale of indulgences.

The following text is adapted from Charles Dickens' 1859 novel *A Tale of Two Cities*. In this passage, the nature of the times is described.

It was the best of times, it was the worst of times, it was the age of wisdom, it was the age of foolishness, it was the epoch of belief, it was the epoch of incredulity, it was the season of Light, it was the season of Darkness, it was the spring of hope, it was the winter of despair.

7 🔖 Mark for Review

Which choice best states the main purpose of the text?

(A) To set the scene for a story about two cities in different parts of the world

(B) To contrast the stark differences and paradoxes of the era described in the novel

(C) To emphasize the hopeful aspects of the time period over the negatives

(D) To provide a historical account of the cities' development during that time period

---

Mikhail Gorbachev, who became the leader of the Soviet Union in 1985, is best known for his policies of glasnost (openness) and perestroika (restructuring). These reforms aimed to increase transparency and reduce the state's control over the economy. While Gorbachev's intentions were to modernize the Soviet system, the rapid changes inadvertently hastened its collapse in 1991. His leadership and the subsequent events significantly altered the geopolitical landscape of the late 20th century.

8 🔖 Mark for Review

Which choice best states the main purpose of the text?

(A) To discuss the entire history of the Soviet Union.

(B) To highlight the geopolitical changes in the late 20th century.

(C) To outline Mikhail Gorbachev's reforms and their global implications.

(D) To analyze the economic structure of the Soviet Union.

The following text is from Rudyard Kipling's 1890 poem "If—."

If you can talk with crowds and keep your virtue,
Or walk with Kings- -nor lose the common touch,
If neither foes nor loving friends can hurt you,
If all men count with you, but none too much:
If you can fill the unforgiving minute
With sixty seconds' worth of distance run,
Yours is the Earth and everything that's in it,
And- -which is more- -you'll be a Man, my son!

9 ☐ Mark for Review

Which choice best states the main purpose of the text?

(A) To describe the characteristics of an ideal man.

(B) To outline the political issues of the late 19th century.

(C) To detail the process of running a successful business.

(D) To explain the workings of the natural world.

In 1991, British computer scientist Tim Berners-Lee introduced the World Wide Web, a system that allowed documents to be linked via hypertext. This innovation was built on top of the existing internet infrastructure. Before this, the internet was primarily used by researchers and the military. Berners-Lee's invention made it possible for the general public to access and share information on a global scale, leading to an explosion of websites and online services.

10 ☐ Mark for Review

Which choice best states the main purpose of the text?

(A) To highlight the military uses of the early internet

(B) To discuss the global impact of the World Wide Web

(C) To explain the technical details of hypertext

(D) To showcase the achievements of British computer scientists

Even though the stain of slavery has mostly been eliminated, our fight is far from ending. People are still imprisoned in bonds, denied their freedom, and subjected to immoral forms of exploitation in some parts of the world. This conflict demands our steadfast dedication and concerted effort. Let's resist getting comfortable with progress. Our shared humanity and beliefs compel us to continue this struggle. We must unite and keep working until every chain is destroyed and until everyone, not just the affluent, is guaranteed the right to freedom.

11 ☐ Mark for Review

Which choice best states the main purpose of the text?

- A) To discuss the history of slavery and its abolition
- B) To analyze the socio-economic factors contributing to modern slavery
- C) To rally a sympathetic audience to continue working against slavery
- D) To criticize governments for their inaction against slavery

As dual-income households became prevalent in the 20th century, the "latchkey kid" phenomenon arose. These children, returning home after school to an empty house due to working parents, carried a house key to let themselves in. Often, they were tasked with self-care, including preparing meals and overseeing their own schedules. While this situation often fostered independence and self-reliance in many, it also sparked concerns about their safety, potential loneliness, and emotional well-being.

12 ☐ Mark for Review

Which choice best states the main purpose of the text?

- A) To explain the origin of the term "latchkey kid"
- B) To discuss the rise of dual-income households
- C) To highlight the responsibilities of latchkey kids
- D) To address the pros and cons of children being left unsupervised

The Great Leap Forward, initiated in 1958 by Mao Zedong, was an ambitious social and economic campaign aimed at rapidly transforming China from an agrarian society into an industrialized nation. Central to this plan was the collectivization of agriculture and the establishment of people's communes. However, the campaign led to widespread famine due to a combination of social, political, and natural factors, resulting in the deaths of millions. By 1962, the initiative was deemed a failure and was eventually abandoned, leaving a lasting impact on Chinese society and its political landscape.

13 ◻ Mark for Review

Which choice best states the main purpose of the text?

(A) To discuss the agricultural practices in China before 1958.

(B) To highlight the leadership style of Mao Zedong.

(C) To outline the intentions and consequences of The Great Leap Forward.

(D) To analyze the political landscape of China post-1962.

The following text is from William Butler Yeats's 1892 poem *The Stolen Child*. In this poem, the speaker is a fairy, talking to a human child.

Come away, O human child!
To the waters and the wild
With a faery, hand in hand,
For the world's more full of
weeping than you can understand.

14 ◻ Mark for Review

Which choice best states the main purpose of the text?

(A) To argue that the child should reject all human relationships

(B) To detail the wonders of the natural world around the child

(C) To express the fairy's contempt for the human world

(D) To persuade the child to escape the sorrows of the human world and join the fairy world

During the Progressive Era in the United States, spanning the late 19th and early 20th centuries, a group of journalists known as the "muckrakers" emerged. These investigative reporters, including figures like Upton Sinclair, Ida Tarbell, and Lincoln Steffens, sought to expose societal issues, corruption, and abuses of power. Their in-depth articles and books, often published in popular magazines, played a pivotal role in raising public awareness and pushing for reforms in areas like labor rights, public health, and corporate malfeasance.

15 🔖 Mark for Review

Which choice best states the main purpose of the text?

(A) To provide a detailed history of the Progressive Era's social movements.

(B) To discuss the literary techniques and styles used by muckrakers.

(C) To highlight the impact and objectives of the muckrakers during the Progressive Era.

(D) To analyze the economic implications of the reforms pushed by muckrakers.

Vincent Van Gogh, a Dutch post-impressionist painter, is renowned for his expressive use of color and bold brushwork. Although he struggled with mental health issues throughout his life and only gained widespread recognition after his death, his works, such as "Starry Night" and "Sunflowers," are now among the most famous and valuable in the art world. Despite his short life, Van Gogh's influence on the world of art is immeasurable, inspiring countless artists and movements.

16 🔖 Mark for Review

Which choice best states the main purpose of the text?

(A) To highlight Vincent Van Gogh's artistic legacy and influence.

(B) To discuss the post-impressionist movement in detail.

(C) To provide a detailed biography of Vincent Van Gogh.

(D) To analyze the economic value of art.

The following text is adapted from Herman Melville's 1851 novel *Moby Dick*. In this passage, Ishmael, the narrator, talks about his reason for going to the sea.

Whenever I find myself growing grim about the mouth; whenever it is a damp, drizzly November in my soul; whenever I find myself involuntarily pausing before coffin warehouses, and bringing up the rear of every funeral I meet; and especially whenever my hypos get such an upper hand of me, that it requires a strong moral principle to prevent me from deliberately stepping into the street, and methodically knocking people's hats off—then, I account it high time to get to the sea as soon as I can.

17 🔲 Mark for Review

Which choice best states the main purpose of the text?

A To detail Ishmael's specific preparations before embarking on a sea journey

B To illustrate Ishmael's deep need for the sea as a way to combat his internal turmoil

C To emphasize the dangers that Ishmael perceives in the city

D To introduce the main antagonist of the novel

In 1989, a pro-democracy movement took shape in Beijing's Tiananmen Square. Initially sparked by the death of a reformist leader, Hu Yaobang, the movement grew as thousands of students called for democratic reforms and an end to government corruption. The peaceful protests culminated in a violent crackdown by the Chinese government on June 4th, resulting in an unknown number of deaths. The event remains a sensitive and censored topic in China.

18 🔲 Mark for Review

Which choice best states the main purpose of the text?

A To outline the events and significance of the 1989 Tiananmen Square protests.

B To discuss the life, legacy, and achievements of Hu Yaobang.

C To provide a comprehensive history of Beijing's landmarks and their significance.

D To analyze the current political climate in China.

CHAPTER 05

Overall Structure

When dealing with questions concerning the "overall structure" of a text, you're required to understand not just the content but also how ideas, themes, and arguments are arranged.
Here's a step-by-step guide:

Step 1: Read the Text Carefully

Begin by reading the provided text, ensuring you understand its literal meaning and themes. Note any significant progression or shifts in ideas or imagery.

Step 2: Identify Key Themes and Ideas

Identify the primary theme or subject matter of the text. This theme can often provide insight into the text's overall structure.

Step 3: Understand the Progression of Ideas

Determine the Organizational Pattern: Consider how the text unfolds. Common structures include:
- Cause and Effect
- Problem and Solution
- Question and Answer
- Comparison and Contrast
- Chronological Sequence
- Introduction and Examples

Step 4: Analyze the Provided Options

Consider each choice and decide how well it matches with your understanding of the text. Which option best describes how ideas or themes are arranged in the text?

Example Question

The following text is adapted from Robert Frost's 1916 poem The Road Not Taken.

> And both that morning equally lay
> In leaves no step had trodden black.
> Oh, I kept the first for another day!
> Yet knowing how way leads on to way,
> I doubted if I should ever come back.
> I shall be telling this with a sigh
> Somewhere ages and ages hence:
> Two roads diverged in a wood, and I—
> I took the one less traveled by,
> And that has made all the difference.

■ ☐ Mark for Review

Which choice best describes the overall structure of the text?

A) The speaker recounts a memory of a journey, then reflects on the meaning of his chosen path.

B) The speaker examines the appearance of two roads, then discusses the wildlife that inhabits the area.

C) The speaker expresses his struggle with indecision, then imagines a future where he is completely decisive.

D) The speaker describes a challenging task he undertook, then discusses the reward he received as a result.

STEP 1 ► Read the Passage Carefully:
The poem speaks of a decision the speaker had to make between two roads, and reflects on the choice that was made.

STEP 2 ► Identify Key Themes and Ideas:
The key theme in this poem is choice and reflection. The poet recounts a past decision between two roads, which metaphorically represent choices or decisions in life, and then reflects on the impact of his decision.

STEP 3 ► Understand the Progression of Ideas:
The poem begins with a memory of a past decision and then moves to a future reflection on that decision.

STEP 4 ► Analyze the Provided Options:

A) This option aligns with the poem. The speaker recounts a memory of a journey and reflects on the choice made.

B) The speaker does not examine the appearance of two roads nor discusses the wildlife inhabiting the area. This is an incorrect depiction of the poem's content.

C) The speaker does not specifically express his struggle with indecision nor imagines a future where he is completely decisive. The focus is more on the choice made and its impact, rather than the struggle of making a decision.

D) The poem does not describe a challenging task nor discusses a reward. It is about a decision made in the past and its lifelong impact.

Max's Note

- **Focus on "How" the Information is Presented:**
  - **Not Just the Content:** The goal is to understand the organization, not just the subject matter.

- **Be Wary of Distractors:**
  - **Partial Matches:** Some options may include correct details but misrepresent the structure.

- **Look for Keywords in Options:**
  - **Match Language:** Words in the options may mirror transition words or structural cues in the text.

Let's Practice!

Overall Structure Problem Set

The following text is adapted from W.B. Yeats's 1919 poem "The Second Coming".

Turning and turning in the widening gyre
The falcon cannot hear the falconer;
Things fall apart; the centre cannot hold;
Mere anarchy is loosed upon the world,
The blood-dimmed tide is loosed, and everywhere
The ceremony of innocence is drowned;
The best lack all conviction, while the worst
Are full of passionate intensity.

1 🔖 Mark for Review

Which choice best describes the overall structure of the text?

- (A) The speaker describes a festive ceremony, then contrasts this with the somber mood of the attendees.

- (B) The speaker laments a lost relationship, then predicts the emotional aftermath of the separation.

- (C) The speaker outlines a series of natural disasters, then considers the role of human behavior in these events.

- (D) The speaker observes the behavior of a falcon, then extrapolates this to comment on the state of the world.

The following text is adapted from Jonathan Swift's *Gulliver's Travels*. Lemuel Gulliver, a ship's surgeon, recounts his adventures as he encounters various extraordinary civilizations during his voyages.

I found myself just in the middle of a vast wilderness, as we may call it, where I saw no glimpse of water nor any sign of houses or inhabitants. I was encompassed with tall, thick trees, which formed a kind of hedge about ten yards distant from me on every side. I walked very circumspectly, for fear of being surprised, or suddenly shot with an arrow from behind or on either side. I then took off my spectacles to get a clearer view of the large object which lay at a small distance, but could make nothing of it. I advanced forward near half a mile, but could not remember to have seen such trees, or the stars to be so big.

2 🔖 Mark for Review

Which choice best describes the overall structure of the text?

(A) It describes Gulliver's initial confusion in a new land, and then focuses on his cautious exploration of the unfamiliar terrain.

(B) It portrays Gulliver's fascination with the night sky, and then delves into his observations of the surrounding wilderness.

(C) It emphasizes Gulliver's isolation, and then contrasts it with the vastness of the unknown world around him.

(D) It sets the scene of a dense forest, and then highlights Gulliver's attempts to understand his surroundings.

William Shakespeare's writing style evolved significantly from his early plays to his later works. His early plays, such as "Romeo and Juliet," often relied on romantic and dramatic tropes, with an emphasis on poetic dialogue and tragic circumstances. As his career progressed, Shakespeare's work became more complex and nuanced, as seen in "Hamlet," where psychological exploration of characters takes center stage. Finally, in his last plays, often referred to as the Romances, such as "The Tempest," Shakespeare combined elements of comedy and tragedy, creating a unique blend of both that resulted in an entirely new genre.

3 🔖 Mark for Review

Which choice best describes the overall structure of the text?

(A) It presents a chronological analysis of Shakespeare's plays, then discusses the impact of his work on contemporary playwrights.

(B) It debates the literary value of Shakespeare's work, then examines the varying public reception of his plays.

(C) It traces the evolution of Shakespeare's writing style throughout his career, highlighting examples from different periods.

(D) It outlines the characteristics of Shakespeare's early plays, then contrasts them with his later works.

The following text is from William Wordsworth's 1807 poem "I Wandered Lonely as a Cloud."

> I wandered lonely as a cloud
> That floats on high o'er vales and hills,
> When all at once I saw a crowd,
> A host, of golden daffodils;
> Fluttering and dancing in the breeze.
>
> Continuous as the stars that shine
> And twinkle on the Milky Way,
> They stretched in never-ending line
> Along the margin of a bay:
> Ten thousand saw I at a glance,
> Tossing their heads in sprightly dance.

4 ☐ Mark for Review

Which choice best describes the overall structure of the text?

(A) The speaker recalls wandering alone, then vividly describes an encounter with a field of daffodils.

(B) The speaker begins with a reflection on his solitary state, then shifts to a criticism of society's disconnection from nature.

(C) The speaker starts with an observation about clouds, then generalizes about the natural world.

(D) The speaker narrates a journey through diverse landscapes, then focuses on the significance of a particular location.

The following text is adapted from Edith Wharton's *Mrs. Manstey's View*. Mrs. Manstey is an elderly woman who finds solace in the view from her apartment window.

Mrs. Manstey lived on the top floor of an old New York house, and from her window could look out over a stretch of back gardens, which, in the spring, blossomed collectively into a blur of green. She was especially fond of the view because it gave her a glimpse of a great church dome, which, because of a bend in the street, appeared almost directly over the nearest house. On the dome was a golden cross, and this cross was Mrs. Manstey's especial joy. It glittered like a golden bird in the sun, it brooded over the twilight like a presence, and when the first lights of evening sprang up in the streets of the city, they were kindled first in the cross.

5 ☐ Mark for Review

Which choice best describes the overall structure of the text?

(A) It describes Mrs. Manstey's living situation, and then focuses on her admiration for a golden cross on a church dome.

(B) It portrays the city's transformation across different times of the day, and then emphasizes Mrs. Manstey's constant view.

(C) It emphasizes the solitude of Mrs. Manstey, and then contrasts it with the bustling life of the city.

(D) It sets the scene of an old New York house, and then delves into the details of its surroundings.

The following text is from Maya Angelou's 1978 poem "Still I Rise."

You may write me down in history
With your bitter, twisted lies,
You may tread me in the very dirt
But still, like dust, I'll rise.

Does my sassiness upset you?
Why are you beset with gloom?
'Cause I walk like I've got oil wells
Pumping in my living room.

Just like moons and like suns,
With the certainty of tides,
Just like hopes springing high,
Still I'll rise.

6 🔖 Mark for Review

Which choice best describes the overall structure of the text?

A) The speaker recounts a personal experience of betrayal, then presents her subsequent recovery.

B) The speaker reflects on historical injustices, then expresses her unwavering resilience.

C) The speaker condemns societal norms, then proposes an alternative way of life.

D) The speaker articulates a universal truth, then illustrates it with personal anecdotes.

The names of characters in J.K. Rowling's Harry Potter series often hint at their personalities or roles in the story. For instance, the villain Voldemort's name, derived from French words meaning "flight from death," underscores his obsession with immortality. Meanwhile, the name of the protagonist, Harry Potter, is more commonplace, suggesting his everyman qualities despite his unique magical abilities. The headmaster Albus Dumbledore's name combines Latin words for "white" and "bumblebee," alluding to his pure nature and Rowling's image of him humming to himself.

7 🔖 Mark for Review

Which choice best describes the overall structure of the text?

A) It first introduces a general observation about Rowling's naming strategy, then provides specific examples that illustrate this point.

B) It provides a chronological overview of how names were chosen throughout the series, then speculates about future naming patterns.

C) It discusses the importance of names in literature, then criticizes Rowling's approach to character naming.

D) It describes the characteristics of various Harry Potter characters, then reveals their names as an afterthought.

The following text is from T.S. Eliot's 1925 poem "The Hollow Men."

We are the hollow men
We are the stuffed men
Leaning together
Headpiece filled with straw. Alas!
Our dried voices, when
We whisper together
Are quiet and meaningless
As wind in dry grass
Or rats' feet over broken glass
In our dry cellar

Shape without form, shade without colour,
Paralysed force, gesture without motion;

8 🔖 Mark for Review

Which choice best describes the overall structure of the text?

A) The speaker describes a group of people living in despair, then imagines their potential redemption.

B) The speaker initially presents a criticism of society, then moves on to describe their personal alienation.

C) The speaker introduces the persona of "hollow men", then contrasts this with images of vitality and richness.

D) The speaker first declares their empty state, then draws unsettling analogies to emphasize their condition.

The following text is adapted from Elizabeth Gaskell's 1855 novel *North and South*. Margaret Hale, the protagonist, finds herself in a new environment after moving from the rural south of England to the industrial north.

Margaret sat sewing by the window in the long drawing-room at Harley Street, looking out on the head of a tree, which felt as near to the open country as she had been for days. She heard a step on the stairs, but it was only one, and she knew it was Dixon's. She lifted up her head, listening; and she heard another, a light footstep, going about the room. She opened the door very softly and listened. It was her mother.

9 🔖 Mark for Review

Which choice best describes the overall structure of the text?

A) It describes Margaret's activity and setting, and then introduces an unexpected visitor.

B) It portrays Margaret's longing for the countryside, and then shifts to her current urban surroundings.

C) It focuses on the sounds and movements in the house, and then reveals the identity of the person.

D) It sets the scene of a quiet afternoon, and then emphasizes the surprise of a familiar presence.

The following text is from Samuel Taylor Coleridge's 1798 poem "The Rime of the Ancient Mariner".

The Sun now rose upon the right
Out of the sea came he,
Still hid in mist, and on the left
Went down into the sea.

And the good south wind still blew behind,
But no sweet bird did follow,
Nor any day for food or play
Came to the mariner's hollo!

10 ☐ Mark for Review

Which choice best describes the overall structure of the text?

(A) The speaker expresses a personal fascination with the sea, then reflects on its potential dangers.

(B) The speaker presents a day in the life of a mariner, highlighting the contrast between his expectations and reality.

(C) The speaker starts with a vivid description of natural phenomena, then transitions to the human condition in this setting.

(D) The speaker depicts a serene ocean sunrise, then shifts to a description of its unsettling aftermath.

Charles Dickens had a knack for choosing names for his characters that reflected their personalities or roles in his novels. In "A Tale of Two Cities," for instance, the virtuous Lucie Manette's name evokes light, underlining her role as a beacon of hope and love in the midst of chaos. Conversely, the name of the miserly protagonist in "A Christmas Carol," Ebenezer Scrooge, has become synonymous with stinginess. Finally, in "Great Expectations," the name of the wealthy spinster Miss Havisham, which suggests "have" and "sham," points to the hollowness of wealth and social status.

11 ☐ Mark for Review

Which choice best describes the overall structure of the text?

(A) It discusses the significance of Dickens's personal history, then applies these insights to his choice of character names.

(B) It presents a theory about the symbolic meaning of names in literature, then criticizes Dickens's deviations from this theory.

(C) It starts by focusing on one specific character's name, then broadens the discussion to include the whole array of Dickens's characters.

(D) It describes the traits and roles of various characters in Dickens's novels, then reveals how their names reflect these aspects.

The following text is from Emily Dickinson's 1862 poem "Success is counted sweetest."

Success is counted sweetest
By those who ne'er succeed.
To comprehend a nectar
Requires sorest need.
Not one of all the purple Host
Who took the Flag today
Can tell the meaning of the Victory,
But he defeated — dying — on whose forbidden ear
The distant strains of triumph
Burst agonized and clear!

12 ☐ Mark for Review

Which choice best describes the overall structure of the text?

A) The speaker first discusses the idea of success, then transitions to the image of a victorious army.

B) The speaker defines success, then contrasts the perception of it between those who succeed and those who don't.

C) The speaker begins with a broad reflection on life, then narrows the focus to personal experiences.

D) The speaker explores the concept of victory in various fields, then focuses on military conquest.

Over the years, the depiction of superheroes in comic books has shifted to reflect societal changes. During the Golden Age of comic books in the 1930s and 1940s, superheroes like Superman and Captain America embodied idealized figures of hope and patriotism, symbolizing the optimism of the era. However, in the Silver Age of the 1960s and 1970s, under the influence of social upheaval and counterculture, superheroes like Spider-Man and the X-Men were portrayed as more relatable and flawed characters dealing with real-world issues. More recently, in the Modern Age, the focus has been on deconstructing the superhero genre, as seen in comics like "Watchmen," where traditional superhero tropes are questioned and subverted.

13 ☐ Mark for Review

Which choice best describes the overall structure of the text?

A) It presents a broad overview of the superhero genre, then zooms in on a particular comic book for detailed analysis.

B) It discusses the cultural significance of superheroes, then argues for a reevaluation of their role in society.

C) It chronologically traces the transformation of superhero portrayal in comic books, providing examples from different periods.

D) It introduces the concept of superheroes, then compares their depiction in comic books and movies.

The following text is adapted from Jane Austen's 1813 novel *Pride and Prejudice*. Elizabeth Bennet and Mr. Darcy are central characters who undergo a transformation in their relationship.

Elizabeth, as they drove along, watched for the first appearance of Pemberley Woods with some perturbation; and when at length they turned in at the lodge, her spirits were in a high flutter. The park was very large, and contained great variety of ground. They entered it in one of its lowest points, and drove for some time through a beautiful wood stretching over a wide extent. Elizabeth's mind was too full for conversation, but she saw and admired every remarkable spot and point of view. Mr. Darcy occasionally looked and smiled at her.

14 ◻ Mark for Review

Which choice best describes the overall structure of the text?

- (A) It portrays Elizabeth's anticipation, followed by her admiration of Pemberley's beauty.
- (B) It emphasizes Mr. Darcy's pride, and then shows Elizabeth's reaction to it.
- (C) It describes the journey to Pemberley, and then focuses on the interactions between Elizabeth and Mr. Darcy.
- (D) It reveals Elizabeth's reservations about visiting Pemberley, and then details the landscape of the estate.

The following text is adapted from Mary Shelley's 1818 novel *Frankenstein*. Victor Frankenstein is the protagonist who creates a creature that he later regrets bringing to life.

The night was dark; the rain fell in torrents, except at occasional intervals, when it was checked by a violent gust of wind which swept up the streets. I remained motionless. The thunder ceased; but the rain still continued, and the scene was enveloped in impenetrable darkness. Suddenly a flash of lightning illuminated the object, and discovered its shape plainly to me; its gigantic stature, and the deformity of its aspect, more hideous than belongs to humanity, instantly informed me that it was the wretch, the filthy demon to whom I had given life.

15 ◻ Mark for Review

Which choice best describes the overall structure of the text?

- (A) It describes a stormy night, and then reveals the sudden appearance of the creature.
- (B) It focuses on Victor's fear, and then details the creature's actions during the storm.
- (C) It portrays the natural elements, and then emphasizes the unnatural creation of Victor.
- (D) It reveals the creature's intentions, and then describes the setting in which it appears.

The following text is from Edgar Allan Poe's 1845 poem "The Raven".

Once upon a midnight dreary, while I pondered, weak and weary,
Over many a quaint and curious volume of forgotten lore—
While I nodded, nearly napping, suddenly there came a tapping,
As of someone gently rapping, rapping at my chamber door.
"'Tis some visitor," I muttered, "tapping at my chamber door—
Only this and nothing more."

And the silken, sad, uncertain rustling of each purple curtain
Thrilled me—filled me with fantastic terrors never felt before;
So that now, to still the beating of my heart, I stood repeating
"'Tis some visitor entreating entrance at my chamber door—
Some late visitor entreating entrance at my chamber door;—
This it is and nothing more."

Which choice best describes the overall structure of the text?

A) The speaker reflects on a mysterious event from his past, then transitions to his emotional reaction to the event.

B) The speaker sets up a haunting atmosphere, then introduces a mysterious occurrence that increases tension.

C) The speaker begins with a lighthearted reminiscence, then introduces a dark twist.

D) The speaker presents a chilling tale, then questions the reliability of his own narrative.

The following text is adapted from Paul Laurence Dunbar's story *The Visiting of Mother Danbury*. The tale revolves around the wisdom of Mother Danbury, a respected elder in the community.

The sun was setting, casting a golden hue over the town. Children's laughter echoed, a sweet sound amidst the evening calm. But as the shadows lengthened, a group of adults formed a line outside a particular house. They waited patiently, each carrying their own burdens of worry. Inside, Mother Danbury, the wise old woman of the village, prepared to listen.

17 ☐ Mark for Review

Which choice best describes the overall structure of the text?

- (A) It describes the setting sun and children playing, and then introduces a gathering at Mother Danbury's house.
- (B) It contrasts the joyous sounds of children with the solemnity of adults seeking counsel.
- (C) It sets the scene of a village evening, and then focuses on the revered role of Mother Danbury.
- (D) It portrays the daily activities of the village, and then emphasizes the importance of seeking guidance.

The following text is from Robert Frost's 1916 poem "Birches."

When I see birches bend to left and right
Across the lines of straighter darker trees,
I like to think some boy's been swinging them.
But swinging doesn't bend them down to stay
As ice-storms do. Often you must have seen them
Loaded with ice a sunny winter morning
After a rain. They click upon themselves
As the breeze rises, and turn many-colored
As the stir cracks and crazes their enamel.

18 ☐ Mark for Review

Which choice best describes the overall structure of the text?

- (A) The speaker begins by describing birch trees, then elaborates on two possible reasons for their bending.
- (B) The speaker reminisces about a past experience, then relates it to his current observations about nature.
- (C) The speaker presents a symbolic reading of birch trees, then questions the validity of his interpretation.
- (D) The speaker observes the effects of a natural event, then makes an environmental appeal.

The following text is adapted from Nathaniel Hawthorne's *The Scarlet Letter*. The novel revolves around Hester Prynne, who is punished for adultery by having to wear a scarlet letter "A".

A crowd of eager and curious schoolboys, understanding little of the matter in hand, and mightily refreshed by the minister's voice, which had always affected them as by the mutterings of an earthquake, or some other terrible phenomenon, listened with wide-opened mouth and stupid eyes. They saw the minister, with a flush of triumph in his face, as one who, in the crisis of acutest pain, had won a victory. Then, down he sank upon the scaffold. Hester partly raised him, and supported his head against her bosom. Old Roger Chillingworth knelt down beside him, with a blank, dull countenance, out of which a life seemed to have departed.

19 ☐ Mark for Review

Which choice best describes the overall structure of the text?

(A) It describes the reaction of schoolboys to a public event, and then shifts focus to the minister's condition and those around him.

(B) It portrays the public punishment of Hester Prynne, and then emphasizes the reactions of key characters.

(C) It focuses on the minister's triumph, and then contrasts it with his subsequent weakness and the reactions of those around him.

(D) It sets the scene of a public gathering, and then delves into the personal struggles of the main characters.

The following text is adapted from Emily Dickinson's 1861 poem "Hope is the thing with feathers."

"Hope" is the thing with feathers -
That perches in the soul -
And sings the tune without the words -
And never stops - at all -
And sweetest - in the Gale - is heard -
And sore must be the storm -
That could abash the little Bird
That kept so many warm -
I've heard it in the chillest land -
And on the strangest Sea -
Yet - never - in Extremity,
It asked a crumb - of me.

20 ☐ Mark for Review

Which choice best describes the overall structure of the text?

(A) The speaker discusses the singing of a bird, then compares it to the singing of people in different parts of the world.

(B) The speaker describes a journey she took, then recalls the sights and sounds she experienced along the way.

(C) The speaker presents a metaphor for hope, then expands upon its characteristics and resilience in various circumstances.

(D) The speaker introduces a rare and beautiful creature, then narrates her attempts to capture it.

CHAPTER 06
The Function of a Sentence

Step 1: Read and Understand the Entire Passage

o Comprehend the Context: Read the entire passage carefully to grasp the main ideas, arguments, and overall flow.

o Identify the Purpose: Determine the author's primary purpose and the main point of the passage.

Step 2: Identify the Sentence's Role

Analyze the sentence in question and categorize its function. Some common functions include:

- Introduction: Introducing a new idea, topic, or argument.
- Thesis Statement: Presenting the main argument or claim of the passage.
- Evidence or Example: Providing support, evidence, or examples for a claim or argument.
- Explanation or Elaboration: Clarifying or expanding on a point previously mentioned.
- Counterargument or Concession: Acknowledging an opposing viewpoint or alternative perspective.
- Rebuttal or Refutation: Challenging or disproving a counterargument.
- Transition or Connection: Linking ideas, signaling a shift in focus, or summarizing previous points.
- Conclusion or Summary: Summing up arguments or drawing a conclusion from the presented information.
- Emphasis or Highlighting: Stressing the importance of a particular point or idea.
- Definition or Clarification: Defining terms or concepts to aid understanding.
- Cause and Effect: Explaining reasons for a situation or the consequences of an action.

Step 3: Understand the Answer Choices

Read all the answer choices carefully. Some of them might sound plausible, but there's usually only one that truly reflects the sentence's function in the context of the entire passage.

Step 4: Eliminate Incorrect Answers

Begin eliminating answer choices that don't fit. This can be the most challenging step since some incorrect options might seem plausible at first glance. Try to look for discrepancies between the answer choices and the text.

Step 5: Choose the Best Answer

After eliminating the incorrect choices, select the answer that best describes the sentence's function. If you're unsure, go back to the sentence and the passage and reassess its role.

Keep in mind that these steps may vary based on the complexity of the text and the sentence in question. It's essential to practice this approach to improve your reading comprehension skills and become proficient in answering these types of questions.

Example Question

According to historian John Lee, African American men played a pivotal role in the development of jazz music during the Harlem Renaissance. During this era, nightclubs and performance venues flourished in Harlem, offering new opportunities for musicians. The increased popularity of jazz music gave these artists greater influence in the music industry: <u>musicians negotiated for better pay and artistic control, and producers, eager to capitalize on the jazz craze, often agreed.</u>

☐ Mark for Review

Which choice best describes the function of the underlined portion in the text as a whole??

- (A) It elaborates on a claim about the music industry's dynamics in a specific era made earlier in the text.

- (B) It offers an example of a trend in the Harlem Renaissance–era culture discussed earlier in the text.

- (C) It notes a possible exception to the historical narrative of musical evolution sketched earlier in the text.

- (D) It provides further details about the musicians' identities discussed earlier in the text.

STEP 1 ▶ Read and Understand the Entire Passage:

The passage describes a young boy named John, living near the St. John River.
The description reveals that John is a dreamy, imaginative child.

STEP 2 ▶ Identify the Sentence's Role:

Context: The sentence follows the statement that the increased popularity of jazz gave artists greater influence in the music industry.
Function: It provides specific details about how musicians used their increased influence:

- Negotiated for better pay
- Sought artistic control
- Producers agreed due to the jazz craze

This sentence **elaborates on how the dynamics of the music industry changed** during the Harlem Renaissance, highlighting the negotiations between musicians and producers.

STEP 3 ▶ Understand the Answer Choices:

A) It elaborates on a claim about the music industry's dynamics in a specific era made earlier in the text.

B) It offers an example of a trend in the Harlem Renaissance–era culture discussed earlier in the text.

C) It notes a possible exception to the historical narrative of musical evolution sketched earlier in the text.

D) It provides further details about the musicians' identities discussed earlier in the text.

STEP 4 ▶ Eliminate Incorrect Answers:

C) The underlined sentence does not mention any exceptions; it describes a general occurrence.

D) The sentence focuses on actions (negotiations and agreements) rather than personal identities.

STEP 5 ▶ Choose the Best Answer:

Now, we need to choose between Option A and Option B.

A) The sentence gives details on how musicians gained leverage in the industry (negotiating better pay and control) and how producers responded. This elaborates on the earlier claim about increased influence.

B) While the sentence could be seen as illustrating a cultural trend, it's more specifically detailing industry negotiations rather than broader cultural trends.

So, the correct answer is A. The underlined sentence elaborates on how the music industry's dynamics changed during the Harlem Renaissance by providing specific examples of musicians negotiating for better conditions and producers agreeing. It directly builds upon the earlier mention of artists gaining greater influence in the industry.

The Function of a Sentence Problem Set

The following passage is based on historical accounts by researcher Amanda Y. Smith, focusing on the roles of African American women during the Civil Rights Movement.

During this period, numerous local businesses were involved in discriminatory practices. This included everything from retail outlets to transport services. Enhanced consumer activism provided increased influence for these businesses' clientele, a significant number of whom were African American women: "the customers demanded improved equal service rights, and business owners, eager to avoid public backlash and maintain their operations, complied." Consequently, the Civil Rights Movement became an arena for African American women to exhibit their influence and impact.

1 ◻ Mark for Review

Which choice best describes the function of the portion in quotation marks in the text as a whole?

- (A) It expands on a statement about customer-business interactions in a specific sector discussed earlier in the text.

- (B) It serves as an illustration of a societal shift during the Civil Rights Movement era mentioned earlier in the text.

- (C) It points out a potential deviation from the broader narrative of the Civil Rights Movement outlined earlier in the text.

- (D) It provides additional information about the identity of the customers referenced earlier in the text.

"The increasing popularity of biodegradable materials for creating art sculptures will lead to the decline of art history preservation." Artists' original sculptures, when made, are intended to be showcased and appreciated in their time, but they later become historians' principal sources for understanding cultural and artistic evolution. In the future, most such sculptures are likely to be made from materials that degrade over time, so the most intricate, valuable artworks will be lost to history unless they are preserved in controlled environments.

2 ◻ Mark for Review

Which choice best describes the function of the portion in quotation marks in the text as a whole?

- (A) It provides a summary of the potential impact of a current trend in art.

- (B) It illustrates the materials used by artists in creating sculptures.

- (C) It offers a critique of modern art preservation techniques.

- (D) It argues for the preservation of historical artworks in controlled environments.

The chestnut blight fungus originated in Asia, where local chestnut species had evolved resistance to it. In 1904, the fungus was unintentionally brought to North America, where the indigenous chestnut species had no such resistance. "But evolutionary connections between pathogens and their hosts can persist over time and geographical distance." Around 1980, the fungus was detected in European chestnut forests where researchers had been monitoring chestnut trees. Within a year, most of the trees had been affected by the fungus.

3 ☐ Mark for Review

Which choice best describes the function of the portion in quotation marks in the text as a whole?

- (A) It states the hypothesis that researchers had planned to test using chestnut trees and the blight fungus.

- (B) It presents a broad concept that is exemplified by the specific case of the chestnut trees and the blight fungus.

- (C) It proposes an alternate interpretation for the results of the researchers' observations.

- (D) It gives background information that explains why the species spread to new locations.

The following excerpt is from *Moby Dick* by Herman Melville.

Whenever I find myself growing grim about the mouth; whenever it is a damp, drizzly November in my soul; whenever I find myself involuntarily pausing before coffin warehouses, and bringing up the rear of every funeral I meet; and especially whenever my hypos get such an upper hand of me, that it requires a strong moral principle to prevent me from deliberately stepping into the street, and methodically knocking people's hats off—then, I account it high time to get to sea as soon as I can. "This is my substitute for pistol and ball." I quietly take to the ship. There is nothing surprising in this. If they but knew it, almost all men in their degree, some time or other, cherish very nearly the same feelings towards the ocean with me.

4 ☐ Mark for Review

Which choice best describes the function of the portion in quotation marks in the text as a whole?

- (A) It introduces a new character to the story.

- (B) It offers a detailed description of the protagonist's surroundings.

- (C) It hints at the upcoming events of the story.

- (D) It indicates the protagonist's coping mechanism.

The following text is from Mark Twain's 1884 novel *Adventures of Huckleberry Finn*.

We was feeling pretty good after breakfast, and took my canoe out on the river. The sunshine sparkled on the water, and made everything look fresh and bright. "When we went by our house, I wished I was there, but I weren't." We went on a three-mile race up the river and floated back. Jim, he couldn't get over the beauty of the morning.

5 ☐ Mark for Review

Which choice best describes the function of the portion in quotation marks in the text as a whole?

A) It highlights the protagonist's sense of adventure.

B) It reveals the protagonist's longing and emotional connection to his home.

C) It provides a vivid description of the river's scenery.

D) It emphasizes the physical exertion of the canoe trip.

The following text is from Mary Shelley's 1818 novel *Frankenstein*.

The weather was serene, and as I was unable to rest, I resolved to visit the spot where my poor William had been murdered. As I went along, the wind whispered through the trees, making them shiver in response. "No birds sang in these woods, for the presence of man, my unnatural self, had scared them away." I continued my journey, hoping for some form of closure. Each step brought back memories of William.

6 ☐ Mark for Review

Which choice best describes the function of the portion in quotation marks in the text as a whole?

A) It emphasizes the peace and tranquility of the forest.

B) It showcases the protagonist's ability to appreciate nature.

C) It symbolizes the protagonist's isolation and the consequences of his actions.

D) It highlights the protagonist's deep connection with William.

The following text is from Charlotte Brontë's 1847 novel *Jane Eyre*.

The red-room was a square chamber, very seldom slept in. Its furniture was of mahogany, covered in deep crimson. "The bed, too, had crimson curtains." The carpet was red, the table at the foot of the bed was covered with a crimson cloth. The walls were a soft fawn color, with a blush of pink in it.

Which choice best describes the function of the portion in quotation marks in the text as a whole?

A. It contrasts with the overall mood and setting of the narrative.

B. It introduces a shift in the narrative's focus.

C. It emphasizes the luxuriousness of the room's furnishings.

D. It underscores the dominant color theme of the room.

The following text is from Jane Austen's 1813 novel *Pride and Prejudice.*

Mrs. Bennet prided herself on being a good judge of character. She had an opinion on every person in town, often shared loudly over tea. "Yet, for all her confidence, she frequently misjudged those around her." Her daughters, especially Elizabeth, often found amusement in her errors. But they rarely corrected her, knowing it would only lead to more dramatic proclamations.

Which choice best describes the function of the portion in quotation marks in the text as a whole?

A. It provides background information on Mrs. Bennet's past decisions.

B. It emphasizes the irony of Mrs. Bennet's self-perception versus reality.

C. It portrays Elizabeth as the primary source of the narrative's humor.

D. It introduces a new character to the narrative.

The following text is from Herman Melville's 1851 novel *Moby-Dick*.

Call me Ishmael. Some years ago—never mind how long precisely—having little or no money in my purse, and nothing particular to interest me on shore, I thought I would sail about a little and see the watery part of the world. "It is a way I have of driving off the spleen and regulating the circulation." Whenever I find myself growing grim about the mouth; whenever it is a damp, drizzly November in my soul; I account it high time to get to sea as soon as I can.

9 ☐ Mark for Review

Which choice best describes the function of the portion in quotation marks in the text as a whole?

A It provides a detailed account of the protagonist's financial situation.

B It offers a humorous reflection on the protagonist's whims and decisions.

C It elucidates the personal remedy the protagonist employs when feeling melancholic.

D It serves as a transition between the protagonist's introduction and his maritime tales.

Pottery fragments discovered in a specific mountainous region of South America correspond to a period when the climate was cold and inhospitable. While there were tribes present during this era, there were no signs of large-scale agriculture. Any natural fertile land available in this region would have attracted more tribes for cultivation. "Unless they have advanced agricultural techniques, tribes are unlikely to settle in a region where there are no naturally fertile lands available to them." Thus, these tribes had developed advanced farming methods, indicating that the inhabitants of the region had transitioned from nomadic lifestyles to settled agricultural communities.

10 ☐ Mark for Review

Which choice best describes the function of the portion in quotation marks in the text as a whole?

A It provides historical context about the agricultural practices of ancient tribes.

B It offers a general principle that supports the conclusion drawn in the text.

C It describes the physical characteristics of the pottery fragments found in the region.

D It highlights the challenges faced by the tribes in adapting to the region's conditions.

The following text is from Lewis Carroll's *Alice's Adventures in Wonderland.*

Alice opened the door and found that it led into a small passage, not much larger than a rat-hole: she knelt down and looked along the passage into the loveliest garden you ever saw. How she longed to get out of that dark hall and wander about among those beds of bright flowers and those cool fountains, but she could not even get her head through the doorway. "And even if my head would go through," thought poor Alice, "it would be of very little use without my shoulders." She went back to the table, hoping she might find another key on it, or at any rate a book of rules for shutting people up like telescopes.

11 ☐ Mark for Review

Which choice best describes the function of the underlined portion in the text as a whole?

- A) It portrays Alice's determination to overcome the obstacles she encounters.
- B) It underscores Alice's realization of the impracticality of her situation.
- C) It emphasizes the physical challenges posed by the environment.
- D) It serves as a transition between her desire and her subsequent actions.

In the dense canopy where they reside, individual parrots are noticeable because of their vibrant colors, which contrast with the green of the surrounding leaves. Yet parrots are often targeted by predators, and eagles that hunt them can see these colors vividly. It's intriguing to think how parrots continue to thrive despite their conspicuous appearance. "When parrots fly in a flock, as they often do when sensing threats, their combined colors create a dazzling display, making it challenging for a predator to focus on a single bird."

12 ☐ Mark for Review

Which choice best describes the function of the portion in quotation marks in the text as a whole?

- A) It provides an extended description of the habitat where parrots live.
- B) It offers an example of a defensive behavior exhibited by parrots.
- C) It explains the main reason why eagles target parrots.
- D) It highlights the individual beauty of each parrot within the flock.

The following text is from Paul Laurence Dunbar's *The Visiting of Mother Danbury*.

Miss Cynthy had been gone away to town for three years, and now she was coming back. The thought of her home-coming had stirred the depths of Mother Danbury's heart. It was the one great subject of conversation. "It ain't so much dat she's been away," said Mother Danbury, "but it's de trouble dat she done gone th'ough." Everyone in town knew what that trouble was.

Which choice best describes the function of the underlined portion in the text as a whole?

A) It highlights the community's lack of knowledge about Miss Cynthy's experiences.

B) It illustrates Mother Danbury's concern about the time duration of Miss Cynthy's absence.

C) It emphasizes the significance of Miss Cynthy's experiences while she was away.

D) It portrays Mother Danbury as being out of touch with the town's gossip.

The following text is adapted from Paul Laurence Dunbar's *The Tragedy of Three Forks*.

In Three Forks, life was simple and uneventful. The ebb and flow of existence was as steady as the current of its river. People came and went, were born, grew up, married, and died, with little variation in the routine. Yet, to those who lived it, it was a life full of interest. "Even the coming of a stranger was an event to be chronicled and discussed." In such a setting, tales and rumors grew, taking on a life of their own.

Which choice best describes the function of the portion in quotation marks in the text as a whole?

A) It underscores the monotonous nature of life in Three Forks.

B) It suggests the tight-knit and close community within Three Forks.

C) It highlights the significance of minor occurrences in a tranquil environment.

D) It portrays Three Forks as an unwelcoming community to outsiders.

The following text is adapted from Edith Wharton's *Mrs. Manstey's View*.

Mrs. Manstey occupied the back room on the third floor of a New York boarding house. Her windows looked out on a series of rear yards lying below the level of the street. She took no interest in the comings and goings of the occupants at the front. She had long ceased to care for the theatrically shifting scenery of the crowded thoroughfare and had come to regard her backyard view as a city spectacle. "The yard was a narrow pocket hemmed in by three tall brick walls."

Which choice best describes the function of the portion in quotation marks in the text as a whole?

(A) It highlights the bustling nature of New York life.

(B) It contrasts the confined nature of Mrs. Manstey's environment with the city's expanse.

(C) It underscores Mrs. Manstey's preference for her specific city view.

(D) It introduces a new character into Mrs. Manstey's narrative.

The following text is adapted from Willa Cather's *O Pioneers!*

On a bright winter morning, Alexandra Bergson was driving her sleigh along the country road. Her white horses trotted along briskly, making their bells jingle merrily. Alexandra sat erect in the seat, her long fur cloak protecting her from the crisp air. The land was smooth and white, and the sky was a brilliant blue. "The fields and meadows were empty, with only the distant silhouette of a lone tree or a barn."

Which choice best describes the function of the portion in quotation marks in the text as a whole?

(A) It evokes a sense of isolation and solitude in the landscape.

(B) It emphasizes the vibrant colors of the morning.

(C) It introduces a major event or turning point in Alexandra's journey.

(D) It highlights Alexandra's enthusiasm for her surroundings.

The following excerpt is from *The Mysterious Portrait* by Nikolai Gogol.

The artist walked along a long corridor, whose walls on both sides were hung with pictures. These specimens of art were destined for a forthcoming exhibition. The young painter, having hung up his own picture, stood still before another, the work of a strange artist. 'How wonderful!' he said, 'what power, what expression! I have never seen such a portrait. How living, how clearly defined against the dark background is that pale face, with its burning eyes.'

17 ☐ Mark for Review

Which choice best describes the function of the underlined portion in the text as a whole?

- (A) It indicates the artist's dissatisfaction with his own work.
- (B) It highlights the artist's recognition of an unfamiliar style.
- (C) It captures the artist's admiration and astonishment for the depicted art.
- (D) It emphasizes the crowded nature of the exhibition.

The following excerpt is from *Sister Carrie* by Theodore Dreiser.

When a girl leaves her home at eighteen, she does one of two things. Either she falls into saving hands and becomes better, or she rapidly assumes the cosmopolitan standard of virtue and becomes worse. "Of an intermediate balance, under the circumstances, there is no possibility." Carrie Meeber was of a fair type, not more clever than her neighbors, nor yet noticeably below them. Intellectually, she was not above the people about her.

18 ☐ Mark for Review

Which choice best describes the function of the portion in quotation marks in the text as a whole?

- (A) It underscores the inevitability of Carrie's choices after leaving home.
- (B) It suggests that Carrie's intellect played a major role in her decisions.
- (C) It emphasizes the importance of home and family in determining character.
- (D) It compares Carrie to other girls of her age and social standing.

The following excerpt is from *Middlemarch* by George Eliot.

Miss Brooke had that kind of beauty which seems to be thrown into relief by poor dress. Her hand and wrist were so finely formed that she could wear sleeves of stiff material with impunity. "Her profile as well as her stature and bearing seemed to gain the more dignity from her plain garments, which by the side of provincial fashion gave her the impressiveness of a fine quotation from the Bible." Dorothea knew many passages of Pascal's 'Pensées' and of Jeremy Taylor by heart.

19 ☐ Mark for Review

Which choice best describes the function of the portion in quotation marks in the text as a whole?

- (A) It emphasizes the contrast between Miss Brooke's natural beauty and the prevailing fashion trends.
- (B) It illustrates Miss Brooke's religious devotion.
- (C) It describes the societal norms regarding women's dress.
- (D) It portrays Miss Brooke's preference for modesty over ostentation.

The following excerpt is from *Mansfield Park* by Jane Austen.

Fanny Price was at this time just ten years old, and though there might not be much in her first appearance to captivate, there was, at least, nothing to disgust her relations. "She was small of her age, with no glow of complexion, nor any other striking beauty; exceedingly timid and shy, and shrinking from notice; but her air, though awkward, was not vulgar, her voice was sweet, and when she spoke, her countenance was pretty." Sir Thomas and Lady Bertram received her very kindly; and Sir Thomas, seeing how much she needed encouragement, tried to be all that was conciliating.

20 ☐ Mark for Review

Which choice best describes the function of the portion in quotation marks in the text as a whole?

- (A) It suggests that Fanny's physical appearance was the sole reason for her acceptance by her relatives.
- (B) It contrasts Fanny's physical characteristics with her gentle nature and demeanor.
- (C) It underscores Fanny's position as an outsider in the Bertram household.
- (D) It highlights the superficial values of the society in which Fanny lives.

CHAPTER 07
Illustrating a Claim

Step 1: Read the Claim Carefully

Read the provided statement, or "claim", carefully and ensure you understand what it is saying. The claim will often express an idea, opinion, or conclusion about a specific topic.

Step 2: Identify Key Points

Identify the main points in the claim. What is the subject of the claim? What is the main argument or conclusion about that subject?

Step 3: Evaluate the Options

Read each of the provided options carefully. Remember, your job is to identify the statement that best illustrates or supports the claim.

Step 4: Compare Options to Claim

Compare each option to the claim and ask yourself, does this option support or exemplify the claim? How directly does it relate to the claim's main points?

Step 5: Check for Relevance

The correct option will be directly relevant to the claim and will typically provide clear support or a clear example for the claim. Be cautious of options that may seem related but do not directly support the claim.

Step 6: Select the Best Option

Based on your analysis, select the option that best illustrates the claim.

Example Question

In his thesis, a scholar criticizes various film historians for perceiving Alfred Hitchcock merely as a suspense master, asserting they often overlook his innovative use of cinematography.

☐ Mark for Review

Which quotation from a film historian's work would best illustrate the scholar's claim?

A) "Hitchcock's films, full of suspense and intrigue, have left an indelible mark on the thriller genre."

B) "Hitchcock's understanding of audience psychology was unparalleled, contributing to his reputation as a master of suspense."

C) "It's not Hitchcock's manipulation of suspense but his revolutionary camera techniques that truly set him apart in cinematic history."

D) "Hitchcock's ability to create tension is exemplary, yet it overshadows his exceptional work in framing and camera movement."

STEP 1 ► Read the Claim Carefully:
The claim here is that film historians have often overlooked Alfred Hitchcock's innovative use of cinematography, focusing mainly on his mastery of suspense.

STEP 2 ► Identify Key Points:
The key points are the overlook of Hitchcock's "innovative use of cinematography" and the focus on his mastery of "suspense".

STEP 3 ► Evaluate the Options:
We now read the options, looking for a quote that showcases this claim.

STEP 4 ► Compare Options to Claim:
- **Option A:** This quote emphasizes Hitchcock's influence on the thriller genre, primarily focusing on his use of suspense, not his cinematography.

- **Option B:** This quote also focuses on Hitchcock's understanding of suspense, rather than his cinematography.

- **Option C:** While this quote recognizes Hitchcock's innovative use of cinematography, it doesn't indicate that this aspect of his work has been overlooked

- **Option D:** This quote mentions both Hitchcock's mastery of suspense and his innovative use of cinematography, and indicates that his cinematographic skills have been overshadowed.

STEP 5 ► Check for Relevance:
Among the options, Option D is the one that aligns with the claim that Hitchcock's mastery of suspense has often led to his cinematographic innovations being overlooked.

STEP 6 ► Select the Best Option:
Based on the analysis, Option D: "Hitchcock's ability to create tension is exemplary, yet it overshadows his exceptional work in framing and camera movement." is the best choice. It directly supports the claim that Hitchcock's mastery of suspense has often caused his innovative cinematographic techniques to be overlooked.

Illustrating a Claim Problem Set

Startups, whether in the technology sector or retail, are companies in their initial stage of operations, usually driven by unique and innovative ideas. Based on recent interviews with various startup founders, a business journalist claims that these early-stage companies can provide immense learning opportunities but can also lead to high-stress levels due to the uncertainty and risk involved.

---

1 🔖 Mark for Review

Which quotation from the interviews best illustrates the journalist's claim?

A) "Building a startup from the ground up has been an incredibly enriching experience. Every day, I am learning something new, but the uncertainty of the future can be quite stressful."

B) "Being part of a startup is very fulfilling. The sense of ownership and the ability to make impactful decisions is unparalleled."

C) "I joined the startup because I was inspired by their mission and vision. It is exciting to work with a team that is making a difference."

D) "Startups allow you to wear many hats. I have been a coder, a manager, and even a HR personnel at times. This variety keeps the job interesting."

Scientific research teams, like those at CERN or NASA, consist of professionals who agree to collaborate, possibly due to shared scientific interests, the need for various expertise, or to pool resources and equipment. Based on a recent series of interviews with various scientific research teams, a science journalist asserts that this collaboration significantly influences the individual scientist's work, who might previously have been accustomed to conducting independent research.

2 ◻ Mark for Review

Which quotation from the interviews best illustrates the journalist's claim?

(A) "My first research team had brilliant scientists, and we enjoyed working together, but due to disagreements on research credits and roles, the team eventually disbanded."

(B) "We work collaboratively, but that doesn't mean that every project involves everyone equally. Many of our projects are primarily driven by whoever proposed the initial research idea."

(C) "Having worked as part of a research team for several years, it's sometimes hard to recall what it was like to conduct research independently. The team's support doesn't stifle my individual ideas but actually fosters them."

(D) "Sometimes a scientist from outside our team collaborates with us on a project, but all of those projects fit within the larger themes of the research our team conducts individually."

Moby-Dick is an 1851 novel by Herman Melville. In the novel, Melville depicts Captain Ahab as a man whose obsession with the great white whale, Moby Dick, consumes his entire existence.

Which quotation from "Moby-Dick" most effectively illustrates the claim?

A. "He piled upon the whale's white hump the sum of all the general rage and hate felt by his whole race from Adam down; and then, as if his chest had been a mortar, he burst his hot heart's shell upon it."

B. "I leave a white and turbid wake; pale waters, paler cheeks, where'er I sail. The envious billows sidelong swell to whelm my track; let them; but first I pass."

C. "For the sea is his; he owns it, as Emperors own empires."

D. "I am madness maddened! That wild madness that's only calm to comprehend itself!"

The Great Gatsby is a 1925 novel by F. Scott Fitzgerald. In the novel, Fitzgerald portrays Jay Gatsby as a character whose life and identity are deeply shaped by his unattainable dreams.

4 🔖 Mark for Review

Which quotation from "The Great Gatsby" most effectively illustrates the claim?

A. "He had come a long way to this blue lawn, and his dream must have seemed so close that he could hardly fail to grasp it."

B. "There are only the pursued, the pursuing, the busy and the tired."

C. "I hope she'll be a fool—that's the best thing a girl can be in this world, a beautiful little fool."

D. "So we beat on, boats against the current, borne back ceaselessly into the past."

Sonnets to Orpheus is a 1922 collection of sonnets by Rainer Maria Rilke. In these sonnets, Rilke muses on the power of art and its capacity to transform and transcend reality.

5 🔖 Mark for Review

Which quotation from "Sonnets to Orpheus" most effectively illustrates the claim?

A. "See, I want a lot. Maybe I want it all: the darkness of each endless fall, the shimmering light of each ascent."

B. "Be ahead of all parting, as though it already were behind you, like the winter that has just gone by."

C. "Be, in this immensity of night, be magic power at your senses' crossroad, the meaning of their strange encounter."

D. "Every happiness is the child of a separation it did not think it could survive."

The Yellow Wallpaper is an 1892 short story by Charlotte Perkins Gilman. In the story, Gilman provides a critique of the limitations imposed on women by a patriarchal society, through the deteriorating mental health of the female protagonist.

Which quotation from "The Yellow Wallpaper" most effectively illustrates the claim?

- (A) "It is the same woman, I know, for she is always creeping, and most women do not creep by daylight."

- (B) "There are things in that paper that nobody knows but me, or ever will."

- (C) "I've got out at last," said I, "in spite of you and Jane. And I've pulled off most of the paper, so you can't put me back!"

- (D) "It does not do to trust people too much."

Ethan Frome is a 1911 novel by Edith Wharton. In the novel, Wharton describes Ethan Frome as a character deeply affected by his oppressive and isolated environment, writing, _____

Which quotation from "Ethan Frome" most effectively illustrates the claim?

A. "There was something bleak and unapproachable in his face, and he was so stiffened and grizzled that I took him for an old man and was surprised to hear that he was not more than fifty-two."

B. "The winter morning was as clear as crystal. The sunrise burned red in a pure sky, the shadows on the rim of the wood-lot were darkly blue, and beyond the white and scintillating fields patches of far-off forest hung like smoke."

C. "He seemed a part of the mute melancholy landscape, an incarnation of its frozen woe, with all that was warm and sentient in him fast bound below the surface."

D. "Ethan, looking slowly about the kitchen, said to himself that it was the room for a man to die in."

The Life of Charles Dickens is an 1874 biography by John Forster. In the biography, Forster details Dickens's profound sense of social justice, arguing that Dickens used his writing as a means of highlighting societal injustices: _____

Which quotation from "The Life of Charles Dickens" most effectively illustrates the claim?

A) "His novels are a mirror of the time, showing us the world as he sees it, full of injustice and suffering, but also of joy and love."

B) "To him, the greatest evil was poverty and its consequent degradation of human nature."

C) "He had a wonderful faculty for the description of life and character, and his sense of the ludicrous was as keen as his sense of the pathetic."

D) "He had seen in his youth, and was never tired of reiterating what he had seen, of the suffering, the horrible and brutalizing suffering, caused by the world's neglect and scorn."

An Encounter is a 1914 short story by James Joyce. In the story, Joyce delves into the complex psyche of a young boy, frequently contrasting the boy's naive worldview with the harsh realities of adult life, as when Joyce writes of the boy, _____

9 🔖 Mark for Review

Which quotation from "An Encounter" most effectively illustrates the claim?

(A) "He knew that he would regret in the morning but at present he was glad of the dark stupor that would cover up his folly."

(B) "He lived in a world of his own, a world bounded by the narrow streets of Dublin."

(C) "I wanted real adventures to happen to myself. But real adventures, I reflected, do not happen to people who remain at home: they must be sought abroad."

(D) "His face wore a look of serious purpose which I had never seen before. It was as if he had been called upon to witness some terrible scene."

Song of Myself is an 1855 poem by Walt Whitman. In the poem, Whitman advocates the idea of self-love and self-acceptance, writing, _____

10 🔖 Mark for Review

Which quotation from "Song of Myself" most effectively illustrates the claim?

(A) "I celebrate myself, and sing myself, / And what I assume you shall assume, / For every atom belonging to me as good belongs to you."

(B) "You shall no longer take things at second or third hand... nor look through the eyes of the dead...nor feed on the spectres in books."

(C) "I am large, I contain multitudes."

(D) "Do I contradict myself? Very well then I contradict myself."

My Antonia is a 1918 novel by Willa Cather. In the novel, Cather paints Antonia Shimerda as a character who is deeply connected and in tune with her natural surroundings: _____

Which quotation from "My Antonia" most effectively illustrates the claim?

A) "She was a natural-born kind of creature and natural things and creatures seemed to feel kinship with her."

B) "Antonia loved to help grandmother in the kitchen and to learn about cooking and housekeeping."

C) "Antonia had the most trusting, responsive eyes in the world; love and credulousness seemed to look out of them with open faces."

D) "Antonia had not lost the fire of life. Her skin was brown and rugged; there was something in the shape of her hands, so many years in the soil had molded them into earthy forms."

Modernist Literature is a 1922 essay by Virginia Woolf. In the essay, Woolf argues that the quality and depth of a society's literature have a profound impact on its collective psyche:

_____

Which quotation from "Modernist Literature" most effectively illustrates the claim?

A) "A society has not fulfilled its potential until it can read and write, until it can record its history and its dreams."

B) "The value of literature is its ability to illuminate the human condition, to allow us to see ourselves reflected and refracted through the lens of the written word."

C) "The vitality and vibrancy of a nation can be measured by the vitality and vibrancy of its literature."

D) "The more cultivated a society is, the more its literature matters. It helps shape societal values and principles."

Miss Brill is a 1920 short story by Katherine Mansfield. In the story, Mansfield characterizes Miss Brill as a lonely woman whose cheerful appearance masks her deep-seated loneliness and desire for companionship, as when Mansfield writes of Miss Brill, _____

Which quotation from "Miss Brill" most effectively illustrates the claim?

A. "Even she had a part and came every Sunday. No doubt somebody would have noticed if she hadn't been there; she was part of the performance after all."

B. "Miss Brill put up her hand and touched her fur."

C. "She felt a tingling in her hands and arms, but that came from walking, she supposed."

D. "And when she breathed, something light and sad—no, not sad, exactly—something gentle seemed to move in her bosom."

The following text is from Emily Brontë's 1847 novel *Wuthering Heights*. Catherine Earnshaw is known to have a deep connection with the wild moors surrounding her home: _____

Which quotation from Wuthering Heights most effectively illustrates the claim?

(A) "She had a love for the boundless moors. She found solace in the whispering wind and the sweeping heather. It was as though her spirit resided there, amidst the skylarks and the endless wild."

(B) "Catherine would talk to the house staff about the weather and the changing seasons. She would spend an entire day discussing the native flora with a visiting naturalist. She had an understanding of the environment."

(C) "Catherine journeyed through the moors alone. The crunching of her footsteps against the untamed earth was the only sound. But the solitude seemed to empower her, made her a vital part of the untamed wild."

(D) "It was Catherine who read the weather reports and anticipated the changing seasons. It was Catherine who could always tell when a storm was about to roll in, and who could name each bird by its song."

In a recent article, a nutritionist claims that many popular diet plans focus too much on short-term weight loss rather than promoting sustainable, long-term health habits.

15 ▢ Mark for Review

Which quotation from a diet book would best illustrate the nutritionist's claim?

A) "Lose 10 pounds in just 10 days with our rapid weight loss program!"

B) "Our diet plan emphasizes the importance of understanding the nutritional value of what you eat, rather than just counting calories."

C) "The key to lifelong health is not just about losing weight, but about understanding and adopting a balanced lifestyle."

D) "This diet is designed for those who want quick results, and it's not intended for long-term use."

In a documentary about urban planning, an architect claims that many modern cities prioritize cars over pedestrians, leading to less walkable and more congested urban areas.

16 ▢ Mark for Review

Which quotation from a city planning document would best illustrate the architect's claim?

A) "The primary goal of our urban development is to ensure smooth traffic flow and ample parking spaces for vehicles."

B) "Our city aims to create a balance between pedestrian walkways, bicycle lanes, and roads for vehicles."

C) "The heart of our city is its people, and we aim to create spaces where they can walk, play, and interact without the interference of vehicles."

D) "Public transportation is a secondary concern; our main focus is on expanding road networks to accommodate the increasing number of cars."

In an article for "Culinary Chronicles," a food critic delves into the world of fusion cuisine, highlighting renowned establishments like "East Meets West" in San Francisco and "Global Bites" in Chicago. The critic posits that while these restaurants offer a tantalizing blend of flavors, they sometimes risk overshadowing the rich traditions from which they draw.

Which quotation from Chef Marco Delgado of "East Meets West" would best illustrate the critic's claim?

A. "At 'East Meets West,' we pride ourselves on crafting a menu that's a culinary journey across continents."

B. "While fusion allows us to innovate, there are times when the essence of a traditional dish might take a backseat to our experimental flair."

C. "Our dishes are a testament to the beauty of blending culinary traditions, showcasing the harmony possible in every bite."

D. "Having trained in both Tokyo and Rome, I bring a unique perspective to the table, but always strive to honor the roots of each dish."

In a recent article, a journalist discusses the challenges independent bookstores face in the online shopping age. The journalist claims that while many people romanticize the idea of a local bookstore, they often overlook the financial and logistical challenges these stores face in the modern era.

Which quotation from an independent bookstore owner would best illustrate the journalist's claim?

A. "Our bookstore has been a cornerstone of this community for decades, and we've seen the landscape of reading habits change dramatically."

B. "Despite the love we receive from our community, the reality is that online giants offer prices and convenience we simply can't match."

C. "We pride ourselves on our curated selection and the personal touch we offer to every customer who walks through our doors."

D. "It's not just about selling books; it's about creating a space where people can come together and share their love for literature."

Journey to the East is a 1932 novel by Hermann Hesse. In the novel, Hesse delves into the spiritual journey of its protagonist, Leo, suggesting that true enlightenment often comes from understanding one's own self and the world around them: _____

Which quotation from "Journey to the East" most effectively illustrates the claim?

A) "Words do not express thoughts very well; everything immediately becomes a little different, a little distorted, a little foolish. And yet it also pleases me and seems right that what is of value and wisdom to one man seems nonsense to another."

B) "I had been and still was on the way; but I was no longer my own master, following my own dark path."

C) "For our goal was not only the East, or rather the East was not only a country and something geographical, but it was the home and youth of the soul, it was everywhere and nowhere, it was the union of all times."

D) "The bird fights its way out of the egg. The egg is the world. Who would be born must destroy a world."

The Dead is a short story from James Joyce's 1914 collection "Dubliners." In the story, Joyce paints a vivid picture of a society trapped by its own traditions and the past, as seen through the protagonist, Gabriel Conroy, during an annual dance and dinner in the Morkan sisters' home: _____

Which quotation from "The Dead" most effectively illustrates the claim?

A. "His soul swooned slowly as he heard the snow falling faintly through the universe and faintly falling, like the descent of their last end, upon all the living and the dead."

B. "One by one, they were all becoming shades. Better pass boldly into that other world, in the full glory of some passion, than fade and wither dismally with age."

C. "I think he died for me."

D. "Generous tears filled Gabriel's eyes. He had never felt like that himself towards any woman, but he knew that such a feeling must be love."

CHAPTER 08

Cross Text

Objective:
To accurately understand and answer cross-text analysis questions by comparing and contrasting the claims, perspectives, or findings presented in two texts.

Step 1: Read the Question Carefully

Look for the keywords in the instruction. Understand what is being asked—is it about agreement, disagreement, or how one author would respond to another's claim?

Step 2: Identify the Claims or Perspectives

Determine the central idea, argument, or claim presented in Text 1, especially focusing on any underlined or highlighted statements. Understand the stance or viewpoint being expressed regarding the keywords from the question.

Step 3: Analyze the Second Text

With your identified keywords in mind, shift your focus to the second text. What are the main points here? How do the key individuals or groups in this text relate to your keywords? What are their findings, arguments, or opinions about these topics?

Step 4: Cross-Referencing

Compare the main points of both texts, focusing on areas of agreement, disagreement, or partial agreement. Analyze how the author of Text 2 might respond to the claims or perspectives presented in Text 1, ensuring your analysis remains centered on the specific claim, statement, or issue highlighted in the question. Avoid being distracted by unrelated details.

Step 5: Review the Response Options

Understand what each response option is suggesting.
Determine how well each option aligns with the perspective of the author in Text 2 regarding the claim in Text 1.

Discard options that:
- Misrepresent the author's viewpoint.
- Introduce information not supported by Text 2.
- Reflect the wrong relationship (e.g., agreement vs. disagreement).

Step 6: Select the Best Response

Choose the response that best aligns with the views or arguments presented in the second text in relation to the claims made about the keywords in the first text. This requires careful analysis and may not be the most obvious answer.

Step 7: Justification

Always be ready to justify your choice. You should be able to explain why the chosen response best represents the stance of the individuals or groups in the second text regarding the keywords.

Max's Note

Stay Objective
Focus on the authors' perspectives, not your personal opinions.

Be Mindful of Tone and Intent
Consider the tone used by the authors—are they critical, supportive, or neutral?

Watch for Subtle Differences
Pay attention to qualifiers like "may," "must," "should," which can affect the meaning.

Time Management
Allocate your time wisely to read, analyze, and choose the best answer without rushing.

Example Question

Text 1

Deep-sea fishing presents numerous environmental challenges, not least of which is bycatch—the unintentional capture of non-target species. Traditional deep-sea fishing methods can devastate marine life, inadvertently catching and killing thousands of sea turtles, dolphins, and sharks. Many argue that current regulations on bycatch are insufficient, pointing to the need for better fishing technology and stricter enforcement of rules.

Text 2

Marine biologist Sandra Huber and her team have developed a fishing method called "precision fishing." By using advanced sonar and machine learning algorithms to identify species before they're caught, this technique aims to drastically reduce bycatch. Huber's method has been successful in early trials, but she emphasizes that the technology is only part of the solution and must be complemented by stronger regulations and a commitment to sustainability from the fishing industry.

⬛ 🔖 Mark for Review

Based on the texts, how would Sandra Huber (Text 2) most likely respond to the problems discussed in Text 1?

- (A) By endorsing the concerns raised and advocating for her precision fishing technique as a part of the solution

- (B) By dismissing the significance of bycatch and asserting the effectiveness of existing fishing methods

- (C) By downplaying the role of technology in addressing bycatch and focusing instead on regulatory changes

- (D) By arguing that the problems of bycatch are overblown and do not require substantial changes to fishing practices

STEP 1 ▶ Read the Main Instruction:

The main instruction is "Based on the texts, how would Sandra Huber (Text 2) most likely respond to the problems discussed in Text 1?" The keywords here are "Sandra Huber," "respond," and "problems discussed in Text 1."

STEP 2 ▶ Identify the Claims or Perspectives:

In Text 1, the main claims presented are that deep-sea fishing results in significant bycatch, causing environmental damage and killing non-target species. The text argues that current regulations are insufficient, and there's a need for better fishing technology and stricter rules.

STEP 3 ▶ Analyze the Second Text:

Text 2 introduces Sandra Huber, who has developed "precision fishing," a method that uses advanced technology to reduce bycatch. Huber suggests that technology is part of the solution, but also stresses the importance of stronger regulations and commitment from the fishing industry.

STEP 4 ▶ Cross-Referencing:

Comparing the two texts, it's clear that Sandra Huber's views align with the concerns raised in Text 1. She acknowledges the issue of bycatch and proposes a solution that includes advanced technology (precision fishing), reinforced regulations, and industry commitment to sustainability.

STEP 5 ▶ Review the Response Options:

Each of the response options suggests a different way Sandra Huber could respond to the issues raised in Text 1.

STEP 6 ▶ Select the Best Response:

Based on the analysis, the best response is: A)By endorsing the concerns raised and advocating for her precision fishing technique as a part of the solution

STEP 7 ▶ Justification:

This response best represents Sandra Huber's stance as presented in Text 2. She acknowledges the issues raised in Text 1 and presents her precision fishing technique as part of the solution. She doesn't dismiss or downplay the issues raised in Text 1, nor does she argue they are overblown, which eliminates options B, C, and D.

Cross Text Problem Set

Text 1

Modern science is still struggling to comprehend the nature of consciousness, despite centuries of inquiry. Traditionally, consciousness has been associated with the functioning of the human brain. However, new research has started to challenge this conception, suggesting that consciousness might not be solely a human characteristic but could extend to other animals and even to non-biological entities.

Text 2

Neuroscientist Dr. Emilia Harper and her team have been studying the potential for consciousness in AI systems. They argue that given the complexity and adaptability of advanced AI, it might be possible for these systems to develop a form of consciousness. However, Harper emphasizes that the kind of consciousness an AI might possess would be very different from human consciousness and cautions against anthropomorphizing AI systems.

---

1 ☐ Mark for Review

Based on the texts, how would Dr. Emilia Harper (Text 2) most likely respond to the claims about consciousness presented in Text 1?

- (A) By agreeing with the possibility of non-human consciousness but highlighting the need for clarity on what consciousness means for AI systems

- (B) By refuting the notion of consciousness in non-biological entities, stressing the uniqueness of human consciousness

- (C) By emphasizing the necessity of further research into the brain before exploring consciousness in non-human entities

- (D) By asserting that the idea of consciousness extending to non-human entities is purely speculative and lacks empirical evidence

Text 1

The archaeological record contains numerous examples of long-distance trade routes that developed in the Bronze Age. Such trade routes allowed civilizations to acquire valuable resources that were unavailable in their local regions. Some scholars believe that these trade networks also promoted cultural exchange and the spread of technological advancements.

Text 2

Historian Dr. Alexander Norton and his team have been studying the implications of Bronze Age trade routes. Their findings suggest that while these networks did indeed facilitate resource acquisition, the claim of significant cultural and technological diffusion might be overstated. Norton emphasizes the importance of not conflating trade of goods with exchange of ideas, as the latter involves a more complex and nuanced process.

Based on the texts, how would Dr. Alexander Norton (Text 2) most likely respond to the assertions about Bronze Age trade routes made in Text 1?

A) By supporting the notion of resource acquisition but questioning the degree of cultural and technological exchange through these trade networks

B) By refuting the existence of extensive Bronze Age trade routes and suggesting a more localized trade system

C) By emphasizing that trade routes were more about political alliances than exchange of resources, ideas, or technology

D) By asserting that the archaeological record does not offer sufficient evidence to support the idea of long-distance trade routes in the Bronze Age

Text 1

Climate change has a significant impact on global biodiversity, affecting the distribution and behavior of many species. As temperatures continue to rise, some species are forced to migrate to cooler areas, while others are unable to adapt to these changes and face extinction. The loss of these species could potentially disrupt the balance of ecosystems and lead to further environmental issues.

Text 2

Environmental scientist Dr. Leah Jensen and her team have been studying the effects of climate change on the shifting ranges of various species. While they agree that climate change forces species to adapt or migrate, they assert that these shifts can also lead to an unexpected increase in local biodiversity in some regions. However, Dr. Jensen cautions that this should not be taken as a positive side effect of climate change, as the overall impact on global biodiversity is still detrimental.

3 ☐ Mark for Review

Based on the texts, how would Dr. Leah Jensen (Text 2) most likely respond to the concerns about biodiversity outlined in Text 1?

(A) By affirming the concerns but adding the possibility of localized increases in biodiversity due to species migration

(B) By rejecting the idea that climate change leads to species migration and extinction, suggesting it has minimal impact on biodiversity

(C) By emphasizing that climate change only affects species unable to adapt, with little impact on overall biodiversity

(D) By arguing that the effect of climate change on biodiversity has been overly dramatized and is not as severe as it is presented.

Text 1

Urban planning in modern cities often involves the concept of creating green spaces. These spaces not only offer areas for recreation but also play a crucial role in improving air quality, reducing heat, and providing habitats for urban wildlife. Many believe that green spaces also enhance the mental well-being of city dwellers and encourage a healthier lifestyle.

Text 2

Architect Lena Simmons and her team have been developing 'blue spaces'—areas that incorporate bodies of water like ponds, lakes, or streams in urban planning. Simmons suggests that blue spaces can provide many of the same benefits as green spaces and, in some instances, even more. For example, blue spaces can help manage urban stormwater and support a diverse range of aquatic ecosystems. However, Simmons emphasizes that both green and blue spaces should be incorporated into city planning for maximum benefits.

---

4 ☐ Mark for Review

Based on the texts, how would Lena Simmons (Text 2) most likely respond to the claims about green spaces made in Text 1?

- (A) By dismissing the advantages of green spaces as insignificant compared to the benefits offered by blue spaces

- (B) By arguing that blue spaces are superior to green spaces in every aspect of urban planning and environmental benefits

- (C) By stating that the focus on green spaces is outdated and that modern urban planning should prioritize blue spaces

- (D) By acknowledging the benefits of green spaces but suggesting that blue spaces can provide additional advantages

Text 1

It is a widely accepted theory that the extinction of dinosaurs was due to a massive asteroid hitting the Earth around 66 million years ago. The collision is believed to have caused catastrophic changes to the Earth's climate, leading to the extinction of dinosaurs and many other species. This event is known as the Cretaceous–Paleogene (K-Pg) extinction event.

Text 2

Paleontologist Dr. Lisa Huang and her team argue that while the asteroid impact certainly played a significant role in the K-Pg extinction, it may not be the sole cause. They have discovered evidence of significant volcanic activity around the same period that could have contributed to the severe climate changes. Dr. Huang suggests that the combination of these two massive geological events is likely responsible for the mass extinction.

Based on the texts, how would Dr. Lisa Huang (Text 2) most likely respond to the theory presented in Text 1?

A) By acknowledging the impact of the asteroid collision but pointing out the potential role of volcanic activity in the K-Pg extinction

B) By challenging the theory and stating that the asteroid impact alone could not have led to the extinction of dinosaurs

C) By refuting the asteroid impact theory altogether and presenting volcanic activity as the primary cause of extinction

D) By endorsing the asteroid impact theory but suggesting that the timeline of the K-Pg extinction event needs to be revised

Text 1

Modern technology has transformed the way we work, enabling increased flexibility and remote work options. This shift is often linked to improved work-life balance and overall job satisfaction. However, it's also argued that it leads to an "always-on" culture, potentially increasing stress levels and impacting mental health.

Text 2

Psychologist Dr. Olivia Ross and her team have been studying the psychological effects of remote work. While they acknowledge the benefits of flexibility, they also emphasize the downside of blurred boundaries between work and personal life. Dr. Ross asserts that the "always-on" culture can lead to burnout, and advises implementing clear work-life boundaries even when working remotely.

Based on the texts, how would Dr. Olivia Ross (Text 2) most likely respond to the discussion on remote work presented in Text 1?

A By supporting the notion of improved work-life balance but stressing the risks of an "always-on" culture and the importance of setting boundaries

B By refuting the idea that remote work leads to increased job satisfaction and proposing that it primarily contributes to burnout

C By suggesting that the impact of remote work on mental health has been overemphasized and that the benefits largely outweigh the drawbacks

D By endorsing the advantages of remote work unconditionally and disregarding the potential negative effects on mental health

Text 1

Artificial intelligence (AI) has dramatically transformed various sectors, from healthcare to transportation. Many argue that AI, with its ability to analyze vast amounts of data and make predictions, can solve complex problems more efficiently than humans. However, critics caution about the risks of relying too heavily on AI, including job displacement and ethical concerns related to privacy and algorithmic bias.

Text 2

Computer scientist Dr. Karen Mitchell and her team specialize in the field of AI ethics. While acknowledging the benefits of AI, they insist that unchecked reliance on AI systems could lead to significant societal issues. Mitchell emphasizes the importance of designing AI with human oversight and robust ethical frameworks to minimize potential harm, such as job displacement and algorithmic bias.

7 🔖 Mark for Review

Based on the texts, how would Dr. Karen Mitchell (Text 2) most likely respond to the points about AI presented in Text 1?

(A) By agreeing with the benefits of AI but emphasizing the need for human oversight and ethical considerations in AI deployment

(B) By challenging the idea that AI can solve complex problems more efficiently than humans, highlighting its potential societal consequences

(C) By dismissing the concerns about job displacement and ethical issues, focusing on the transformative potential of AI

(D) By questioning the transformational impact of AI across various sectors, given the ethical and societal issues it presents

Text 1

Advancements in renewable energy technologies, such as solar and wind power, have made it possible to decrease our reliance on fossil fuels. These forms of energy are considered sustainable and environmentally friendly, as they do not contribute to greenhouse gas emissions. However, they are often criticized for their intermittent nature and reliance on specific geographical and weather conditions.

Text 2

Energy scientist Dr. Carlos Moreno and his team have been investigating the use of energy storage systems to mitigate the limitations of renewable energy sources. They argue that these systems, which store excess energy produced during optimal conditions for later use, could help overcome the intermittent nature of solar and wind power. Dr. Moreno, however, emphasizes that further research and innovation are needed to improve the efficiency and cost-effectiveness of these storage systems.

8 🔖 Mark for Review

Based on the texts, how would Dr. Carlos Moreno (Text 2) most likely respond to the discussion on renewable energy presented in Text 1?

- (A) By confirming the criticisms but suggesting that energy storage systems could address the intermittency of renewable energy sources

- (B) By disputing the limitations of renewable energy, asserting that the intermittency issue is overblown and can be readily managed

- (C) By insisting that the focus should be on improving the efficiency of renewable energy sources rather than on developing energy storage systems

- (D) By arguing that despite their environmental benefits, renewable energy sources cannot replace fossil fuels due to their inherent limitations

CHAPTER 09
Supporting/Weakening a Claim

Supporting claim questions aim to identify information or new findings that bolster or validate a stated hypothesis or claim. To efficiently tackle these questions, adhere to the following strategy:

STEP 1 : Read the Question Carefully

- Identify the Task: Determine whether the question asks you to support or weaken a claim.
- Highlight the Claim or Hypothesis: Note exactly what claim or hypothesis you need to evaluate.

STEP 2: Understand the Claim or Hypothesis

- Paraphrase the Claim: Restate it in your own words to ensure comprehension.
- Identify Key Components: Pinpoint the main ideas, assumptions, or relationships within the claim.
- Determine the Underlying Reasoning: Understand the logic or evidence the claim is based on.

STEP 3: Predict the Type of Evidence Needed

- For Supporting: Think about what evidence would strengthen the claim or provide additional justification.
- For Weakening: Consider what evidence would undermine the claim, expose flaws, or present exceptions.

STEP 4: Analyze Each Answer Choice

- Relevance: Does the option directly relate to the claim?
- Impact on the Claim:
  - Supports: Provides evidence that strengthens or validates the claim.
  - Weakens: Introduces information that challenges or contradicts the claim.
- Eliminate Irrelevant or Neutral Options: Discard choices that do not affect the claim.

STEP 5: Select the Best Answer

> o Direct Effect: Choose the option that has the most immediate and significant impact on the claim.
>
> o Logical Consistency: Ensure the choice logically supports or weakens the claim without requiring unreasonable assumptions.

Example Question

At the peak of the Himalayas, two moss species, Bryum argenteum and Sanionia uncinata, are known to survive in harsh, freezing temperatures with limited nutrient availability. Botanist Dr. Alan Peterson and his team conducted detailed studies of these mosses and discovered that they have an unusual cellular structure in their chloroplasts. Further examination suggested that these unique structures may help the plants survive in low temperatures by enhancing photosynthetic efficiency. Dr. Peterson hypothesizes that these mosses have evolved this unique adaptation to thrive in the harsh Himalayan environment.

🔖 Mark for Review

Which finding, if true, would most directly support Dr. Peterson's hypothesis?

A	Other moss species from temperate climates, when brought to the Himalayas, showed signs of chloroplast damage and decreased photosynthetic efficiency.
B	Bryum argenteum and Sanionia uncinata, when transplanted to warmer climates, showed alterations in their chloroplast structures over several generations.
C	In freezing temperatures, Bryum argenteum and Sanionia uncinata exhibited higher photosynthetic efficiency compared to mosses with normal chloroplast structures.
D	Bryum argenteum and Sanionia uncinata showed higher growth rates compared to other moss species when grown in controlled laboratory conditions mimicking the Himalayan environment.

STEP 1 ▶ **Read the Question Carefully**

Task: The question asks us to identify the finding that most directly supports Dr. Peterson's hypothesis.

Highlight the Claim or Hypothesis: Dr. Peterson hypothesizes that Bryum argenteum and Sanionia uncinata have evolved unique chloroplast structures to enhance photosynthetic efficiency, allowing them to thrive in the harsh Himalayan environment.

STEP 2 ► **Understand the Claim or Hypothesis**

Paraphrase the Claim: The mosses' unique chloroplast structures help them survive in freezing temperatures by improving photosynthesis.

Key Components:
- The mosses have unique chloroplast structures.
- These structures enhance photosynthetic efficiency.
- This adaptation is linked to their survival in the Himalayan environment.

Underlying Reasoning: If these chloroplast structures provide a specific advantage in freezing temperatures, it supports the hypothesis.

STEP 3 ► **Predict the Type of Evidence Needed**

Look for evidence that links:
- The unique chloroplast structures to increased photosynthetic efficiency.
- This photosynthetic efficiency to survival in freezing temperatures.

STEP 4 ► **Analyze Each Answer Choice**

A: Highlights temperate moss struggles but doesn't link Himalayan mosses' unique chloroplasts to survival. Indirectly relevant, not the best.

B: Suggests adaptability in warmer climates but doesn't address freezing conditions or photosynthesis. Not directly relevant.

C: Directly links unique chloroplasts to higher photosynthetic efficiency in freezing conditions. Strongly supports hypothesis. Best choice.

D: Shows growth rate differences but doesn't explicitly connect chloroplasts to photosynthesis or survival in freezing temperatures. Weaker than C.

STEP 5 ► **Step 5: Select the Best Answer**

C directly links the unique chloroplast structures to higher photosynthetic efficiency in freezing temperatures, directly supporting the hypothesis. No unreasonable assumptions are required; the evidence aligns with the claim.

Max's Note

Focus on Direct Evidence: The correct answer should have a clear and direct effect on the claim.

Ignore Outside Knowledge: Base your answer solely on the information provided in the passage and question.

Beware of Common Traps:
- Irrelevant Information: Options that are true but do not impact the claim.
- Opposite Effect: Choices that have the reverse impact (support instead of weaken, or vice versa).

Supporting/ Weakening a Claim Problem Set

In the urban community of Metroville, two neighborhoods, Oakwood and Brookside, display different levels of community engagement. Oakwood, characterized by high-density housing and frequent community events, and Brookside, known for its low-density housing and fewer community gatherings, share the city with the Metroville Community Center, which sends out emergency alerts during city-wide crises. Sociologist Dr. Linda Evans and her team, who studied the social dynamics of these neighborhoods, hypothesized that there is an inverse relationship between neighborhood density and responsiveness to emergency alerts from the community center.

1 🔖 Mark for Review

Which finding, if true, would most directly support Dr. Evans and her team's hypothesis?

A) When Dr. Evans and her team sent out emergency alerts from the community center, residents of Oakwood and Brookside displayed no reaction, whereas the staff of the community center took immediate action.

B) Many neighborhoods with similar housing density to that of Oakwood displayed no reaction when Dr. Evans and her team sent out emergency alerts, whereas Oakwood displayed high levels of emergency preparedness.

C) Some residents of Brookside took immediate action when Dr. Evans and her team sent out emergency alerts, whereas nearly all residents did when Oakwood's neighborhood alerts were sent out.

D) Brookside displayed no reaction when Dr. Evans and her team sent out emergency alerts, whereas Oakwood displayed high levels of emergency preparedness in response to the alerts.

Marine biologists Dr. Serena Turner and Dr. Owen Fletcher investigated the impact of coral reef degradation on marine biodiversity in the Pacific Ocean. By comparing the variety of fish species in areas with healthy coral reefs to areas with degraded coral, they found a noticeable decline in species diversity in the latter. Dr. Turner and Dr. Fletcher argue that preserving and rehabilitating coral reefs is essential not just for the corals but also for maintaining marine biodiversity in the region.

Which finding, if true, would most directly support Dr. Turner and Dr. Fletcher's argument?

(A) Coral reefs also act as a natural barrier against coastal erosion, providing another reason for their preservation.

(B) Fish species in the Pacific Ocean are primarily influenced by water temperature, not the state of the coral reefs.

(C) Regions with degraded coral reefs also experience a decline in tourism-related activities like snorkeling and scuba diving.

(D) Areas where coral reefs have been rehabilitated show a gradual return of diverse fish species over time.

Megalodons were enormous sharks that roamed the oceans millions of years ago. Their massive size has led to theories about their migratory patterns. Dr. Helena Mitchell, Dr. Erik Lawson, and Dr. James O'Reilly analyzed trace elements in megalodon teeth to estimate the various oceanic temperatures these creatures might have encountered during their lives. Based on their findings, the scientists claim that megalodons likely migrated vast distances, from warm equatorial waters to colder northern and southern waters, in search of prey.

3 🔖 Mark for Review

Which finding, if true, would most directly support Dr. Mitchell, Dr. Lawson, and Dr. O'Reilly's claim?

A) The trace elements in megalodon teeth are best analyzed when compared to those of smaller, non-migratory shark species.

B) Teeth from juvenile megalodons primarily show evidence of warm water temperatures, while adult teeth show a mix of warm and cold water markers.

C) Several megalodon teeth have been discovered in areas known to be cold during their era, while similar large predatory sharks' teeth are rarely found in those regions.

D) During the era of megalodons, large prey species such as whales often migrated between warm breeding grounds and cold feeding areas.

In the late nineteenth century, historians delved deep into the origins of Australian Aboriginal art. While they all acknowledged the ancient traditions, they debated its influences. Dr. Marcus Owen believed that Australian Aboriginal art was majorly influenced by neighboring Southeast Asian cultures due to trading interactions. Dr. Linda Farley, on the other hand, believed that the art was uniquely Australian, evolving mostly independently with minimal external influences. The focus here is on Dr. Farley's claim that Australian Aboriginal art has evolved primarily within Australia with little influence from outside.

4 🔖 Mark for Review

Which finding, if true, would most directly support Dr. Farley's argument?

A) The art pieces studied from the era had notable similarities to the batik paintings of Indonesia.

B) Across different Australian regions, the art pieces displayed a common theme of dreamtime stories.

C) A large portion of the art pieces were of types and themes previously not seen in any other culture.

D) Many of the art pieces were centered around local wildlife and landscape, utilizing techniques not found in Southeast Asian art traditions.

The Tyrannosaurus rex, one of the most iconic dinosaurs, is often depicted as a fearsome predator. Paleontologists have debated whether this massive theropod was primarily a predator or a scavenger. Dr. Emily Thompson from the Dinosaur Research Institute conducted a study examining the bone structure and dental patterns of T. rex fossils to determine its primary feeding habits. She hypothesized that the T. rex's physical attributes would align more with those of a predator than a scavenger.

5 🔖 Mark for Review

Which finding, if true, would most directly support Dr. Thompson's hypothesis?

A) The T. rex's teeth showed wear patterns consistent with biting through bone, suggesting active hunting and feeding on large prey.

B) The T. rex fossils were often found near water sources, indicating they might have scavenged for dead animals near these areas.

C) The leg bones of the T. rex suggest it had a relatively slow walking speed compared to other theropods of its time.

D) Many herbivorous dinosaur fossils were found in the same regions as the T. rex, indicating a potential food source.

Kimchi, a traditional Korean fermented dish primarily made from cabbage and various spices, is touted for its health benefits. Many believe that the fermentation process of kimchi introduces beneficial probiotics into the digestive system, aiding in gut health and digestion. Dr. Soo-Min Lee from the Seoul Nutrition Institute conducted a study to determine if regular consumption of kimchi has a positive effect on gut flora and overall digestive health. She hypothesized that individuals who consume kimchi daily would show a more diverse and healthy gut microbiome compared to those who don't.

6 ☐ Mark for Review

Which finding, if true, would most directly support Dr. Lee's hypothesis?

A) Upon consumption, kimchi was observed to significantly reduce levels of harmful bacteria in the gut, enhancing nutrient absorption from digested food.

B) Individuals who consumed kimchi daily had a notable increase in beneficial gut bacteria such as Lactobacillus and Bifidobacterium, while those who didn't consume kimchi showed no such increase.

C) The fermentation process of kimchi was determined to produce specific enzymes believed to assist in breaking down complex carbohydrates, resulting in reduced calorie intake.

D) Both individuals who consumed kimchi daily and those who didn't showed similar levels of beneficial gut bacteria, but the former group reported a slightly tangier flavor preference.

During the late 18th century, governments across Europe experimented with various systems of taxation to fund their growing administrative and military needs. Historian Andrew Collier analyzed three types of tax systems: proportional (tax rate constant regardless of income), regressive (higher tax burden on lower-income groups), and progressive (higher tax burden on higher-income groups). Collier observed that in economies with large wealth disparities, progressive taxation systems were better able to maintain social stability by reducing economic grievances. Based on these findings, historian Julia Tan hypothesized that societies with progressive taxation systems during the late 18th century were more likely to avoid significant uprisings compared to those with proportional or regressive systems.

Which finding, if true, would most directly support Julia Tan's hypothesis?

(A) A study of late 18th-century England found that despite the implementation of a progressive taxation system, several small uprisings occurred among rural laborers.

(B) A study of late 18th-century France found that regions with regressive taxation systems experienced more frequent peasant revolts than regions with progressive taxation systems.

(C) A study of late 18th-century Prussia found that areas with proportional taxation systems saw the same frequency of protests as areas with progressive taxation systems.

(D) A study of late 18th-century Spain found that wealthier citizens in regions with progressive taxation systems contributed significantly more to state revenues than in regions with proportional systems.

K-pop, a genre of popular music originating in South Korea, has seen a meteoric rise in global popularity over the past decade. Beyond its catchy melodies and impressive choreographies, many attribute its success to the strategic use of social media and dedicated fan bases known as "fandoms". Dr. Ji-Yoon Park from the Seoul Music Academy conducted a study to determine the impact of fandom activities, such as streaming and social media campaigns, on the international chart performance of K-pop songs. She hypothesized that active and coordinated fandom efforts significantly influence a K-pop song's position on global music charts.

8 🔖 Mark for Review

Which finding, if true, would most directly support Dr. Park's hypothesis?

(A) K-pop songs that were actively promoted by fandoms on social media platforms consistently ranked higher on international music charts compared to those with less fandom engagement.

(B) The majority of K-pop fans use social media daily, with many reporting that they follow their favorite artists' official accounts.

(C) K-pop concerts in international locations often sell out within minutes, indicating a strong global fan presence.

(D) Both K-pop songs with high and low fandom engagement utilized similar marketing strategies, such as music video releases and television appearances.

Octopuses are known for their remarkable ability to change skin color and texture, a trait that has long been associated with camouflage. However, marine biologist Dr. Maya Srinivasan and her team proposed that this unique ability might also serve as a sophisticated form of communication among octopuses. To test this idea, the team placed octopuses in an environment with various marine creatures and observed their color-changing patterns. Some of the interactions were with potential predators, while others were with neutral or non-threatening marine animals.

9 🔖 Mark for Review

Which finding, if true, would most directly support the team's idea?

(A) Octopuses changed their skin color and patterns more frequently when interacting with non-threatening marine animals compared to when potential predators were present.

(B) Octopuses predominantly displayed a darkened color when potential predators were nearby, suggesting a primary use of camouflage.

(C) The majority of octopuses showed no change in color or pattern when left alone in the observation tank but showed various colors and patterns when with another octopus.

(D) Some octopuses exhibited rapid, pulsating color changes when in close proximity to certain marine creatures, regardless of the threat level.

Hypothesizing that upbeat, rhythmic music universally energizes individuals during exercise, Dr. Kevin Miller and his team conducted an experiment. They had participants exercise while listening to upbeat, rhythmic music and then while listening to slow, relaxing music. Participants exercised for longer durations and at higher intensities when listening to upbeat, rhythmic music. Since exercise duration and intensity are linked to energy levels, the team concluded that upbeat, rhythmic music energized the participants. A critic, however, argued that the upbeat music merely distracted participants from fatigue rather than genuinely increasing their energy. To address this, Dr. Miller's team also measured the participants' heart rates, as elevated heart rates are typically associated with increased energy levels rather than distraction.

10 🔖 Mark for Review

Which finding, if true, would most directly support the team's idea?

A) Participants listening to upbeat, rhythmic music had consistently higher heart rates during exercise compared to those listening to slow, relaxing music.

B) Participants reported feeling more motivated when exercising with upbeat, rhythmic music compared to slow, relaxing music.

C) Participants who regularly listened to upbeat, rhythmic music during exercise showed no difference in results compared to those who did not.

D) Fitness trainers commonly use upbeat, rhythmic music to encourage their clients during workouts.

Weakening a Claim Problem Set

In their study on gratitude, sociologists Matthew Bloom and Jessica Pryce proposed that expressing gratitude—a feeling of thankfulness typically stimulated by an act of kindness or generosity—can enhance our sense of well-being and therefore encourage us to engage more positively with our community. In their experiment, participants were asked to either write a thank you note to someone who had positively impacted their life (expected to inspire feelings of gratitude) or write a grocery list. Following this, a research assistant "accidentally" dropped a stack of papers in front of the participants.

1 ☐ Mark for Review

Which finding from the researchers' study, if true, would most strongly weaken their claim?

(A) Participants who were asked to write a thank you note were no more likely to help pick up the dropped papers than those who were asked to write a grocery list.

(B) Participants who were asked to write a thank you note reported feeling more positive emotions than those who wrote a grocery list.

(C) Participants who were asked to write a thank you note were significantly more likely to engage in a conversation with the research assistant after helping pick up the papers.

(D) Participants who were asked to write a thank you note felt more thankful and reported a higher sense of well-being than those who wrote a grocery list.

In a 2020 study, cultural historians Elena R. Vasquez and Liam P. O'Connor examined the use of folk songs as tools for political resistance during colonial occupations. They proposed that the thematic content and widespread popularity of folk songs made them effective in rallying communities and communicating subversive messages without drawing the attention of colonial authorities. The researchers hypothesized that the adoption of folk songs as a resistance strategy obviated the need for more explicit and dangerous forms of written political communication, which were often censored or confiscated by colonial regimes.

2 ☐ Mark for Review

Which finding, if true, would most directly weaken the hypothesis presented in the text?

(A) Folk songs used in political resistance during colonial occupations often contained coded messages understood only by members of specific communities.

(B) Many folk songs created during colonial occupations were later adopted as anthems in post-colonial nation-building efforts.

(C) Colonial authorities often banned certain folk songs, leading to the imprisonment of individuals caught singing them publicly.

(D) Communities engaged in resistance during colonial occupations relied heavily on underground newspapers to organize protests and disseminate information.

The Indus Valley Civilization flourished in South Asia around 4,500 years ago. Archaeological evidence shows that they produced a distinctive type of pottery with intricate geometric designs. Similar pottery styles have also been found in Mesopotamian cities dating to the same period. Trade routes between the Indus Valley and Mesopotamia are well-documented, while no evidence of direct connections between the Indus Valley and Central Asia exists from this time. Therefore, the pottery style in Mesopotamia was likely influenced by trade with the Indus Valley.

---

3 ▢ Mark for Review

Which finding, if true, would most directly weaken the underlined claim?

(A)	Differences in vocal cord structures were found to be a common variation among all Scarlet Ibises, not just between subspecies.
(B)	Non-migratory Scarlet Ibis males were observed to occasionally travel a similar distance as the migratory males.
(C)	Offspring of non-migratory Scarlet Ibis males and female Scarlet Ibises were found to be born with vocal cords that resemble those of migratory Scarlet Ibis males.
(D)	The migratory Scarlet Ibis males' distinctive call was found to be more due to the environment they migrate to than to genetic differences.

Dr. Elena Vargas and her team studied how ancient Egyptians conceptualized political authority. The researchers analyzed inscriptions on temple walls and stelae, focusing on terms like *maat*, a principle associated with order and justice, and *nesu*, a term referring to the divine kingship. Previous studies have shown that many ancient cultures represented political authority using hierarchical spatial metaphors, such as the association of rulers with height or elevation (e.g., "the throne is above all"). In a history seminar, a student claims that hierarchical spatial metaphors for political authority are universal across ancient civilizations.

---

4 ▢ Mark for Review

Which finding from the researchers' study, if true, would most strongly weaken Clark's hypothesis?

(A)	Inscriptions from other ancient cultures, such as Mesopotamia, include terms similar to *maat* that emphasize moral principles like justice rather than elevation.
(B)	Some Egyptian inscriptions depict rulers seated at the same height as their subjects during public ceremonies.
(C)	Certain Egyptian texts describe rulers as protectors of balance and harmony.
(D)	Depictions of rulers in ancient Egypt often focus on their symbolic alignment with divine principles rather than emphasizing height or hierarchical spatial metaphors.

Many coaches are eager for their athletes to excel in their chosen sport. However, instead of providing a well-rounded training regimen, coaches often focus on tailoring their athletes' development to their own preferred techniques and strategies. Because athletes inherently possess a passion and drive to improve, they make significant progress by immersing themselves in the sport and adapting to various challenges. Therefore, a critic asserts this kind of specialized coaching is unlikely to enhance an athlete's overall performance.

Which finding from the researchers' study, if true, would most strongly weaken the critic's hypothesis?

A) Athletes who received specialized coaching had a higher level of satisfaction and motivation compared to athletes who followed a generic, well-rounded training regimen.

B) Athletes who received specialized coaching tailored to their coaches' techniques and strategies consistently achieved better overall performance compared to athletes who followed a generic, well-rounded training regimen.

C) Athletes who received specialized coaching reported fewer injuries and a lower rate of burnout compared to athletes who followed a generic, well-rounded training regimen.

D) Athletes who received specialized coaching outperformed their peers in key performance metrics that are crucial for success in their chosen sport, such as speed, strength, or accuracy.

Research has shown that regular physical exercise not only improves physical health but also has a significant impact on mental well-being. To better understand this connection, researchers designed a study comparing individuals who engaged in at least 150 minutes of moderate exercise per week with those who did not exercise regularly. Initial results indicated that the exercisers reported 40 percent lower levels of stress and anxiety compared to the non-exercisers. However, the researchers hypothesized that other factors, such as diet and sleep quality, might also contribute to the observed differences in mental well-being.

Which of the following, if true, would most weaken the researchers' hypothesis?

A) Participants who engaged in regular exercise reported no significant changes in their diet or sleep quality during the study period.

B) Non-exercisers in the study were more likely to consume processed foods and report poor sleep quality compared to exercisers.

C) A follow-up study found that both exercisers and non-exercisers with similar dietary and sleep patterns reported comparable levels of mental well-being.

D) Participants in the study who exercised regularly also reported higher levels of social interaction, which is known to improve mental well-being.

In a recent survey conducted by epidemiologist Dr. Sarah Johnson on coffee consumption, researchers discovered that individuals who regularly consume more than three cups of coffee per day are more prone to reporting heightened levels of anxiety and restlessness. The survey's findings suggest a direct link between high coffee consumption and an increase in feelings of anxiety. As a result, the survey recommends that, in order to alleviate anxiety, individuals should contemplate reducing their coffee intake.

Which one of the following statements, if true, most seriously weakens the argument?

A) Many of the survey respondents who reported high coffee consumption also reported high levels of stress at work.

B) The caffeine content in coffee can vary widely depending on the type and preparation of the coffee.

C) Some people drink coffee primarily in social settings, which can be relaxing and reduce feelings of anxiety.

D) There are many other sources of caffeine, like tea and energy drinks, which lead to happiness.

In Lireo, a detailed five-year study was conducted to assess the impact of vehicular emissions on urban air quality. As the number of vehicles on the roads increased by 30%, levels of airborne pollutants correspondingly rose by 25%. Concurrently, the city's health department reported a 20% rise in respiratory illnesses among residents. Based on this data, researchers concluded that the significant surge in vehicles is the primary cause behind the deteriorating air quality and associated health issues. They strongly recommend adopting stricter emission standards and actively promoting public transport.

8 🔖 Mark for Review

Which one of the following statements, if true, most seriously weakens the argument?

- (A) Lireo's rapidly growing industrial sector expanded significantly during the study, leading to increased emissions.

- (B) Lireo's public transport system is consistently ranked among the country's best.

- (C) A notable portion of Lireo residents have transitioned to electric vehicles, which produce minimal emissions.

- (D) The health department also observed a rise in non-respiratory illnesses during the same period.

Studying the growth rates of Procoptodon, an extinct marsupial, is challenging. Counting annual leg bone growth rings, the usual method to determine age, is complex due to bone structural changes with age, including hollowness and tissue remodeling. Yet, a promising discovery was made during recent Australian outback excavations by paleontologist Dr. Amelia Harper from the University of Queensland. She found distinct dental growth rings in Procoptodon, particularly in molars. Dental structures are less affected by weight-bearing stresses, offering an alternative approach to studying Procoptodon's growth rates.

9 🔖 Mark for Review

What discovery, if accurate, would most significantly challenge Dr. Amelia Harper's theory about the growth rates of Procoptodon?

- (A) As marsupials evolved into more advanced species, their growth rates increased.

- (B) Growth rates for individual Procoptodon varied based on differences in dietary habits.

- (C) Procoptodon had a significantly longer life span compared to other marsupials of its era.

- (D) Dental growth ring formation in Procoptodon is a random event.

CHAPTER 10
Completing a Text

Step 1: Read the Text Carefully

Read the text carefully: Begin by reading the entire passage thoroughly. Pay attention to all the details and make sure you understand the main idea, point of view, and any conclusions or implications presented. Understanding the overall context is critical to make a logical guess about the missing information.

Step 2: Identify the Clues

Go back to the sentence or sentences immediately preceding the blank, as these often provide clues about what the answer should be. Look for any hints or leading phrases that might give away the expected direction of the concluding statement.

Step 3: Formulate a Prediction

Based on your understanding of the text and the clues you've identified, try to predict what the missing text could say before looking at the choices. This pre-emptive answer doesn't have to match the choices word-for-word, but it will guide you in the right direction.

Step 4: Review All Choices

Even if you feel confident about a choice immediately, make sure to read through all of the options. Sometimes a later option might fit the text better than the first one you felt was correct.

Step 5: Eliminate Wrong Choices

Rule out any choices that are clearly not correct based on the context provided. These might contradict the overall message, stray from the topic, or make illogical leaps.

Step 6: Select the Best Fit

Out of the remaining choices, select the one that best fits the context, aligns with the clues identified and follows logically from the points made in the text.

Example Question

Early astronomical models, such as those proposed by Aristotle in the 4th century BCE and Ptolemy in the 2nd century CE, placed Earth at the center of the universe. During the 16th century, Copernicus presented a heliocentric model, but even his work did not include the concept of elliptical orbits for planets. It was not until the early 17th century, when Johannes Kepler used Tycho Brahe's meticulous observational data, that the idea of planets moving in elliptical orbits was introduced and accepted. No surviving texts predating Kepler's Astronomia Nova (1609) contain explicit reference to elliptical planetary paths, but his work and later Newtonian physics do. It can therefore be inferred that _____

▮ 🔖 Mark for Review

Which choice completes the text with the most logical and precise word or phrase?

(A) Copernicus was familiar with Kepler's idea of elliptical orbits but chose to ignore it for political reasons.

(B) Kepler, while building on Copernicus's heliocentric view, introduced a fundamentally new concept of planetary motion not found in earlier models.

(C) Newton's laws of motion were inspired directly by Aristotle's original geocentric model.

(D) Aristotle's and Ptolemy's lack of references to elliptical orbits proves that they were aware of the concept but decided not to publish it.

STEP 1 ► Read the Text Carefully:
The passage provides a historical overview of astronomical models:
- Aristotle (4th century BCE) and Ptolemy (2nd century CE) had Earth-centered (geocentric) models with no mention of elliptical orbits.
- Copernicus (16th century) introduced the heliocentric model but still maintained circular orbits.
- Kepler (early 17th century), using Tycho Brahe's data, introduced elliptical orbits.
- No texts before Kepler's Astronomia Nova (1609) mention elliptical orbits; after Kepler, elliptical orbits are accepted and even supported by Newtonian physics.

STEP 2 ► Identify the Clues:
The key clue is that elliptical orbits are a "new concept" that appear for the first time in Kepler's work. Aristotle, Ptolemy, and Copernicus did not mention elliptical orbits, implying this idea was not part of earlier astronomical frameworks.

STEP 3 ► Formulate a Prediction:
Since no prior sources mention elliptical orbits, but Kepler's work does, it can be inferred that Kepler introduced a new idea that was absent from all previous models.

STEP 4 ► Review All Choices:
A) This doesn't follow logically because Copernicus died decades before Kepler published Astronomia Nova. There's no evidence Copernicus knew of elliptical orbits.

B) This fits the evidence perfectly. Kepler's elliptical orbits were indeed not found in earlier models by Aristotle, Ptolemy, or Copernicus.

C) Newton's laws were formulated long after Aristotle and are based on mathematical principles and Kepler's findings, not Aristotle's geocentric model. This is not supported.

D) This is an unfounded speculation. The passage suggests they simply didn't have this idea, not that they withheld it.

STEP 5 ► Eliminate Wrong Choices:
(A) is impossible historically and logically.
(C) and (D) are not supported by the passage.

STEP 6 ► Select the Best Fit:
(B) directly matches the new concept (elliptical orbits) with Kepler's introduction of it, aligning perfectly with the passage's content.

Let's Practice!

Completing a Text Problem Set

Like many urban shoppers, residents of the city of Brookfield contribute to the growth of local businesses by making purchases at neighborhood stores and markets. Sociologists have found that while some residents do patronize small, traditional shops—businesses that are struggling to remain viable in the face of competition—most consumers make more frequent purchases at large, well-established chain supermarkets. The reason is straightforward: these large chains are more numerous, offer a wider range of products, and are often more conveniently located. Therefore, it isn't surprising that _____

1 ☐ Mark for Review

Which choice most logically completes the text?

(A) the overall growth rate of large chain supermarkets in Brookfield surpasses that of smaller, traditional shops struggling to remain open.

(B) smaller, traditional shops on Brookfield's outskirts have recently begun to offer fewer product choices than large supermarkets.

(C) large chain supermarkets in Brookfield originally modeled their business strategies on small, traditional shops.

(D) residents of Brookfield view both small, traditional shops and large chain supermarkets as equally important to the local economy.

During the European Middle Ages, written materials were highly prized, but not all forms of documentation were equally common. Everyday records, like simple accounts of trade or basic legal agreements, were relatively plentiful; these could be compiled on cheaper parchment and produced by local scribes. Illuminated manuscripts, on the other hand, were exceptionally rare. These lavishly decorated volumes were painstakingly crafted by skilled artisans, and the gold leaf, vibrant pigments, and intricate calligraphy used in their creation made them far more valuable than ordinary documents. Monastic libraries and a few noble households were known to preserve collections of such exquisite texts. Given how costly and time-consuming it was to produce illuminated manuscripts, it is not surprising that _____.

2 ☐ Mark for Review

Which choice most logically completes the text?

A) some monastic libraries contained primarily simple, unadorned writings with no illuminated manuscripts.

B) most households in medieval Europe possessed numerous illuminated manuscripts.

C) the creation of illuminated manuscripts required far fewer resources than producing common documents.

D) local scribes frequently gave illuminated manuscripts away for free to neighboring villages.

In a popular online streaming platform, viewers help content creators gain visibility by watching and sharing their videos. Analysts have found that viewers engage with some videos from niche, independent creators who struggle to grow their audience, such as those making educational content. However, viewers engage with a higher number of videos from well-known, mainstream creators, likely because there are so many more of those videos available. Therefore, it isn't surprising that _____

3 ☐ Mark for Review

Which choice most logically completes the text?

A) on the platform, the subscriber growth rate is higher for well-known mainstream creators than it is for niche, independent creators.

B) well-known mainstream creators only recently began to outnumber niche, independent creators on the platform.

C) on the platform, niche, independent creators are already producing content in most of the genres where viewers are engaged.

D) both niche, independent creators and well-known mainstream creators are equally likely to gain new subscribers on the platform.

Throughout history, various cultures have used storytelling as a means to convey their values and traditions. For instance, the ancient Greek epic "The Odyssey" tells the tale of Odysseus's journey home from the Trojan War, but it also serves as a vessel for conveying Greek ideals of heroism and cleverness. Similarly, the African folktales of Anansi the Spider are not just entertaining stories but also contain moral lessons and cultural insights. Therefore, it can be inferred that _____.

4   🔖 Mark for Review

Which choice most logically completes the text?

A storytelling has been a universal form of entertainment across all cultures.

B storytelling has evolved significantly over time to adapt to changing cultural values.

C storytelling serves as more than a form of entertainment.

D storytelling is a dying art form in the modern era with the rise of technology.

Cities in the southeastern region of the country have traditionally categorized their neighborhoods into well-defined zones—residential, commercial, industrial—based on decades-old population and economic data. Many other municipalities follow similar models, relying on stability and long-standing assumptions. However, urban planners Carmen Ramirez and David Wu have observed that changing workplace dynamics, an increase in remote employment, and shifts in local demographics are now challenging these static zoning distinctions. Areas once considered unsuitable for residential life may suddenly become desirable due to improved transportation options or the rise of home-based businesses. Traditional zoning categories, they argue, no longer capture the complexity of modern urban development. These observations suggest that _____.

5   🔖 Mark for Review

Which choice most logically completes the text?

A municipalities that rely solely on old data may overlook new opportunities for growth.

B most cities have always had stable populations and do not need to rethink their zoning.

C the concept of zoning will remain unchanged despite shifting demographics.

D urban planners should limit their research to historical data rather than current trends.

The Scandinavian region of Europe is widely recognized for its high levels of gender equality, but a recent study revealed a surprising trend: Scandinavian women are less likely to be entrepreneurs than their counterparts in other Western countries. The researchers hypothesized that generous family leave policies and extensive public childcare in Scandinavia could be a factor. If true, this suggests that _____

6 ☐ Mark for Review

Which choice most logically completes the text?

(A) Scandinavian women are less ambitious than their counterparts in other Western countries.

(B) these family-friendly policies may unintentionally discourage women from pursuing entrepreneurship.

(C) family leave policies and public childcare are less effective in promoting gender equality than previously believed.

(D) women in other Western countries are more likely to start businesses because they lack access to public childcare and family leave.

Two chemists, Dr. Evans and Dr. Martinez, were investigating how solution acidity affects the activity of two different catalysts—Catalyst Iron (Fe) and Catalyst Platinum (Pt)—used in a chemical reaction that converts substrate molecules into a valuable product. They tested the reactions across a range of pH levels, from strongly acidic to moderately basic conditions, as well as under different concentrations of a particular ligand that can bind to the catalysts. The data showed that Catalyst Iron's activity increases substantially under more acidic conditions, while Catalyst Platinum's activity remains relatively unchanged regardless of pH. Based on these results, the researchers concluded that making the reaction mixture more acidic is less likely to _____ .

7 ☐ Mark for Review

Which choice most logically completes the text?

(A) ncrease Catalyst Platinum's activity than it is to increase Catalyst Iron's activity.

(B) inhibit Catalyst Iron's activity than it is to promote Catalyst Platinum's activity.

(C) yield any product at all than it is to affect either Catalyst Iron or Catalyst Platinum.

(D) maintain the current reaction rate than it is to diminish the importance of pH in the reaction.

Chemists Dr. Nguyen and Dr. Patel investigated how varying reaction conditions—such as temperature, solvent polarity, and catalyst presence—affect the yield of a particular organic synthesis. While controlled laboratory tests are useful for isolating variables, real-world industrial processes often involve fluctuating conditions that can alter reaction outcomes. Given this, it's not altogether surprising that when Nguyen and Patel analyzed results from both strictly controlled lab experiments and large-scale industrial runs, they found that _____.

8 🔖 Mark for Review

Which choice most logically completes the text?

A) the reaction yield was significantly different in industrial settings than in the tightly controlled laboratory environment.

B) the reaction's yield remained identical regardless of whether the reaction was performed in a lab or an industrial plant.

C) lowering the temperature in industrial settings did not affect the reaction yield, contrary to all laboratory data.

D) changing solvent polarity had no effect in either the lab or industrial scenarios, suggesting that conditions are irrelevant.

Researchers have noted that people with deeply held scientific beliefs tend to perceive data that aligns with those beliefs as more conclusive than data of the same evidential strength that contradicts their worldview. In a recent study, Dr. Jane Smith and colleagues presented participants with two sets of experimental results—one supporting a widely accepted scientific theory and another supporting a less conventional hypothesis. Although both sets of findings were matched in terms of their statistical rigor and methodology, participants generally judged the evidence in favor of the established theory as more credible. The researchers' conclusions suggest that if a participant was shown equally compelling evidence for both the established theory and the unconventional hypothesis, the participant likely would have ____.

9 🔖 Mark for Review

Which choice most logically completes the text?

A) judged the evidence for the established theory as more credible than the evidence for the unconventional hypothesis.

B) dismissed both sets of evidence as equally inconclusive.

C) perceived the evidence for the unconventional hypothesis as stronger than it actually was.

D) found the evidence for the unconventional hypothesis more persuasive than the evidence for the established theory.

Anthropologists have observed that cultural practices often influence how individuals perceive and respond to environmental challenges. In a recent study, Dr. Maria Lopez and colleagues examined agricultural techniques among two communities—one using traditional, labor-intensive farming methods and another employing modern, mechanized practices. Despite similar environmental conditions, the traditional farming community reported higher levels of satisfaction with their agricultural yield, attributing their success to ancestral knowledge and spiritual practices. In contrast, the mechanized farming community emphasized technology and efficiency as the key factors for success. These findings suggest that if members of both communities were exposed to identical farming outcomes, they likely would have _____.

10 ☐ Mark for Review

Which choice most logically completes the text?

(A) perceived their own community's approach as more effective regardless of the actual yield.

(B) questioned the environmental conditions rather than their methods.

(C) agreed that mechanized farming offers better long-term results.

(D) shown a preference for adopting elements of the other community's techniques.

Historians have noted that during periods of economic instability, communities often developed systems of mutual aid and informal trade to mitigate the effects of scarcity. To investigate the prevalence of these practices—which researchers had thought were exclusive to rural areas—Dr. Sarah Whitaker and her team examined records from 200 urban and rural communities across 18th-century Europe. These records included personal letters, tax accounts, and local decrees. They found that in 63 of the communities, including several densely populated urban centers, informal trade networks and mutual aid societies flourished during economic downturns. This result suggests that _____

11 ☐ Mark for Review

Which choice most logically completes the text?

(A) informal trade and mutual aid networks may have been more common in urban areas during economic instability than researchers previously believed.

(B) communities relied on informal trade networks and mutual aid societies primarily as a response to economic instability rather than for other social or cultural reasons.

(C) rural communities likely developed more robust systems of mutual aid than urban communities during times of scarcity.

(D) urban communities were less likely to rely on formal economic structures during times of scarcity compared to rural areas.

Smartphones, a revolutionary technology, became widely available as traditional flip phones phased out. These devices offer a wide array of applications and features that simplify daily tasks and enhance communication. While many users embrace smartphones for their convenience and versatility, some individuals may struggle to adapt. These users may find the multitude of apps and functions overwhelming, making it challenging to navigate and fully utilize the potential of their smartphones. Despite this learning curve for some users, ___

12 ☐ Mark for Review

Which choice most logically completes the text?

(A) smartphones are a passing trend, and their widespread adoption will likely decline as people rediscover the benefits of traditional communication methods.

(B) the popularity of flip phones is experiencing a resurgence, with some users opting for their simplicity and nostalgic appeal.

(C) smartphones have undeniably transformed the way we live and connect with the world around us.

(D) users who struggle with smartphones should avoid using them altogether and rely solely on older, less complex technology for their daily tasks.

The ancient civilization of the Mayans, from whom several modern groups in Central America have descended, developed sophisticated city-states around 750 B.C.E. in the region now known as Guatemala and Mexico. These cities were suddenly abandoned around 900 C.E., leaving behind complex systems of agriculture, including maize cultivation. Recent studies comparing maize remains from the ancient city of Tikal to present-day maize in the Veracruz region of Mexico revealed similarities not inherent to the maize cultivated at Tikal. This has led researchers to deduce that _____

13 🔖 Mark for Review

Which choice most logically completes the text?

A) the climate conditions in Veracruz and Tikal were remarkably similar during ancient times.

B) some Mayans likely migrated to Veracruz around the 10th century and brought their agricultural techniques with them.

C) the indigenous people living in Veracruz primarily harvested other crops and didn't start cultivating maize until around the 10th century.

D) the Mayans at Tikal had adopted the agricultural practices of other indigenous groups in different regions.

Many eco-conscious consumers are excited about new "green packaging" solutions designed to make products more environmentally friendly, with reduced waste and carbon footprints. However, those who expect these eco-friendly packaging alternatives to significantly lower overall environmental impact may be disappointed. Research has shown that ___

14 ◻ Mark for Review

Which choice most logically completes the text?

(A) consumers often overcompensate for the perceived eco-friendliness of the packaging by using more of the product or generating additional waste in other areas of their lives, potentially offsetting the intended environmental benefits.

(B) these eco-friendly packaging alternatives are universally embraced and endorsed by all consumers, leading to a rapid and substantial decrease in environmental impact.

(C) consumers have shown an unwavering commitment to eco-friendly packaging, resulting in a complete elimination of all environmental issues related to packaging.

(D) supporting and adopting these innovative "green packaging" solutions can contribute positively to a more sustainable and environmentally responsible future.

The writings of ancient philosopher Socrates have influenced countless individuals throughout history, despite the fact that Socrates himself never wrote a single word. Instead, his student, Plato, wrote down Socrates' teachings. Therefore, those who credit Socrates as the author of certain philosophical works ___

15 ◻ Mark for Review

Which choice most logically completes the text?

(A) may be inadvertently attributing the works of Plato to Socrates.

(B) are overlooking the significant contributions of Plato to the philosophical canon.

(C) are likely misinterpreting the meaning behind Socrates' teachings.

(D) are wrong because Socrates never actually wrote anything himself.

CHAPTER 11

Infographics

Type 1 — **Using the data from the table to support/ undermine the researchers' claim.**

The primary goal for this type of question is to evaluate the reader's ability to understand and interpret data presented in tables, charts, or other visual representations in order to validate or refute a researcher's claim.

Example Instructions:
- Read the researcher's claim carefully to understand what is being stated.

- Study the data presented in the infographic carefully. Pay attention to the labels, units, categories, or any other descriptive element associated with the data.

- Compare the data from the table with the researcher's claim. The correct answer will be the one that best aligns the data from the table with the researcher's claim

Type 2 — **Using the data from the table to complete the text.**

The main goal for this type of question is to assess the reader's ability to accurately and succinctly convey information from a table or infographic in text form.

Example Instructions:
- Read the text to understand the context of the data that needs to be completed.

- Examine the infographic carefully. Pay special attention to details that seem most relevant to completing the text.

- The correct choice will be the one that accurately uses the data from the table to fill the missing part of the text.

Step 1: Understand the Question

The first step in solving infographic questions is to carefully read and understand the question. Make sure you fully understand what the question is asking before moving on to analyze the infographic.

Step 2: Study the Infographic

Examine the infographic carefully. Look for data that relates directly to the question asked. This could involve reading the labels and captions, studying the charts and graphs, or considering the layout and organization of the information presented.

Step 3: Interpret the Data

Infographic questions often require you to interpret data. This could involve performing simple calculations, recognizing patterns or trends, comparing and contrasting data, or drawing inferences from the data. Make sure you understand what the data is showing before trying to answer the question.

Step 4: Link the Data to the Question

After interpreting the data, it's important to connect it back to the question asked. You should look for data that directly addresses the question and provides a clear and concise answer.

Step 5: Answer the Question

Once you have analyzed the data and linked it to the question, you should be able to answer the question. Ensure your answer is based on the data presented in the infographic and directly addresses the question asked.

Step 6: Check Your Answer

Finally, take the time to review your answer and check it against the infographic. Make sure your answer is accurate and supported by the data.

Example Question

Evolution of Bicycle Design Over the Years

Year	Design Changes	Material	Average Weight (lbs)
1817	Running Machine	Wood	48
1865	High Wheel	Steel and Iron	37
1885	Safety Bicycle	Srteel	32
1933	Streamlined	Steel and Aluminum	29
1970	10-Speed	Aluminum	25
1990	Mountain Bike	Aluminum and Carbon Fiber	22
2020	Electric Bike	Aluminum, Carbon Fiber, Lithium	50

As the bicycle evolved from the "running machine" of the early 19th century to the e-bikes of today, a variety of design modifications were made to improve the user's riding experience. These changes often involved utilizing different materials to construct the bicycle, ultimately affecting its weight. The researcher claimed that with the evolution of bicycles, while the design has become more sophisticated, the average weight also reduced until the introduction of the e-bikes.

☐ Mark for Review

Which choice best describes data from the table that support the researcher's claim?

A) The weight of bicycles has significantly increased from the 'Running Machine' of 1817 to the 'Electric Bike' of 2020.

B) Despite the changes in materials from wood to combinations of steel, aluminum, and carbon fiber, the bicycle's weight has remained fairly constant over the years.

C) The transition from steel and iron 'High Wheel' bicycles to the steel 'Safety Bicycle' resulted in a notable decrease in weight.

D) There is a consistent trend of decreasing weight from the 'Running Machine' of 1817 through to the 'Mountain Bike' of 1990, before a significant weight increase with the 'Electric Bike' in 2020.

STEP 1 ▸ Understand the Question:
The question is asking for the choice that best supports the researcher's claim that as bicycles have evolved and become more sophisticated in design, their average weight has decreased until the introduction of e-bikes.

STEP 2 ▸ Study the Infographic:
Looking at the data table, we can see changes in bicycle design over the years, the materials used, and the corresponding average weight.

STEP 3 ▸ Interpret the Data:
We can see from the data that the weight of bicycles generally decreased from 1817 to 1990, with the 'Running Machine' at 48 lbs and the 'Mountain Bike' at 22 lbs. However, with the introduction of the 'Electric Bike' in 2020, the weight increased significantly to 50 lbs. This is largely due to the use of lithium in e-bikes, which is a heavy material.

STEP 4 ▸ Link the Data to the Question:
Comparing this interpretation with the researcher's claim, it's clear that the trend in the data supports the claim - the weight decreased as the design became more sophisticated, but increased with the introduction of e-bikes.

STEP 5 ▸ Answer the Question:
Therefore, the answer is D) There is a consistent trend of decreasing weight from the 'Running Machine' of 1817 through to the 'Mountain Bike' of 1990, before a significant weight increase with the 'Electric Bike' in 2020.

STEP 6 ▸ Check Your Answer:
Checking this against the data, it is clear that this choice accurately reflects the trend described in the table and supports the researcher's claim.

Infographic Problem Set

Mother of Brood	Known Sire(s) of Brood	Male(s) Feeding Brood
Female A	Male 1	Male 1
Female B	Male 2, Male 3	Male 3
Female C	Male 4	Male 4, Male 5
Female D	Male 6, Male 7	Male 7
Female E	Male 8, Male 9	Male 8, Male 11, Male 9, Male 12
Female F	Male 10	Male 10
Female G	Male 11	Male 13, Male 14, Male 11

Foraging and Feeding Relationships among Blue Rock Thrush in the Apennines, Italy, have attracted the attention of ornithologists globally. Intriguingly, these avian species exhibit a unique pattern of brood care, where the males involved in feeding the offspring aren't necessarily their biological fathers. This atypical behavior diverges from the commonly observed practices in many bird species. The extensive data gathered so far highlights this complexity but also raises more questions. For instance, it's entirely conceivable that _____

1 ◻ Mark for Review

Which choice most effectively uses data from the table to complete the example?

- A) Male 3 fed the brood of Female B, despite not being the only known sire.

- B) Female E's brood was fed by Male 8 and Male 9 only.

- C) Female G's brood was fed by males who weren't the known sires.

- D) Female C's brood was fed by Male 4 and Male 5, who were both the known sires.

Job Type	Job Openings, 2018-2019	Percent Increase in Jobs, 2015-2019
Solar Power	70,000	145%
Wind Energy	35,500	120%
Hydroelectric Power	20,000	78%
Bioenergy	24,000	150%
Geothermal Energy	5,000	100%
All Renewable Energy Jobs	500,000	89%

The renewable energy sector in the United States has seen a significant increase in jobs between 2015 and 2019. Researchers have highlighted that these job openings and their respective growth percentage represent the importance and prioritization of renewable energy industries. Based on the data, they suggest that some sectors despite having fewer job openings have seen a higher percentage increase in jobs.

Which choice best describes data from the table that supports the researchers' suggestion?

A) The Solar Power sector, having the most job openings, also has one of the highest percentages of job increase.

B) The Bioenergy sector, despite having fewer job openings than Solar Power and Wind Energy, has the highest percentage increase in jobs.

C) The Geothermal Energy sector, having the least job openings, also shows the least percentage increase in jobs.

D) The Hydroelectric Power sector, despite having more job openings than Bioenergy and Geothermal Energy, has the lowest percentage increase in jobs.

Average Number of Mistakes Made During Driving Test

Driving Skill	Traditional Training (mistakes)	Combined Traditional and Simulator Training (mistakes)
Parallel Parking	3.7	2.5
Turning and Intersections	2.8	2.1
Highway Driving	3	2.4
Emergency Procedures	2.9	2.2

A group of driving instructors conducted a study comparing traditional driving training to a combination of traditional and driving simulator training. The average number of mistakes made during a driving test was recorded for each type of training in four critical driving skills. The instructors hypothesize that the combined traditional and simulator training reduces the average number of mistakes compared to the traditional training method alone.

Which choice best supports the instructors' claim based on the data from the table?

A) The skill with the most mistakes in both training methods is parallel parking, suggesting that the combined training method does not reduce mistakes.

B) For each driving skill, the average number of mistakes made during the driving test is lower for those who underwent the combined traditional and simulator training compared to those who had only traditional training.

C) The skills of turning and intersections and emergency procedures saw a similar number of mistakes in both training methods, suggesting there is no significant difference in mistake reduction between the training methods.

D) The highway driving skill saw fewer mistakes in the traditional training method, implying that the traditional method is more effective in reducing mistakes.

Age Group	Immediate Recall % (Names)	Delayed Recall % (Names)	Immediate Recall % (Places)	Delayed Recall % (Places)
20-29	90.10%	85.00%	80.90%	76.20%
30-39	86.30%	81.10%	78.30%	71.30%
40-49	83.50%	78.20%	74.70%	66.60%
50-59	79.80%	74.10%	72.00%	62.30%
60-69	76.20%	70.10%	67.00%	58.50%
70-79	71.80%	65.30%	62.60%	54.50%
80+	67.50%	61.00%	58.10%	49.20%

Researchers have conducted a study on recall abilities for names and places in different age groups, both immediately after exposure and following a delay. The results suggest that there is a decline in memory performance with aging, seen in both immediate and delayed recall tasks. However, the decline pattern differs based on the type of information (names vs places) and recall conditions. This can be most effectively observed by comparing the immediate and delayed recall percentages for names and places in _____

Which choice most effectively uses data from the table to complete the statement?

(A) the age group 20-29 with the age group 80+.

(B) the age group 40-49 with the age group 50-59.

(C) the age group 30-39 with the age group 60-69.

(D) the age group 70-79 with the age group 80+.

Music Festival Event-Related Spending (average per person per event)

Expense Category	Local Fan Spending	Visitor Fan Spending	Combined Fan Spending
Festival Pass	$60.24	$81.45	$70.35
Food & Beverage	$32.78	$48.60	$38.94
Camping & Accommodation	$24.15	$36.78	$29.57
Merchandise	$16.90	$21.37	$18.74
Transportation	$13.56	$22.40	$16.38
Other	$12.30	$17.65	$14.48

Music festivals often stimulate local economies by attracting visitors from other areas. A recent study compared the average event-related spending per person per event of local fans versus visiting fans. The categories of spending include festival passes, food & beverage, camping & accommodation, merchandise, transportation, and other expenses. Not surprisingly, the amount spent in each category varies between local and visiting fans.

5 ▢ Mark for Review

Which of the following statements is most strongly supported by the data in the table?

(A) Local fans spend more on festival passes than visiting fans.

(B) Visiting fans spend more on every category of expenses than local fans.

(C) The combined average spending on merchandise is higher than that on transportation.

(D) Local fans spend more on food & beverage than on camping & accommodation.

Investment decision factor	Average rating (scale of 1 to 4)
Company's financial performance	3.45
Market trends	3.35
Economic conditions	3.30
Company's leadership and management	3.22
Government policy	3.20
Investor's risk tolerance	3.15
Product/Service innovation	3.12
Company's ESG factors	3.08
Competitors' performance	3.01
Industry growth rate	2.98
Interest rates	2.85

Making an investment decision can be a complex process, given the various factors that can influence the potential success of an investment. A study published in 2025 in the Journal of Investment and Portfolio Management asked portfolio managers to rate (from 1 to 4) the factors they consider when making investment decisions. As expected, the company's financial performance received the highest rating at 3.45. Other top-rated factors reflect the multi-faceted expertise that portfolio managers must bring to their work. For instance, understanding market trends (3.35), economic conditions (3.30), and company leadership (3.22) all received high average ratings. Managers also rated investor's risk tolerance (3.15) and _____.

Which choice most effectively uses data from the graph to complete the example?

(A) government policy (3.20) quite high, demonstrating that they must pay attention to both individual investor profiles and broader economic policy.

(B) product/service innovation (3.12) quite high, illustrating that they must pay attention to both individual investor profiles and creative business strategies.

(C) competitors' performance (3.01) quite high, indicating that they must pay attention to both individual investor profiles and market competition.

(D) interest rates (2.85) quite high, signifying that they must pay attention to both individual investor profiles and economic indicators.

Sheila's Grandma's Recipes and Michael's Recipes

■ 2020 Sheila's Grandma   ▨ 2022 Michael

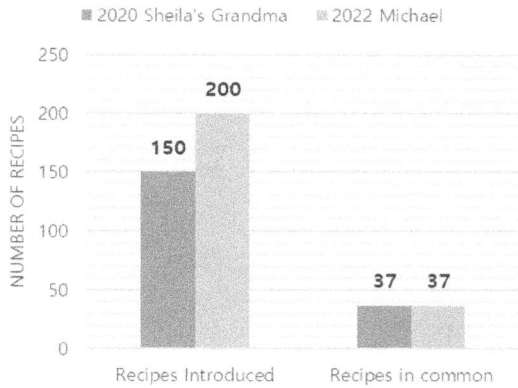

Michael's secret recipe book, published in 2022, boasts 200 different recipes. Some of these recipes bear a striking resemblance to those found in Sheila's grandma's recipe book, which was published in 2020. Given the uniqueness of some of these recipes, it's improbable that two different authors would have independently created them. Thus, it's highly probable that Michael was influenced by Sheila's grandma's earlier recipes.

Which one of the following, if true, most weakens the argument?

(A) A family recipe collection, likely known to both Sheila's grandma and Michael, was passed down through generations and contains some of the same unique recipes.

(B) The recipes in Michael's book that resemble those in Sheila's grandma's book cater to a completely different cuisine style.

(C) Both Sheila's grandma's and Michael's recipe books were targeted at the same audience of home cooks.

(D) Sheila's grandma added a new edition to her recipe book in 2023, which included recipes that were not present in Michael's 2022 book.

Melatonin Production, Activity Period, and Exposure to Predators in Selected Mammal Species

	Species	Specific Melatonin Production* (pg/mL)	Eating Location/ Exposure to Predators
Nocturnal Mammals	Raccoon	80	Urban areas/high exposure
	Common Opossum	120	Woodland areas/ medium exposure
	Striped Skunk	150	Open grasslands/ high exposure
	Virginia Opossum	200	Near water bodies/ low exposure
Diurnal Mammals	Eastern Gray Squirrel	10	Forest canopy/low exposure
	European Rabbit	20	Burrows/low exposure
	Brown Rat	30	Urban areas/high exposure
	House Mouse	40	Domestic buildings/high exposure

A group of researchers recently conducted a study on the melatonin production of different mammal species and their exposure to predators. They observed that nocturnal mammals generally have higher melatonin production compared to diurnal mammals. Furthermore, they suggested that melatonin production could be associated with survival mechanisms in areas with higher predator exposure. However, this conclusion doesn't seem to apply universally, as evidenced by _____

---

8 🔖 Mark for Review

Which choice most effectively uses data from the table to complete the statement?

(A) The Virginia Opossum, a nocturnal mammal, produces the highest amount of melatonin but has low predator exposure.

(B) The Brown Rat, a diurnal mammal, living in urban areas with high exposure to predators but producing relatively low melatonin.

(C) The Eastern Gray Squirrel and the European Rabbit, both diurnal mammals, producing less melatonin while living in areas with low exposure to predators.

(D) The Striped Skunk, a nocturnal mammal, producing high amounts of melatonin and living in open grasslands with high exposure to predators.

Percent of Customer Satisfaction

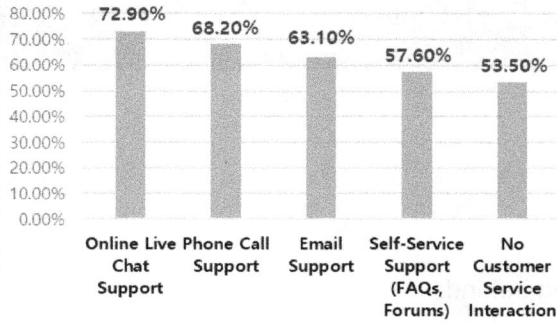

72.90%	68.20%	63.10%	57.60%	53.50%
Online Live Chat Support	Phone Call Support	Email Support	Self-Service Support (FAQs, Forums)	No Customer Service Interaction

A team of business researchers conducted a study to evaluate the influence of various types of customer service on customer satisfaction. The customer service types ranged from no interaction to various direct customer service methods, such as online live chat, phone call, and email, as well as indirect methods like self-service support. The researchers hypothesized that direct, personalized customer service interaction would lead to significantly higher customer satisfaction compared to indirect methods or no interaction.

9 🔖 Mark for Review

Which choice best describes data from the table that support the researchers' hypothesis?

(A) The highest customer satisfaction rate was reported for online live chat support, a direct method of customer service

(B) The group of customers who had no customer service interaction reported higher satisfaction than those who used self-service support.

(C) The customers who interacted with customer service via email reported lower satisfaction than those who used self-service methods.

(D) The customers who received phone call support, a direct method of customer service, reported nearly the same satisfaction rate as those who used email support.

CHAPTER 12
Vocabulary list

A

Abandon [əˈbændən] (ab- "away" + bandon "control")
(v.) To give up completely; to leave someone or something behind.
She abandoned her plans to move abroad.

Absorb [əbˈzɔːrb] (ab- "away" + sorbere "to suck in")
(v.) To take in or soak up; to fully engage or occupy.
The sponge absorbed the spilled water.

Abundant [əˈbʌndənt] (ab- "away, from" + unda "wave, flow")
(adj.) Present in great quantity; more than sufficient.
The garden was abundant with vibrant flowers.

Accelerate [əkˈsɛləreɪt] (ac- "to, toward" + celer "swift")
(v.) To increase in speed or rate.
The car accelerated quickly on the highway.

Accentuate [ækˈsɛntʃueɪt] (ad- "to" + centus "song, tone")
(v.) To emphasize or make more noticeable.
The dress accentuated her elegant figure.

Accidental [ˌæksɪˈdɛntl] (ad- "to" + cadere "to fall")
(adj.) Happening by chance or unintentionally.
The accidental discovery led to groundbreaking research.

Acclaim [əˈkleɪm] (ad- "to" + clamare "to shout")
(v.) To praise enthusiastically; (n.) enthusiastic praise.
The critics acclaimed her latest novel.
The film received widespread acclaim.

Accumulate [əˈkjuːmjʊleɪt] (ad- "to" + cumulus "heap")
(v.) To gather or collect over time.
He accumulated a vast collection of rare books.

Accurate [ˈækjʊrət] (ad- "to" + cura "care")
(adj.) Correct in all details; exact.
The scientist's measurements were highly accurate.

Achieve [əˈtʃiːv] (ad- "to" + capere "to take")
(v.) To successfully reach a goal or objective.
She achieved her dream of becoming an astronaut.

Adapt [əˈdæpt] (ad- "to" + aptus "fit, suited")
(v.) To adjust to new conditions or environments.
Animals adapt to survive in harsh climates.

Adequate [ˈædɪkwət] (ad- "to" + aequare "to make equal")
(adj.) Sufficient for a specific need or requirement.
The accommodations were adequate for our stay.

Advance [ədˈvæns] (ad- "to" + ante "before")
(v.) To move forward or make progress; (n.) progress or forward movement.
Technology continues to advance rapidly.
The team's advance was unstoppable.

Advancement [ədˈvænsmənt] (ad- "to" + ante "before")
(n.) Progress or development in a field or area.
His advancement in the company was well-deserved.

Advice [ədˈvaɪs] (ad- "to" + visum "to see")
(n.) Guidance or recommendations given to someone.
She sought advice from her mentor.

Aesthetics [iːsˈθɛtɪks] (aisth- "to perceive" + -ikos "pertaining to")
(n.) A set of principles concerned with beauty and artistic taste.
The aesthetics of the room were modern and elegant.

Affecting [əˈfɛktɪŋ] (ad- "to" + facere "to do, make")
(adj.) Emotionally moving or touching.
The affecting story brought tears to the audience.

Alter [ˈɔːltər] (alter- "other, another")
(v.) To change or modify something.
She decided to alter the design of her dress.

Ambiguity [ˌæmbɪˈgjuːɪti] (ambi- "both" + agere "to drive")
(n.) Uncertainty or inexactness of meaning.
The ambiguity in his statement caused confusion.

Ambiguous [æmˈbɪgjuəs] (ambi- "both" + agere "to drive")
(adj.) Open to more than one interpretation; unclear.
Her ambiguous response left everyone puzzled.

Ambivalence [æmˈbɪvələns] (ambi- "both" + valere "to be strong")
(n.) Mixed feelings or contradictory attitudes toward something.
His ambivalence about the decision was evident.

Amplify [ˈæmplɪfaɪ] (ampli- "large" + facere "to make")
(v.) To increase in size, strength, or importance.
The speaker amplified his voice to reach the large crowd.

Analogical [ˌænəˈlɒdʒɪkəl] (ana- "up, back" + logos "word, reason")
(adj.) Relating to or based on analogy.
The analogical reasoning helped clarify the concept.

Analyses [əˈnælɪsiːz] (ana- "up" + lysis "loosening, breaking apart")
(n.) Detailed examinations of the elements or structure of something.
Her analyses of the data revealed significant trends.

Analytically [ˌænəˈlɪtɪkli] (ana- "up" + lytikos "able to untie")
(adv.) In a manner involving detailed analysis or logical reasoning.
He approached the problem analytically.

Annotate [ˈænəteɪt] (ad- "to" + notare "to mark, note")
(v.) To add explanatory notes or comments to a text.
She annotated her textbook to highlight key points.

Antagonistic [ænˌtægəˈnɪstɪk] (anti- "against" + agon "struggle")
(adj.) Showing hostility or opposition.
Their antagonistic behavior worsened the conflict.

Anticipate [ænˈtɪsɪpeɪt] (anti- "before" + capere "to take")
(v.) To expect or predict something.
We anticipated a large turnout for the event.

Apathy [ˈæpəθi] (a- "without" + pathos "emotion")
(n.) Lack of interest, enthusiasm, or concern.
The students' apathy toward the project was disappointing.

Appraising [əˈpreɪzɪŋ] (ad- "to" + pretium "price, value")
(adj.) Evaluating or assessing something critically.
Her appraising gaze made him self-conscious.

Approve [əˈpruːvd] (ad- "to" + probare "to test, prove")
(v.) Officially agree to or accept as satisfactory.
The board approved the new policy unanimously.

Approximately [əˈprɒksɪmətli] (ad- "to" + proximus "nearest")
(adv.) Close to or around a specific number or value.
The event attracted approximately 500 attendees.

Arcane [ɑːˈkeɪn] (arcanus "secret, hidden")
(adj.) Understood by only a few; mysterious or obscure.
The professor shared arcane knowledge about ancient rituals.

Arduous [ˈɑːdjʊəs] (arduus "steep, difficult")
(adj.) Involving or requiring strenuous effort; very difficult.
Climbing the mountain was an arduous task.

Arguably [ˈɑːgjuəblɪ] (arguere "to argue")
(adv.) It may be argued; used to qualify a statement or opinion.
She is arguably the best player on the team.

Assent [əˈsɛnt] (ad- "to" + sentire "to feel, think")
(n.) Agreement or approval; (v.) to agree to or approve of something.
The proposal received her assent.
He assented to the plan after much consideration.

Assert [əˈsɜːt] (ad- "to" + serere "to join, connect")
(v.) To state a fact or belief confidently and forcefully.
He asserted his authority over the team.

Assertive [əˈsɜːtɪv] (ad- "to" + serere "to join, connect")
(adj.) Having or showing a confident and forceful personality.
She was assertive in expressing her opinions.

Assess [əˈsɛs] (ad- "to" + sedere "to sit")
(v.) To evaluate or estimate the nature, ability, or quality of something.
The teacher assessed the students' progress.

Assistance [əˈsɪstəns] (ad- "to" + sistere "to stand, place")
(n.) Help or support provided to someone.
The organization offered financial assistance to those in need.

Associative [əˈsəʊʃiətɪv] (ad- "to" + sociare "to join, unite")
(adj.) Relating to or resulting from association.
The brain's associative process linked the smell to childhood memories.

Attainable [əˈteɪnəbl] (ad- "to" + tangere "to touch")
(adj.) Capable of being achieved or reached.
With hard work, her goals were attainable.

Attractive [əˈtræktɪv] (ad- "to" + trahere "to draw, pull")
(adj.) Pleasing or appealing to the senses or mind.
The city has many attractive tourist destinations.

Authentic [ɔːˈθɛntɪk] (autos "self" + hentes "doer, being")
(adj.) Genuine; not false or copied.
The document was confirmed to be authentic.

Available [əˈveɪləbl] (ad- "to" + valere "to be strong, effective")
(adj.) Able to be used or obtained; at someone's disposal.
The book is available in both print and digital formats.

Avoid [əˈvɔɪdɪd] (ab- "away" + videre "to see")
(v.) Keep away from or prevent from happening.
She avoided discussing the controversial topic.

B

Banal [bəˈnɑːl] (ban "proclamation, decree")
(adj.) So lacking in originality as to be obvious and boring.
The movie's plot was predictable and banal.

Begin [bɪˈgɪn] (be- "about" + ginnan "to open, begin")
(v.) To start or commence.
The concert will begin at 8 PM.

Beneficial [ˌbɛnɪˈfɪʃəl] (bene- "well" + facere "to do, make")
(adj.) Producing good or helpful results; advantageous.
Regular exercise is beneficial to health.

Benevolent [bəˈnɛvələnt] (bene- "well" + volens "wishing")
(adj.) Well-meaning and kindly.
Her benevolent nature made her loved by everyone.

Bias [ˈbaɪəs] (bias "slant, oblique")
(n.) Prejudice in favor of or against one thing, person, or group; (v.) to influence unfairly.
His bias prevented him from seeing the truth.
The report was biased against the opposing party.

Blame [bleɪm] (blasphemare "to reproach, revile")
(v.) To assign responsibility for a fault or wrong; (n.) responsibility for a fault or wrong.
She blamed him for the mistake.
The blame lay with both parties.

Blend [blɛnd] (Old Norse blanda "to mix")
(v.) To mix or combine together; (n.) a mixture of different things.
The artist blended colors to create a masterpiece.
The tea is a blend of several herbs.

Breadth [brɛdθ] (Old English brædu "width")
(n.) The extent or range of something; width.
The breadth of her knowledge is impressive.

Brood [bruːd] (Old English brod "offspring, hatchling")
(n.) A group of young animals born at the same time; (v.) to think deeply about something.
The hen protected her brood from predators.
He brooded over the decision all night.

Buttress [ˈbʌtrɪs] (Old French bouter "to support")
(n.) A support for a structure; (v.) to reinforce or strengthen.
The ancient cathedral was held up by stone buttresses.
The evidence buttressed his argument.

Bypassed [ˈbaɪpɑːst] (by- "near" + passer "to pass")
(v.) Avoided or went around an obstacle or problem.
The new road bypassed the congested city center.

C

Calibration [ˌkælɪˈbreɪʃən] (calibrum "gauge")
(n.) The process of adjusting or marking a tool or instrument for accuracy.
The technician ensured the calibration of the machine was precise.

Candor [ˈkændər] (candor "whiteness, purity")
(n.) The quality of being open, honest, and straightforward.
Her candor in admitting her mistakes earned everyone's respect.

Categorically [ˌkætəˈgɒrɪkli] (kategoria "assertion, accusation")
(adv.) In a way that is unambiguously explicit and direct.
He categorically denied all allegations against him.

Ceremoniously [ˌsɛrəˈmoʊniəsli] (caerimonia "ritual, sacredness")
(adv.) With great formality or respect.
The medal was ceremoniously presented to the winner.

Challenge [ˈtʃælɪndʒ] (Old French chalenge "accusation, claim")
(n.) A task or situation requiring great effort; (v.) to invite someone to engage in competition or conflict.
The project posed a significant challenge.
She challenged him to a debate.

Cheap [tʃiːp] (Old English ceap "bargain, trade")
(adj.) Low in price or cost; (adv.) at a low price.
The store offers cheap products of decent quality.
You can buy it cheap at the market.

Circumvent [ˌsɜːrkəmˈvɛnt] (circum- "around" + venire "to come")
(v.) To find a way around an obstacle; to avoid by cleverness.
They circumvented the security system with ease.

Clash [klæʃ] (imitative origin)
(n.) A conflict or disagreement; (v.) to come into conflict.
There was a clash of opinions during the meeting.
Their personalities clashed from the very beginning.

Clumsily [ˈklʌmzɪli] (clumsy "awkward" + -ly "manner")
(adv.) In an awkward or uncoordinated way.
He clumsily dropped the vase, shattering it into pieces.

Coincide [ˌkoʊɪnˈsaɪd] (com- "together" + incidere "to fall upon")
(v.) To occur at the same time or place; to agree exactly.
Their schedules coincided, allowing them to meet.

Coincidence [koʊˈɪnsɪdəns] (com- "together" + incidere "to fall upon")
(n.) A remarkable occurrence of events at the same time, seemingly by chance.
It was pure coincidence that they both chose the same outfit.

Collaboration [kəˌlæbəˈreɪʃən] (com- "together" + laborare "to work")
(n.) The action of working with someone to produce or achieve something.
The success of the project was due to effective collaboration.

Collaborator [kəˈlæbəreɪtər] (com- "together" + laborare "to work")
(n.) A person who works jointly on an activity or project.
She was a key collaborator on the groundbreaking research.

Commend [kəˈmɛnd] (com- "with" + mandare "to entrust, commit")
(v.) To praise formally or officially.
The teacher commended her for her excellent performance.

Commendable [kəˈmɛndəbl] (com- "with" + mandare "to entrust, praise")
(adj.) Deserving praise; praiseworthy.
Her efforts in organizing the event were commendable.

Commensurately [kəˈmɛnʃərətli] (com- "together" + mensura "measure")
(adv.) In proportion or corresponding in size or degree.
Their salaries increased commensurately with their experience.

Common [ˈkɒmən] (com- "together" + munis "public, shared")
(adj.) Occurring frequently or shared by many; (n.) a shared resource or space.
It's common to feel nervous before a presentation.
The village had a common where people gathered.

Commonplace [ˈkɒmənpleɪs] (com- "together" + placea "place")
(adj.) Ordinary or unremarkable; (n.) an ordinary thing or saying.
Smartphones are now commonplace in society.

Comparable [ˈkɒmpərəbl] (com- "together" + parare "to prepare, arrange")
(adj.) Similar enough to be compared.
The two cities are comparable in size and population.

Compensate [ˈkɒmpɛnseɪt] (com- "together" + pensare "to weigh, consider")
(v.) To make up for a loss or deficiency.
He worked extra hours to compensate for his earlier mistakes.

Complaint [kəmˈpleɪnt] (com- "together" + plangere "to lament, mourn")
(n.) An expression of dissatisfaction or grievance.
The company received several complaints about their service.

Complexity [kəmˈplɛksɪti] (com- "together" + plexus "intertwined, braided")
(n.) The state of being intricate or complicated.
The complexity of the puzzle challenged even the experts.

Complicated [ˈkɒmplɪkeɪtɪd] (com- "together" + plicare "to fold")
(adj.) Consisting of many interconnecting parts; difficult to understand.
The instructions were so complicated that few could follow them.

Compound ['kɒmpaʊnd] (com- "together" + ponere "to place, put")
(n.) A mixture of two or more elements; (v.) to combine or intensify.
Water is a compound of hydrogen and oxygen.
The issue was compounded by poor communication.

Comprehensive [ˌkɒmprɪˈhɛnsɪv] (com- "together" + prehendere "to seize, grasp")
(adj.) Complete and including all aspects.
She wrote a comprehensive report on the topic.

Conceal [kənˈsiːl] (com- "together" + celare "to hide")
(v.) To hide or keep something secret.
He concealed the truth about his whereabouts.

Concealment [kənˈsiːlmənt] (com- "together" + celare "to hide")
(n.) The act of hiding something or keeping it secret.
The concealment of evidence hindered the investigation.

Conceivably [kənˈsiːvəblɪ] (com- "together" + capere "to take, grasp")
(adv.) In a manner that can be imagined or believed.
The plan could conceivably succeed with enough effort.

Concerns [kənˈsɜːnz] (com- "together" + cernere "to sift, separate")
(n.) Worries or anxieties; (v.) to relate to or affect.
Her main concerns were about safety.
The matter concerns everyone in the community.

Concludes [kənˈkluːdz] (com- "together" + claudere "to shut, close")
(v.) Brings to an end or finishes.
The study concludes that exercise improves mental health.

Conclusively [kənˈkluːsɪvli] (com- "together" + claudere "to shut, close")
(adv.) In a way that is decisive or convincing.
The evidence conclusively proved his innocence.

Concrete ['kɒŋkriːt] (com- "together" + crescere "to grow")
(adj.) Specific or definite; (n.) a hard, strong building material.
She gave concrete examples to support her argument.
The structure was made of reinforced concrete.

Concurrent [kənˈkʌrənt] (com- "together" + currere "to run")
(adj.) Happening at the same time; simultaneous.
The conference featured concurrent sessions on different topics.

Confident ['kɒnfɪdənt] (com- "together" + fidere "to trust")
(adj.) Feeling or showing certainty.
She was confident in her ability to succeed.

Conflate [kənˈfleɪt] (com- "together" + flare "to blow")
(v.) To combine two or more ideas, texts, or elements into one.
The report conflated two separate issues.

Confusion [kənˈfjuːʒən] (com- "together" + fundere "to pour")
(n.) A lack of clarity or understanding.
The instructions caused a lot of confusion among the team.

Conjectures [kənˈdʒɛktʃərz] (com- "together" + iacere "to throw")
(n.) Opinions or conclusions formed on incomplete information.
His conjectures about the outcome were proven wrong.

Consequence [ˈkɒnsɪkwəns] (com- "together" + sequi "to follow")
(n.) A result or effect of an action or condition.
Her actions had unforeseen consequences.

Consequential [ˌkɒnsɪˈkwɛnʃəl] (com- "together" + sequi "to follow")
(adj.) Significant or important; resulting from an action.
The policy change had consequential effects on the economy.

Consistently [kənˈsɪstəntli] (com- "together" + sistere "to stand, place")
(adv.) In a steady or reliable manner.
She consistently delivered excellent results.

Conspicuous [kənˈspɪkjʊəs] (com- "together" + specere "to look at")
(adj.) Clearly visible or attracting attention.
His bright red coat made him conspicuous in the crowd.

Constrain [kənˈstreɪn] (com- "together" + stringere "to bind, tighten")
(v.) To force or restrict.
Time constraints limited the scope of the project.

Constrict [kənˈstrɪkt] (com- "together" + stringere "to bind, tighten")
(v.) To make narrower by encircling pressure; to limit or restrict.
The tight collar constricted his neck.

Contemplate [ˈkɒntəmpleɪt] (com- "together" + templum "place for observation")
(v.) To think deeply or carefully about something.
She spent hours contemplating her future.

Contentious [kənˈtɛnʃəs] (com- "together" + tendere "to stretch, strive")
(adj.) Causing or likely to cause disagreement or controversy.
The topic was highly contentious during the debate.

Contingent [kənˈtɪndʒənt] (com- "together" + tangere "to touch")
(adj.) Dependent on certain conditions; (n.) a group of people representing a larger group.
Her approval was contingent on the committee's decision.
A contingent of students attended the conference.

Continuity [ˌkɒntɪˈnjuːɪti] (com- "together" + tenere "to hold")
(n.) The consistent existence or operation of something over time.
The movie lacked continuity between scenes.

Continuously [kənˈtɪnjuəsli] (com- "together" + tenere "to hold")
(adv.) Without interruption or break.
The machine operated continuously for eight hours.

Contribution [ˌkɒntrɪˈbjuːʃən] (com- "together" + tribuere "to assign, allot")
(n.) A gift or effort provided to help achieve or build something.
Her contribution to the project was invaluable.

Controversial [ˌkɒntrəˈvɜːʃəl] (contra- "against" + vertere "to turn")
(adj.) Causing disagreement or debate.
The new policy was highly controversial.

Controversy [ˈkɒntrəvɜːsi] (contra- "against" + vertere "to turn")
(n.) Disagreement, often prolonged and public.
The book sparked a major controversy among scholars.

Convenient [kənˈviːnjənt] (com- "together" + venire "to come")
(adj.) Fitting well with one's needs or plans; easily accessible.
The store's location is very convenient for me.

Conventional [kənˈvɛnʃənəl] (com- "together" + venire "to come")
(adj.) Based on or in accordance with general agreement or traditional standards.
The design was plain but conventional.

Converge [kənˈvɜːdʒ] (com- "together" + vergere "to bend, incline")
(v.) To come together from different directions to meet at a point.
The two roads converge near the city center.

Convert [kənˈvɜːt] (com- "together" + vertere "to turn")
(v.) To change or transform something into a different form or use; (n.) a person who has been converted.
She converted the attic into a cozy study.
He became a convert to the new religion.

Convey [kənˈveɪ] (com- "together" + via "way, road")
(v.) To communicate or transport something.
The message was conveyed through email.

Convincingly [kənˈvɪnsɪŋli] (com- "together" + vincere "to conquer")
(adv.) In a manner that causes someone to believe something.
She argued convincingly for her proposal.

Corroborate [kəˈrɒbəreɪt] (com- "together" + roborare "to strengthen")
(v.) To confirm or give support to a statement or finding.
The witness corroborated the suspect's alibi.

Counteract [ˌkaʊntərˈækt] (contra- "against" + agere "to do")
(v.) To act against something to reduce or neutralize its effect.
The medication counteracted the symptoms effectively.

Counterbalance [ˌkaʊntərˈbæləns] (contra- "against" + bilancia "scales")
(v.) To offset the weight or effect of something; (n.) a weight or force that balances another.
The new policy was designed to counterbalance the economic impact.

Counterfactual [ˌkaʊntərˈfæktʃuəl] (contra- "against" + factum "fact")
(adj.) Relating to or expressing what has not happened or is not the case.
The historian explored counterfactual scenarios in his analysis.

Credible [ˈkrɛdɪbl] (credere "to believe")
(adj.) Capable of being believed; plausible.
Her explanation was credible and convincing.

Critique [krɪˈtiːk] (kritikos "able to judge")
(n.) A detailed analysis or assessment of something; (v.) to evaluate or analyze critically.
The professor's critique highlighted several flaws in the argument.

Curiosity [ˌkjʊərɪˈɒsɪti] (curiosus "careful, inquisitive")
(n.) A strong desire to learn or know something.
Her curiosity about the world led her to travel extensively.

D

Definitively [dɪˈfɪnɪtɪvli] (de- "completely" + finire "to limit, end")
(adv.) In a way that provides a final or conclusive answer.
The issue was definitively resolved after the meeting.

Defunct [dɪˈfʌŋkt] (de- "away" + fungi "to perform, execute")
(adj.) No longer existing or functioning.
The factory has been defunct for over a decade.

Demand [dɪˈmɑːnd] (de- "away" + mandare "to order")
(v.) To ask forcefully or require; (n.) the need or desire for something.
The workers demanded better wages.
The demand for electric cars is increasing rapidly.

Demarcate [ˌdiːˈmɑːkeɪt] (de- "away" + marcare "to mark")
(v.) To set the boundaries or limits of something.
The survey was conducted to demarcate the property lines.

Denigrate [ˈdɛnɪgreɪt] (de- "completely" + niger "black, dark")
(v.) To criticize unfairly or belittle.
She refused to denigrate her competitor's achievements.

Denounce [dɪˈnaʊns] (de- "down" + nuntiare "to report")
(v.) To publicly declare something to be wrong or evil.
The leader denounced corruption in his speech.

Dependable [dɪˈpɛndəbl] (de- "from" + pendere "to hang")
(adj.) Reliable and trustworthy.
She is one of the most dependable members of the team.

Dependence [dɪˈpɛndəns] (de- "from" + pendere "to hang")
(n.) The state of relying on or being controlled by something or someone.
His dependence on caffeine increased during finals week.

Depicted [dɪˈpɪktɪd] (de- "down" + pingere "to paint, portray")
(v.) Represented in a drawing, painting, or description.
The painting depicted a serene landscape.

Derive [dɪˈraɪv] (de- "down, away" + rivus "stream")
(v.) To obtain something from a source.
She derived great satisfaction from helping others.

Deserving [dɪˈzɜːvɪŋ] (de- "completely" + servire "to serve")
(adj.) Worthy of reward or praise.
Her efforts were deserving of recognition.

Designate [ˈdɛzɪgneɪt] (de- "out" + signare "to mark, sign")
(v.) To appoint or assign someone to a specific role; (adj.) specified for a particular purpose.
She was designated as the team leader.
The designated area is reserved for guests.

Desultory [ˈdɛsəltəri] (de- "down" + salire "to jump, leap")
(adj.) Lacking a clear plan or purpose; random or disconnected.
His desultory approach to studying made him fall behind.

Detect [dɪˈtɛkt] (de- "away" + tegere "to cover")
(v.) To discover or identify the presence of something.
The sensor can detect even the smallest movements.

Detractors [dɪˈtræktərz] (de- "down" + trahere "to draw")
(n.) People who criticize or belittle someone or something.
Despite her detractors, she continued to pursue her dreams.

Difficult [ˈdɪfɪkəlt] (dis- "apart" + facere "to do, make")
(adj.) Needing much effort or skill to accomplish.
The exam was more difficult than anyone expected.

Diminish [dɪˈmɪnɪʃ] (de- "away" + minuere "to lessen")
(v.) To make or become less.
The medicine diminished her pain significantly.

Disagree [ˌdɪsəˈɡriː] (dis- "apart" + agrere "to please")
(v.) To have a different opinion; to fail to agree.
The two scientists disagreed on the results of the study.

Discern [dɪˈsɜːrn] (dis- "apart" + cernere "to separate, distinguish")
(v.) To recognize or perceive something clearly.
He could discern the faint outline of a ship on the horizon.

Discover [dɪsˈkʌvə] (dis- "apart" + cooperire "to cover")
(v.) To find or uncover something previously unknown.
She discovered a hidden talent for painting.

Discretion [dɪsˈkrɛʃən] (dis- "apart" + cernere "to separate, distinguish")
(n.) The quality of behaving or speaking carefully to avoid offense or revealing private information;
freedom to make decisions.
She handled the delicate matter with discretion.

Disengage [ˌdɪsɪnˈgeɪdʒ] (dis- "apart" + engager "to pledge, engage")
(v.) To release or detach oneself; to withdraw.
The gear disengaged automatically after the engine stopped.

Disfavored [ˌdɪsˈfeɪvəd] (dis- "apart" + favor "approval, support")
(v.) Regarded or treated with disapproval or dislike.
The idea was disfavored by the majority of the group.

Disguise [dɪsˈgaɪz] (dis- "apart" + guise "style, appearance")
(v.) To change the appearance of something to conceal its identity; (n.) a means of altering one's
appearance.
She disguised herself as a tourist to avoid being recognized.
His disguise was so convincing that no one noticed him.

Disingenuous [ˌdɪsɪnˈdʒɛnjʊəs] (dis- "not" + ingenuus "honest, freeborn")
(adj.) Not sincere or straightforward; pretending to know less than one actually does.
Her disingenuous apology failed to convince anyone.

Dismissal [dɪsˈmɪsəl] (dis- "apart" + mittere "to send")
(n.) The act of removing someone from a position or rejecting something as unworthy.
The employee's sudden dismissal shocked everyone.

Disparage [dɪˈspærɪdʒ] (dis- "apart" + parage "rank, equality")
(v.) To speak of in a slighting or disrespectful way; to belittle.
The critics disparaged the artist's latest work.

Displayed [dɪsˈpleɪd] (dis- "apart" + plicare "to fold")
(v.) Showed or exhibited something clearly.
The gallery displayed several new paintings by local artists.

Dispute [dɪsˈpjuːt] (dis- "apart" + putare "to reckon, think")
(v.) To argue about something; to question its validity; (n.) a disagreement or argument.
They disputed the results of the election.
The dispute over land ownership lasted for years.

Disregarded [ˌdɪsrɪˈgɑːdɪd] (dis- "apart" + regard "to look, pay attention to")
(v.) Ignored or paid no attention to.
He disregarded the warnings and continued with his plan.

Dissolve [dɪˈzɒlv] (dis- "apart" + solvere "to loosen, free")
(v.) To mix a solid substance into a liquid until it becomes part of it; to end or disappear.
The sugar dissolved quickly in the hot water.
The committee decided to dissolve after achieving its objectives.

Distinctive [dɪˈstɪŋktɪv] (dis- "apart" + tinguere "to mark, dye")
(adj.) Having a unique or characteristic quality that makes it different.
The singer's voice is distinctive and instantly recognizable.

Distinctively [dɪˈstɪŋktɪvli] (dis- "apart" + tinguere "to mark, dye")
(adv.) In a way that distinguishes something clearly from others.
Each artist in the exhibit painted distinctively.

Distrust [dɪsˈtrʌst] (dis- "apart" + trust "confidence, belief")
(n.) Lack of trust or confidence in someone or something; (v.) to doubt or mistrust.
There was a growing distrust of the government.
He distrusted the stranger's intentions.

Distrustful [dɪsˈtrʌstfʊl] (dis- "apart" + trust "confidence, belief")
(adj.) Inclined to doubt or not trust others.
She was distrustful of people she had just met.

Dogmatic [dɒgˈmætɪk] (dogma "opinion, belief")
(adj.) Asserting opinions in an arrogant or rigid manner, often without evidence.
His dogmatic attitude alienated those who disagreed with him.

Doubts [daʊts] (dubitare "to waver, be uncertain")
(n.) Feelings of uncertainty or lack of confidence; (v.) to question or be unsure about something.
She had doubts about accepting the offer.
He doubted the accuracy of the report.

Duplicated [ˈdjuːplɪkeɪtɪd] (dupli- "double" + plicare "to fold")
(v.) Made an exact copy of something.
The document was duplicated for everyone in the meeting.

Dwindling [ˈdwɪndlɪŋ] (Old English dwinen "to waste away")
(v.) Gradually decreasing in size, strength, or number.
The supply of resources was dwindling rapidly.

Dynamic [daɪˈnæmɪk] (dynamis "power, force")
(adj.) Characterized by constant change or activity; (n.) a force that stimulates growth or change.
She played a dynamic role in the company's success.
The dynamics of the market are difficult to predict.

E

Earnest ['ɜːnɪst] (Old English eornost "seriousness")
(adj.) Showing deep sincerity or seriousness.
He was earnest in his efforts to help others.

Eccentric [ɪkˈsɛntrɪk] (ec- "out" + kentron "center")
(adj.) Unconventional or slightly strange; (n.) a person with unconventional behavior.
His eccentric behavior often puzzled his coworkers.
The artist was known for being an eccentric.

Efficacy [ˈɛfɪkəsi] (efficere "to accomplish, produce")
(n.) The ability to produce the desired result or effect.
The efficacy of the new medicine was evident in the trial results.

Elicit [ɪˈlɪsɪt] (e- "out" + lacere "to entice, lure")
(v.) To draw out or evoke a response, reaction, or fact.
Her question elicited a thoughtful answer from the speaker.

Embrace [ɪmˈbreɪs] (em- "in" + bracchium "arm")
(v.) To accept willingly; to hold closely in one's arms as a sign of affection.
She embraced the challenges of her new role.
(n.) A close, affectionate hold; a hug.
Their embrace lasted longer than expected.

Emphatically [ɪmˈfætɪkli] (em- "in" + phatos "clear, obvious")
(adv.) In a forceful or definite way.
He emphatically denied the accusations.

Empty [ˈɛmpti] (Old English æmettig "at leisure, unoccupied")
(adj.) Containing nothing; lacking substance or value; (v.) to remove contents.
The room was completely empty.
She emptied her bag to find the missing key.

Encourage [ɪnˈkʌrɪdʒ] (en- "in" + cor "heart")
(v.) To inspire confidence, hope, or courage in someone.
Her kind words encouraged him to keep going.

Enduring [ɪnˈdjʊərɪŋ] (en- "in" + durare "to last")
(adj.) Lasting over a long period; (v.) persisting through hardship.
Their enduring friendship stood the test of time.

Engender [ɪnˈdʒɛndər] (en- "in" + generare "to generate, produce")
(v.) To cause or give rise to a feeling, situation, or condition.
The policy engendered a lot of public debate.

Enhance [ɪnˈhɑːns] (en- "in" + altus "high")
(v.) To improve or increase the quality, value, or extent of something.
The new design enhanced the car's performance.

Enhancement [ɪnˈhɑːnsmənt] (en- "in" + altus "high")
(n.) The process of improving something's quality, value, or performance.
The software update included several key enhancements.

Enlist [ɪnˈlɪst] (en- "in" + liste "roll, catalog")
(v.) To enroll or engage someone in a cause, effort, or service.
She enlisted in the army right after college.

Enroll [ɪnˈrəʊl] (en- "in" + rotulus "roll")
(v.) To officially register or sign up for something.
He enrolled in a creative writing course.

Entail [ɪnˈteɪl] (en- "in" + tail "cutting, division")
(v.) To involve or require as a necessary consequence.
The project entails significant time and financial commitments.

Entice [ɪnˈtaɪs] (en- "in" + titare "to set on fire, incite")
(v.) To attract or tempt by offering something desirable.
The advertisement was designed to entice potential customers.

Envision [ɪnˈvɪʒən] (en- "in" + visio "sight")
(v.) To imagine or conceive of something as a possibility or future event.
She envisioned herself as a successful entrepreneur.

Equalize [ˈiːkwəlaɪz] (aequus "equal")
(v.) To make things equal or balanced.
The team worked to equalize the distribution of resources.

Equitable [ˈɛkwɪtəbl] (aequus "equal, fair")
(adj.) Fair and impartial.
The agreement provided an equitable solution for both parties.

Equivocal [ɪˈkwɪvəkl] (equi- "equal" + vocare "to call, speak")
(adj.) Open to more than one interpretation; ambiguous.
His equivocal statement left everyone confused.

Erratic [ɪˈrætɪk] (erraticus "wandering, straying")
(adj.) Irregular, unpredictable, or inconsistent in behavior or movement.
Her erratic driving worried her passengers.

Establish [ɪˈstæblɪʃ] (ex- "out" + stare "to stand")
(v.) To set up or create something on a firm or permanent basis.
The company was established over 50 years ago.

Esteem [ɪsˈtiːm] (aestimare "to value, appraise")
(n.) Respect or admiration for someone; (v.) to regard highly.
She holds her colleagues in high esteem.

Evidently [ˈɛvɪdəntli] (e- "out" + videre "to see")
(adv.) Clearly or obviously.
He was evidently surprised by the news.

Exaggerate [ɪɡˈzædʒəreɪt] (ex- "out" + aggerare "to heap up")
(v.) To represent something as being greater, better, or worse than it really is.
He exaggerated the size of the fish he caught.

Examine [ɪɡˈzæmɪn] (ex- "out" + aminari "to inspect, look at")
(v.) To inspect or analyze something closely and carefully.
The doctor examined the patient for signs of illness.

Exceptionally [ɪkˈsɛpʃənəli] (ex- "out" + capere "to take")
(adv.) To an unusually high degree; unusually well.
She performed exceptionally well on the test.

Excessive [ɪkˈsɛsɪv] (ex- "out" + cedere "to go")
(adj.) More than is necessary, reasonable, or appropriate.
The excessive noise disrupted the meeting.

Exemplar [ɪɡˈzɛmplər] (ex- "out" + emere "to take, obtain")
(n.) A person or thing serving as an excellent model.
Her behavior is an exemplar of professionalism.

Exemplification [ɪɡˌzɛmplɪfɪˈkeɪʃən] (ex- "out" + emere "to take, obtain")
(n.) The act of showing or illustrating by example.
The teacher used a case study as an exemplification of the concept.

Exhaustive [ɪɡˈzɔːstɪv] (ex- "out" + haurire "to draw, drain")
(adj.) Thorough and comprehensive.
The report provided an exhaustive analysis of the issue.

Exhibition [ˌɛksɪˈbɪʃən] (ex- "out" + habere "to hold")
(n.) A public display of works or objects.
The art exhibition attracted visitors from around the world.

Exorbitant [ɪɡˈzɔːbɪtənt] (ex- "out" + orbita "track, course")
(adj.) Unreasonably high or excessive.
The prices in the luxury store were exorbitant.

Expand [ɪkˈspænd] (ex- "out" + pandere "to spread")
(v.) To increase in size, volume, or scope.
The company plans to expand its operations overseas.

Experience [ɪkˈspɪərɪəns] (ex- "out" + periri "to try, test")
(n.) Practical contact with and observation of facts or events; (v.) to encounter or feel.
She has years of experience in the field.
They experienced a mix of emotions during the trip.

Explain [ɪkˈspleɪn] (ex- "out" + planus "flat, clear")
(v.) To make something clear or understandable.
He explained the process step by step.

Explanation [ˌɛkspləˈneɪʃən] (ex- "out" + planus "flat, clear")
(n.) A statement or account that makes something clear.
Her explanation clarified the confusion.

Explicable [ˈɛksplɪkəbl] (ex- "out" + plicare "to fold")
(adj.) Capable of being explained or understood.
The phenomenon was scientifically explicable.

Explicitly [ɪkˈsplɪsɪtli] (ex- "out" + plicare "to fold")
(adv.) In a clear and detailed manner, leaving no room for confusion.
The instructions explicitly stated the rules.

Exploiting [ɪkˈsplɔɪtɪŋ] (ex- "out" + plicare "to fold, deploy")
(v.) Taking advantage of something unfairly for one's own benefit.
They were accused of exploiting the workers' labor.

Exposure [ɪkˈspəʊʒə] (ex- "out" + ponere "to place")
(n.) The state of being exposed to contact with something.
Prolonged exposure to sunlight can damage the skin.

Extend [ɪkˈstɛnd] (ex- "out" + tendere "to stretch")
(v.) To stretch out or make something longer or larger.
They decided to extend their stay by a few days.

Extensively [ɪkˈstɛnsɪvli] (ex- "out" + tendere "to stretch")
(adv.) Over a wide area or to a great degree.
He traveled extensively during his career.

Extract [ɪkˈstrækt] (ex- "out" + trahere "to pull")
(v.) To remove or take out something; (n.) a concentrated form of something.
They extracted valuable minerals from the mine.
The vanilla extract added a rich flavor to the dessert.

Extraneous [ɪkˈstreɪniəs] (extra- "outside" + anus "pertaining to")
(adj.) Not relevant or unrelated to the subject being dealt with.
The report was filled with extraneous details.

Extricate [ˈɛkstrɪkeɪt] (ex- "out" + tricae "perplexities, hindrances")
(v.) To free someone or something from a difficult situation.
The firefighters extricated the passengers from the wrecked car.

F

Fabrications [ˌfæbrɪˈkeɪʃənz] (fabricare "to construct, build")
(n.) The act of inventing false information; things that are made or constructed.
His story was a complete fabrication.
The fabrications were sturdy and well-designed.

Familiarize [fəˈmɪljəraɪz] (familiare "domesticate, make familiar")
(v.) To make someone acquainted with or aware of something.
He took a few minutes to familiarize himself with the controls.

Favorably [ˈfeɪvərəbli] (favor "approval, support" + -ably "in a manner of")
(adv.) In a way that shows approval or support.
Her application was reviewed favorably by the committee.

Feasible [ˈfiːzəbl] (facere "to do, make")
(adj.) Possible to do or accomplish.
The plan is feasible given the available resources.

Firmness [ˈfɜːmnəs] (firmus "strong, stable")
(n.) The quality of being strong, resolute, or unyielding.
The firmness of the foundation ensured the building's stability.

Fluctuation [ˌflʌktʃuˈeɪʃən] (fluctuare "to flow like a wave")
(n.) An irregular rising and falling in number, amount, or level.
The fluctuation in temperatures made it hard to plan activities.

Foresight [ˈfɔːsaɪt] (fore- "before" + sight "vision")
(n.) The ability to predict or plan for the future.
Her foresight in saving money helped during tough times.

Fragile [ˈfrædʒaɪl] (fragilis "easily broken")
(adj.) Easily broken, damaged, or destroyed.
The vase was beautiful but extremely fragile.

Fraudulent [ˈfrɔːdjʊlənt] (fraudulentus "deceitful")
(adj.) Involving deception, especially criminal deception.
He was accused of making fraudulent claims.

Frequently [ˈfriːkwəntli] (frequens "crowded, repeated")
(adv.) Happening often or at short intervals.
She frequently visits her family on weekends.

Fundamentally [ˌfʌndəˈmɛntəli] (fundamentum "foundation")
(adv.) At the most basic or essential level.
The problem is fundamentally a lack of communication.

Fusion [ˈfjuːʒən] (fundere "to melt, pour")
(n.) The process or result of combining two or more things into one.
The cuisine is a fusion of different culinary traditions.

G

Gathering [ˈgæðərɪŋ] (gather "to bring together")
(n.) A meeting or collection of people or things.
The family gathering was full of laughter and stories.

Generally [ˈdʒɛnərəli] (generalis "pertaining to a whole class")
(adv.) In most cases or usually.
He generally arrives at work by 9 a.m.

Generous [ˈdʒɛnərəs] (generosus "noble, magnanimous")
(adj.) Willing to give more than is usual or expected; unselfish.
She was known for her generous donations to charity.

Genuine [ˈdʒɛnjuɪn] (genuinus "native, natural")
(adj.) Authentic, real, or sincere.
The artifact was confirmed to be genuine.

Gradually [ˈgrædʒuəli] (gradus "step")
(adv.) Slowly or by degrees over time.
The temperature gradually increased throughout the day.

Grudgingly [ˈgrʌdʒɪŋli] (grudge "reluctance" + -ly "in a manner of")
(adv.) In a reluctant or unwilling manner.
He grudgingly agreed to help with the chores.

Guessed [gɛst] (Old Norse giska "to guess, estimate")
(v.) Made an estimate or assumption without sufficient information.
She guessed the answer to the riddle correctly.

Guidance [ˈgaɪdəns] (guide "to lead" + -ance "action or process")
(n.) Advice or direction provided to solve a problem or make a decision.
The teacher offered guidance on how to complete the assignment.

H

Haphazard [ˌhæpˈhæzərd] (hap "chance" + hazard "risk, danger")
(adj.) Lacking any obvious principle of organization; random.
The papers were piled on the desk in a haphazard manner.

Harbinger [ˈhɑːbɪndʒər] (here "army" + berga "shelter")
(n.) A person or thing that signals the approach of something.
The robin is often considered a harbinger of spring.

Hesitant [ˈhɛzɪtənt] (haesitare "to stick, hesitate")
(adj.) Unsure or slow in acting or speaking.
She was hesitant to accept the job offer without more information.

Hideous [ˈhɪdiəs] (hide "hide, conceal" + -ous "full of")
(adj.) Extremely ugly or unpleasant.
The monster in the movie was portrayed as hideous.

Highlight [ˈhaɪlaɪt] (high "of great vertical extent" + light "brightness")
(v.) To emphasize or make something stand out; (n.) the most important or interesting part.
She highlighted the key points in her presentation.
The highlight of the trip was visiting the Grand Canyon.

Humble [ˈhʌmbl] (humilis "lowly, modest")
(adj.) Having or showing a modest opinion of one's own importance; (v.) to lower in dignity or importance.
Despite his success, he remained humble.
The experience humbled her.

I

Idealistic [ˌaɪdiəˈlɪstɪk] (idea "form, pattern" + -istic "of or pertaining to")
(adj.) Believing in or aiming for perfection or high ideals, often unrealistically.
His idealistic vision inspired his team to dream big.

Idealized [ˈaɪdiəlaɪzd] (idea "form, pattern" + -ize "to make")
(v.) Represented as perfect or better than reality.
The novel idealized rural life.

Ideally [aɪˈdiːəli] (idea "form, pattern" + -ly "in the manner of")
(adv.) In the best possible way.
Ideally, we would finish the project by next week.

Ignore [ɪgˈnɔːr] (in- "not" + gnorare "to know")
(v.) To deliberately pay no attention to something or someone.
He chose to ignore the warning signs.

Illuminate [ɪˈluːmɪneɪt] (in- "in" + luminare "to light up")
(v.) To light up or make something clear and understandable.
The teacher used examples to illuminate the complex topic.

Illusory [ɪˈluːsəri] (illusio "deceit, mockery" + -ory "pertaining to")
(adj.) Based on illusion; not real.
His hopes of winning the lottery were illusory.

Imaginable [ɪˈmædʒɪnəbl] (imaginari "to picture to oneself" + -able "capable of")
(adj.) Possible to be imagined or conceived.
The movie was set in the most fantastic world imaginable.

Imaginative [ɪˈmædʒɪnətɪv] (imaginari "to picture to oneself" + -ive "pertaining to")
(adj.) Having or showing creativity or resourcefulness.
Her imaginative storytelling captivated the audience.

Imitate ['ɪmɪteɪt] (imitari "to copy, imitate")
(v.) To copy or mimic someone's actions or style.
Children often imitate the behavior of adults.

Immediately [ɪˈmiːdiətli] (in- "not" + medius "middle")
(adv.) At once; without delay.
She left immediately after receiving the news.

Immutable [ɪˈmjuːtəbl] (in- "not" + mutare "to change")
(adj.) Unchanging over time or unable to be changed.
The laws of physics are considered immutable.

Impart [ɪmˈpɑːrt] (in- "in" + partire "to share, divide")
(v.) To give, convey, or communicate information or qualities.
The teacher imparted wisdom to her students.

Impartiality [ˌɪmpɑːrʃiˈælɪti] (in- "not" + partialis "partial, biased")
(n.) Fairness; lack of bias or favoritism.
Judges are expected to maintain impartiality during trials.

Imperative [ɪmˈpɛrətɪv] (imperare "to command")
(adj.) Of vital importance; necessary; (n.) a command or essential action.
It is imperative to follow the safety guidelines.
The teacher's imperative was clear: finish the assignment by tomorrow.

Implausible [ɪmˈplɔːzɪbl] (in- "not" + plaudere "to applaud")
(adj.) Not seeming reasonable or probable; unconvincing.
His excuse for being late sounded implausible.

Imply [ɪmˈplaɪ] (in- "in" + plicare "to fold")
(v.) To suggest or indicate something indirectly.
His tone implied that he was not happy with the decision.

Imposing [ɪmˈpəʊzɪŋ] (in- "in" + ponere "to place")
(adj.) Grand and impressive in appearance.
The imposing mansion stood at the top of the hill.

Imprecise [ˌɪmprɪˈsaɪs] (in- "not" + precise "exact")
(adj.) Not exact or accurate.
The imprecise measurements led to errors in the experiment.

Impressively [ɪmˈprɛsɪvli] (in- "in" + premere "to press")
(adv.) In a way that evokes admiration or respect.
She performed impressively in her first competition.

Inaccurate [ɪnˈækjərət] (in- "not" + accuratus "done with care")
(adj.) Not correct or precise.
The map was inaccurate, leading us in the wrong direction.

Inadvertently [ˌɪnədˈvɜːtəntli] (in- "not" + advertere "to turn toward")
(adv.) Without intention; accidentally.
She inadvertently deleted the important file.

Incentives [ɪnˈsɛntɪvz] (in- "in" + cantare "to sing")
(n.) Things that motivate or encourage someone to do something.
The company offered financial incentives to increase productivity.

Incident [ˈɪnsɪdənt] (in- "in" + cadere "to fall")
(n.) An event or occurrence, often unpleasant or unusual.
The incident caused a delay in the project timeline.

Inconclusive [ˌɪnkənˈkluːsɪv] (in- "not" + concludere "to close, finish")
(adj.) Not leading to a definite result or conclusion.
The results of the experiment were inconclusive.

Incongruity [ˌɪnkənˈgruːɪti] (in- "not" + congruere "to agree")
(n.) The state of being out of place or inconsistent.
The incongruity between his words and actions was striking.

Incongruous [ɪnˈkɒngruəs] (in- "not" + congruere "to agree")
(adj.) Not in harmony or keeping with the surroundings or other aspects.
Her brightly colored outfit was incongruous at the formal event.

Inconsequential [ˌɪnkɒnsɪˈkwɛnʃəl] (in- "not" + sequi "to follow")
(adj.) Not important or significant.
The typo in the document was inconsequential to the overall message.

Inconsistent [ˌɪnkənˈsɪstənt] (in- "not" + consistere "to stand firm")
(adj.) Not staying the same throughout; acting at variance with previous behavior.
His explanations were inconsistent and confusing.

Inconspicuous [ˌɪnkənˈspɪkjuəs] (in- "not" + conspicere "to look at")
(adj.) Not easily seen or attracting attention.
She chose an inconspicuous spot to observe the crowd.

Incontrovertible [ˌɪnkɒntrəˈvɜːtəbl] (in- "not" + controversus "turned against")
(adj.) Not able to be denied or disputed.
The evidence presented in court was incontrovertible.

Increase [ɪnˈkriːs] (in- "into" + crescere "to grow")
(v.) To make greater in size, amount, or degree; (n.) the act of becoming larger.
The company plans to increase its workforce next year.
There has been a significant increase in sales this quarter.

Independent [ˌɪndɪˈpɛndənt] (in- "not" + dependere "to hang from")
(adj.) Free from outside control; not influenced by others.
She has always been an independent thinker.

Indications [ˌɪndɪˈkeɪʃənz] (in- "into" + dicare "to declare")
(n.) Signs or pieces of information that suggest something.
There were clear indications that the project would be successful.

Indifferent [ɪnˈdɪfərənt] (in- "not" + differre "to differ")
(adj.) Having no particular interest or sympathy; unconcerned.
He was indifferent to the outcome of the election.

Indispensable [ˌɪndɪˈspɛnsəbl] (in- "not" + dispendere "to pay out")
(adj.) Absolutely necessary or essential.
Her expertise made her an indispensable member of the team.

Indubitably [ˌɪnˈdjuːbɪtəbli] (in- "not" + dubitare "to doubt")
(adv.) Without a doubt; unquestionably.
She is indubitably one of the greatest athletes of all time.

Induce [ɪnˈdjuːs] (in- "into" + ducere "to lead")
(v.) To cause, bring about, or persuade someone to do something.
The medication was used to induce sleep.

Ineffectual [ˌɪnɪˈfɛktʃuəl] (in- "not" + effectus "effect")
(adj.) Not producing the desired result; lacking effectiveness.
His efforts to fix the situation were ineffectual.

Ineluctable [ˌɪnɪˈlʌktəbl] (in- "not" + eluctari "to struggle out of")
(adj.) Impossible to avoid or escape.
Death is an ineluctable part of life.

Inevitable [ɪnˈɛvɪtəbl] (in- "not" + evitare "to avoid")
(adj.) Certain to happen; unavoidable.
The collapse of the bridge was inevitable due to its age.

Inextricable [ˌɪnɪkˈstrɪkəbl] (in- "not" + extricare "to disentangle")
(adj.) Impossible to separate or disentangle.
Their lives became inextricable after years of working together.

Infeasible [ɪnˈfiːzəbl] (in- "not" + facere "to do")
(adj.) Not possible or practical to accomplish.
Building a bridge in that location is infeasible due to environmental concerns.

Influence [ˈɪnfluəns] (in- "into" + fluere "to flow")
(n.) The capacity to affect the character, development, or behavior of someone or something; (v.) to have an effect on.
Her influence on the project was undeniable.
The teacher influenced his choice of career.

Infrequent [ɪnˈfriːkwənt] (in- "not" + frequens "crowded, repeated")
(adj.) Occurring rarely or at irregular intervals.
Visits to the cabin became infrequent after they moved away.

Ingenious [ɪnˈdʒiːniəs] (ingenium "natural talent")
(adj.) Clever, original, and inventive.
Her ingenious solution saved the company thousands of dollars.

Inhibited [ɪnˈhɪbɪtɪd] (in- "in" + habere "to hold")
(adj.) Held back or restrained; (v.) to prevent or restrict.
She was inhibited in social situations due to shyness.
The drug inhibited the growth of harmful bacteria.

Innovation [ˌɪnəˈveɪʃən] (in- "into" + novus "new")
(n.) The introduction of something new, such as an idea or method.
The company is known for its groundbreaking innovations in technology.

Innovative [ˈɪnəveɪtɪv] (in- "into" + novus "new")
(adj.) Featuring or introducing new ideas, methods, or devices.
The innovative product revolutionized the industry.

Insightful [ˈɪnsaɪtfʊl] (in- "into" + sight "vision, understanding")
(adj.) Showing a deep understanding or perceptiveness.
Her insightful comments added great value to the discussion.

Insignificant [ˌɪnsɪgˈnɪfɪkənt] (in- "not" + significare "to signify")
(adj.) Too small or unimportant to be worth considering.
The cost of the pen was insignificant compared to the total expenses.

Inspired [ɪnˈspaɪəd] (in- "into" + spirare "to breathe")
(adj.) Filled with creative or divine influence; (v.) to motivate or fill with enthusiasm.
The inspired artist created a masterpiece.
The story inspired her to pursue her dreams.

Instructing [ɪnˈstrʌktɪŋ] (in- "in" + struere "to build")
(v.) Teaching or directing someone to do something.
The coach was instructing the players on new strategies.

Insufficient [ˌɪnsəˈfɪʃənt] (in- "not" + sufficere "to suffice")
(adj.) Not enough; inadequate.
There was insufficient evidence to support the claim.

Insuperable [ɪnˈsuːpərəbl] (in- "not" + superare "to overcome")
(adj.) Impossible to overcome.
The team faced insuperable odds but never gave up.

Insurmountable [ˌɪnsəˈmaʊntəbl] (in- "not" + surmontare "to surpass")
(adj.) Too great to overcome.
The challenges seemed insurmountable at first.

Intangible [ɪnˈtændʒəbl] (in- "not" + tangere "to touch")
(adj.) Unable to be touched or grasped; not having a physical presence.
The company's success was largely due to intangible factors like team spirit.

Intense [ɪnˈtɛns] (in- "in" + tendere "to stretch")
(adj.) Of extreme force, degree, or strength.
The competition was intense, with teams vying for the top spot.

Intensely [ɪnˈtɛnsli] (in- "in" + tendere "to stretch")
(adv.) To an extreme or strong degree.
She listened intensely to every word of the lecture.

Interdependent [ˌɪntəˈdɪpəndənt] (inter- "among, between" + dependere "to hang from")
(adj.) Mutually dependent; reliant on each other.
The economies of the two countries are deeply interdependent.

Intermediate [ˌɪntəˈmiːdiət] (inter- "between" + medius "middle")
(adj.) Coming between two things in time, place, or order; (n.) a person at a middle level of knowledge or skill.
The course is designed for intermediate learners.
There was an intermediate step before final approval.

Intermittent [ˌɪntəˈmɪtənt] (inter- "between" + mittere "to send")
(adj.) Occurring at irregular intervals; not continuous.
The intermittent rain made it difficult to plan outdoor activities.

Intricate [ˈɪntrɪkət] (in- "in" + tricare "to perplex, entangle")
(adj.) Very complicated or detailed.
The design of the ancient tapestry was intricate and beautiful.

Intrinsic [ɪnˈtrɪnsɪk] (intra- "within" + secus "alongside")
(adj.) Belonging naturally; inherent.
The intrinsic value of the gemstone made it a prized possession.

Intuitively [ɪnˈtjuːɪtɪvli] (in- "into" + tuere "to look at, guard")
(adv.) In a way that is based on instinctive understanding without the need for reasoning.
She intuitively knew something was wrong.

Invaluable [ɪnˈvæljʊəbl] (in- "not" + valere "to be strong, worth")
(adj.) Extremely useful; indispensable.
His advice was invaluable to the success of the project.

Irreconcilable [ˌɪrɛkənˈsaɪləbl] (in- "not" + reconciliare "to bring together")
(adj.) Impossible to reconcile or bring into harmony.
The couple had irreconcilable differences and decided to separate.

Irrefutable [ˌɪrɪˈfjuːtəbl] (in- "not" + refutare "to refute, disprove")
(adj.) Impossible to deny or disprove.
The prosecutor presented irrefutable evidence of the crime.

Irrelevant [ɪˈrɛlɪvənt] (in- "not" + relevare "to raise, lighten")
(adj.) Not connected to or applicable to the matter at hand.
The comment was irrelevant to the discussion.

Irreproachable [ˌɪrɪˈprəʊtʃəbl] (in- "not" + reproach "to blame")
(adj.) Beyond criticism; faultless.
Her conduct was irreproachable throughout the investigation.

Irresolvable [ˌɪrɪˈzɒlvəbl] (in- "not" + resolvare "to resolve")
(adj.) Impossible to solve or settle.
The issue seemed irreconcilable and irreprovable.

J

Jointly [ˈdʒɔɪntli] (joint "together" + -ly "in the manner of")
(adv.) Together with one or more others.
The project was jointly managed by both departments.

L

Lean [liːn] (hleonian "to incline")
(v.) To incline or rest on something for support; (adj.) thin or lacking fat.
He leaned against the wall to catch his breath.
She followed a lean diet for health reasons.

Lift [lɪft] (lyftan "to raise, heave")
(v.) To raise to a higher position or level; (n.) an upward force or motion.
They lifted the heavy box onto the shelf.
The plane gained lift and soared into the sky.

M

Magnify [ˈmæɡnɪfaɪ] (magnus "great" + facere "to make")
(v.) To make something appear larger or more important.
The microscope magnified the image of the tiny organism.

Magnitude [ˈmæɡnɪtjuːd] (magnus "great" + -tude "state, condition")
(n.) The great size or extent of something.
The magnitude of the earthquake was unprecedented.

Managing [ˈmænɪdʒɪŋ] (manus "hand" + agere "to drive")
(v.) Directing, controlling, or handling something effectively.
She is skilled at managing large teams under tight deadlines.

Mandatory [ˈmændətəri] (mandare "to command, entrust")
(adj.) Required by law or rules; compulsory.
Wearing helmets is mandatory for motorcyclists in this country.

Match [mætʃ] (mætcha "mate, companion")
(v.) To correspond or be equal to; (n.) a thing that equals or complements another.
The curtains perfectly match the color of the walls.
They were a perfect match in terms of skills and experience.

Meager [ˈmiːɡər] (macer "thin, lean")
(adj.) Lacking in quantity or quality.
The meal was meager, barely enough to satisfy their hunger.

Measure [ˈmɛʒər] (metiri "to measure")
(v.) To determine the size, amount, or degree of something; (n.) a standard unit used for comparison.
He measured the length of the table.
The plan included measures to reduce costs.

Meticulous [məˈtɪkjʊləs] (metus "fear" + -culus "small")
(adj.) Showing great attention to detail; very careful and precise.
She is meticulous in her research, leaving no detail unchecked.

Minimize [ˈmɪnɪmaɪz] (minimus "smallest")
(v.) To reduce something to the smallest possible amount or degree.
The goal is to minimize waste in the production process.

Misanthropic [ˌmɪzənˈθrɒpɪk] (misein "to hate" + anthropos "human")
(adj.) Disliking or avoiding human society.
His misanthropic tendencies made him retreat to a remote cabin.

Misconstrued [ˌmɪskənˈstruːd] (mis- "wrongly" + construere "to construct, arrange")
(v.) Interpreted something incorrectly.
Her intentions were misconstrued as selfish.

Misinformed [ˌmɪsɪnˈfɔːmd] (mis- "wrongly" + informare "to inform")
(v.) Given incorrect information.
They were misinformed about the new policy.

Misunderstandings [ˌmɪsʌndəˈstændɪŋz] (mis- "wrongly" + understand)
(n.) Failures to understand correctly.
The argument arose from a series of misunderstandings.

Misunderstood [ˌmɪsʌndəˈstʊd] (mis- "wrongly" + understand)
(v.) Failed to understand someone or something correctly.
She felt misunderstood by her peers.

Mitigate [ˈmɪtɪgeɪt] (mitis "soft" + agere "to drive")
(v.) To make something less severe or serious.
Efforts were made to mitigate the damage caused by the storm.

Mock [mɒk] (mocquer "to deride, scoff at")
(v.) To ridicule or make fun of something; (adj.) not authentic or real.
The students mocked the teacher's outdated teaching methods.
She gave a mock interview to prepare for the real one.

Modest [ˈmɒdɪst] (modestus "keeping within measure")
(adj.) Humble in appearance, behavior, or achievement.
Despite his fame, he remained modest about his accomplishments.

Momentous [məˈmɛntəs] (momentum "importance, consequence")
(adj.) Of great importance or significance.
The signing of the treaty was a momentous occasion.

Monetizing [ˈmɒnɪtaɪzɪŋ] (moneta "money" + -ize "to make")
(v.) Turning something into a source of revenue.
The platform is exploring ways of monetizing its content.

N

Nebulous ['nɛbjʊləs] (nebula "cloud, mist")
(adj.) Vague, unclear, or ill-defined.
His plans for the future remain nebulous and undefined.

Neglect [nɪˈglɛkt] (neglegere "to disregard, not heed")
(v.) To fail to care for or pay attention to something; (n.) the state of being uncared for.
She neglected her studies and failed the exam.
The building fell into neglect after it was abandoned.

Neglected [nɪˈglɛktɪd] (neglegere "to disregard, not heed")
(adj.) Suffering from a lack of care or attention.
The neglected garden was overgrown with weeds.

Neutrally ['nju:trəli] (neutralis "of neuter gender, impartial")
(adv.) In an unbiased or impartial manner.
She spoke neutrally to avoid escalating the conflict.

Nominally ['nɒmɪnəli] (nominalis "pertaining to names")
(adv.) In name only; not in reality.
He was nominally in charge, but the decisions were made by someone else.

Notably ['nəʊtəbli] (nota "mark, sign" + -ably "in a manner of")
(adv.) In a way that is worthy of attention.
The new policy notably improved employee morale.

Noteworthy ['nəʊtwɜ:ði] (note "mark, sign" + worthy "deserving attention")
(adj.) Deserving attention or recognition.
Her achievements in the field are noteworthy.

Notional ['nəʊʃənəl] (notio "concept, idea")
(adj.) Based on an idea or theory; not real or actual.
His notional plan lacked practical details.

Nullify ['nʌlɪfaɪ] (nullus "none" + facere "to make")
(v.) To make something legally void or without effect.
The court nullified the previous ruling.

Nurture ['nɜ:tʃər] (nutrire "to nourish, feed")
(v.) To care for and encourage the growth or development of something; (n.) the act of caring for or fostering growth.
Parents play a vital role in nurturing their children.
The nurture of young talent is essential for the industry.

O

Objective [əbˈdʒɛktɪv] (ob- "toward" + iacere "to throw")
(adj.) Unbiased or not influenced by personal feelings; (n.) a goal or aim.
The judge must remain objective during the trial.
Her main objective is to improve customer satisfaction.

Objectively [əbˈdʒɛktɪvli] (ob- "toward" + iacere "to throw")
(adv.) In a way that is not influenced by personal feelings or opinions.
The report was written objectively, without bias.

Obligated [ˈɒblɪɡeɪtɪd] (ob- "to" + ligare "to bind")
(v.) Bound to do something morally or legally.
She felt obligated to attend the meeting.

Obscure [əbˈskjʊər] (ob- "over" + scurus "covered")
(adj.) Not clearly understood or expressed; (v.) to make something less visible or unclear.
The meaning of the poem is obscure.
The fog obscured the view of the mountains.

Observe [əbˈzɜːv] (ob- "over" + servare "to watch, keep")
(v.) To watch, notice, or adhere to rules or customs.
She observed the behavior of the animals closely.

Obsolete [ˈɒbsəliːt] (ob- "away" + solere "to be accustomed")
(adj.) No longer in use; outdated.
The typewriter has become obsolete in modern workplaces.

Obvious [ˈɒbvɪəs] (ob- "against" + via "way, road")
(adj.) Easily perceived or understood; clear.
The solution to the problem was obvious to everyone.

Occasional [əˈkeɪʒənəl] (occasio "a falling or happening")
(adj.) Happening or appearing at irregular intervals.
He made occasional visits to his hometown.

Oddity [ˈɒdɪti] (odd "strange, unusual" + -ity "state or quality")
(n.) Something strange or unusual.
The oddity of his behavior puzzled his friends.

Offered [ˈɒfəd] (ob- "toward" + ferre "to bring, carry")
(v.) Presented or made available for someone to accept or refuse.
She offered to help with the cleanup after the party.

Organize [ˈɔːɡənaɪz] (organon "instrument, tool" + -ize "to make")
(v.) To arrange systematically; to plan or coordinate.
The event was well-organized and ran smoothly.

Orientation [ˌɔːrɪɛnˈteɪʃən] (orientare "to set or arrange")
(n.) The determination of the relative position of something or someone; a program introducing new members to an organization.
The orientation session helped new employees understand their roles.

Originality [əˌrɪdʒɪˈnælɪti] (originem "beginning, source" + -ity "state or quality")
(n.) The quality of being new, unique, or inventive.
The artist was praised for her originality and creativity.

Orthodox [ˈɔːθədɒks] (orthos "right, true" + doxa "opinion")
(adj.) Conforming to traditional beliefs or practices; conventional.
His views on education were considered orthodox and widely accepted.

Outsized [ˈaʊtsaɪzd] (out- "beyond" + size "dimension, measure")
(adj.) Much larger than usual or expected.
The company's outsized profits surprised the market.

Outstrip [aʊtˈstrɪp] (out- "beyond" + strip "move quickly")
(v.) To exceed or surpass someone or something.
The athlete outstripped all her competitors in the final lap.

Overlook [ˌəʊvəˈlʊk] (over- "above" + look "to see")
(v.) To fail to notice something; to have a view from above.
He overlooked a crucial detail in the report.
The hotel overlooks the ocean.

Overreach [ˌəʊvəˈriːtʃ] (over- "beyond" + reach "to extend")
(v.) To go beyond what is reasonable or achievable.
The company overreached itself with the ambitious project.

Oversees [ˌəʊvəˈsiːz] (over- "above" + see "to look")
(v.) Supervises or manages an activity or operation.
She oversees the entire marketing department.

Overwhelmingly [ˌəʊvəˈwɛlmɪŋli] (over- "above" + whelmen "to turn over, capsize")
(adv.) To a very great degree or with a strong effect.
The vote was overwhelmingly in favor of the new policy.

P

Pay [peɪ] (pacare "to appease, pacify")
(v.) To give money in exchange for goods, services, or to settle a debt; (n.) money given for work or services.
She paid for the groceries with her credit card.
The workers demanded fair pay for their labor.

Perceptible [pəˈsɛptɪbl] (percipere "to seize, understand")
(adj.) Able to be seen, heard, or felt; noticeable.
There was a perceptible change in the atmosphere after the announcement.

Perceptibly [pəˈsɛptəbli] (percipere "to seize, understand")
(adv.) In a way that can be perceived or noticed.
The temperature dropped perceptibly as the sun set.

Permanent [ˈpɜːmənənt] (per- "through" + manere "to remain")
(adj.) Lasting or intended to last indefinitely without change.
The changes to the system are meant to be permanent.

Permissible [pəˈmɪsɪbl] (permittere "to allow")
(adj.) Allowed by law or rules.
It is permissible to park in this area for two hours.

Persistent [pəˈsɪstənt] (per- "through" + sistere "to stand")
(adj.) Continuing firmly or obstinately despite difficulty or opposition.
Her persistent efforts eventually led to success.

Persuasive [pəˈsweɪsɪv] (per- "through" + suadere "to advise")
(adj.) Good at convincing someone to believe or do something.
Her argument was highly persuasive and swayed the audience.

Pervasive [pəˈveɪsɪv] (per- "through" + vadere "to go")
(adj.) Spreading widely throughout an area or group.
The influence of social media is pervasive in modern society.

Petitioned [pəˈtɪʃənd] (petere "to seek, request")
(v.) Formally requested something, especially in writing.
The citizens petitioned the government for better healthcare.

Physical [ˈfɪzɪkl] (physica "natural things")
(adj.) Relating to the body or material world; (n.) a medical examination.
The physical demands of the job were challenging.
She had a physical last week.

Plausibly [ˈplɔːzɪbli] (plausibilis "deserving applause")
(adv.) In a way that seems reasonable or believable.
The story was plausibly explained by the scientist.

Popularity [ˌpɒpjʊˈlærɪti] (popularis "belonging to the people")
(n.) The state of being widely liked or admired.
The singer's popularity skyrocketed after her latest album.

Positions [pəˈzɪʃənz] (positio "a placing")
(n.) Locations or arrangements; (v.) to place something in a particular spot.
The positions of the soldiers were strategically planned.
She positioned the vase in the center of the table.

Positively [ˈpɒzɪtɪvli] (positivus "settled, certain")
(adv.) In a confident or affirmative way; favorably.
She spoke positively about the company's future.

Possess [pəˈzɛs] (possidere "to hold, occupy")
(v.) To own or have something; to control.
He possesses a rare talent for music.

Possible [ˈpɒsəbl] (possibilis "able to be done")
(adj.) Capable of being done or achieved.
It's possible to finish the project by next week with extra effort.

Practicality [ˌpræktɪˈkælɪti] (practicus "active, fit for action")
(n.) The quality of being useful, sensible, or realistic.
The practicality of the design made it an instant success.

Praised [preɪzd] (preisen "to value, prize")
(v.) Expressed approval or admiration for something or someone.
The teacher praised her students for their hard work.

Precedes [prɪˈsiːdz] (prae- "before" + cedere "to go")
(v.) Comes before something in time, order, or position.
The meeting precedes the lunch break.

Precipitating [prɪˈsɪpɪteɪtɪŋ] (prae- "before" + caput "head")
(v.) Causing something to happen suddenly or unexpectedly.
The decision to cut funding precipitated the project's collapse.

Precisely [prɪˈsaɪsli] (prae- "before" + caedere "to cut")
(adv.) In an exact and accurate manner.
She explained her plan precisely and clearly.

Preclude [prɪˈkluːd] (prae- "before" + cludere "to close")
(v.) To prevent something from happening or make it impossible.
Her injury precludes her from participating in the race.

Precursors [prɪˈkɜːsəz] (prae- "before" + currere "to run")
(n.) Things or people that come before and indicate the approach of something else.
These small tremors are often precursors to larger earthquakes.

Predict [prɪˈdɪkt] (prae- "before" + dicere "to say")
(v.) To say or estimate that something will happen in the future.
The meteorologist predicted rain for the weekend.

Predictable [prɪˈdɪktəbl] (prae- "before" + dicere "to say")
(adj.) Capable of being anticipated or expected.
The ending of the movie was so predictable.

Predominant [prɪˈdɒmɪnənt] (prae- "before" + dominari "to rule")
(adj.) Present as the strongest or main element.
English is the predominant language in many countries.

Preeminent [priːˈɛmɪnənt] (prae- "before" + eminere "to stand out")
(adj.) Surpassing all others; very distinguished in some way.
She is one of the preeminent scholars in her field.

Preliminary [prɪˈlɪmɪnəri] (prae- "before" + limen "threshold")
(adj.) Coming before the main event or activity; (n.) an introductory step.
The preliminary results are promising.
The team held a preliminary meeting to discuss the project.

Presaged [ˈprɛsɪdʒd] (prae- "before" + sagire "to perceive keenly")
(v.) Indicated or warned of a future event.
Dark clouds presaged the approaching storm.

Presenting [prɪˈzɛntɪŋ] (prae- "before" + sentire "to place, offer")
(v.) Showing or offering something for consideration.
She is presenting her findings at the conference tomorrow.

Prestige [prɛsˈtiːʒ] (praestigium "illusion, glamour")
(n.) Widespread respect and admiration based on achievement or quality.
The university has great prestige in academic circles.

Presuppose [ˌpriːsəˈpəʊz] (prae- "before" + supponere "to suppose")
(v.) To assume something in advance as a basis for argument or action.
The plan presupposes that we will have enough funding.

Pretentious [prɪˈtɛnʃəs] (prae- "before" + tendere "to stretch")
(adj.) Attempting to impress by affecting greater importance or merit than is actually possessed.
His pretentious attitude annoyed his colleagues.

Prevail Over [prɪˈveɪl ˈəʊvə] (prae- "before" + valere "to be strong")
(v.) To triumph or gain mastery over something.
Good ultimately prevails over evil in the story.

Prevalent [ˈprɛvələnt] (prae- "before" + valere "to be strong")
(adj.) Widespread or commonly occurring.
This type of plant is prevalent in tropical climates.

Pervasive [pəˈveɪsɪv] (per- "through" + vadere "to go")
(adj.) Spreading widely or being present throughout something.
The influence of technology is pervasive in modern society.

Precedent [ˈprɛsɪdənt] (prae- "before" + cedere "to go")
(n.) An earlier event or action that is regarded as an example or guide.
The court's decision set a legal precedent for future cases.

Primarily [ˈpraɪmərɪli] (primus "first")
(adv.) Mainly or for the most part.
The program is designed primarily for advanced learners.

Prioritize [praɪˈɒrɪtaɪz] (prior "former" + -ize "to make")
(v.) To arrange or deal with in order of importance.
You should prioritize your tasks based on their deadlines.

Pristine [ˈprɪstiːn] (pristinus "former, original")
(adj.) In its original condition; unspoiled.
The pristine beaches attracted tourists from around the world.

Probability [ˌprɒbəˈbɪlɪti] (probare "to test, prove" + -bility "state or quality")
(n.) The likelihood of something happening or being true.
The probability of rain tomorrow is high.

Profound [prəˈfaʊnd] (pro- "forth" + fundus "bottom")
(adj.) Very great or intense; having deep insight or understanding.
The book left a profound impact on its readers.

Prohibitive [prəˈhɪbɪtɪv] (pro- "before" + habere "to hold")
(adj.) Serving to prevent something; excessively high in cost.
The prohibitive cost of the house deterred potential buyers.

Prohibitively [prəˈhɪbɪtɪvli] (pro- "before" + habere "to hold")
(adv.) In a way that is too costly or excessive to be afforded.
The land in the city center is prohibitively expensive.

Prolific [prəˈlɪfɪk] (proles "offspring" + facere "to make")
(adj.) Producing much fruit, foliage, or offspring; highly productive.
She is a prolific writer, having published over 50 books.

Prolong [prəˈlɒŋ] (pro- "forth" + longus "long")
(v.) To extend the duration of something.
They decided to prolong their vacation by a few days.

Promote [prəˈməʊt] (pro- "forth" + movere "to move")
(v.) To support or encourage something; to raise someone to a higher rank or position.
The campaign was designed to promote healthy eating habits.

Prudence [ˈpruːdəns] (prudens "foreseeing, wise")
(n.) The quality of being cautious and wise in making decisions.
Her financial prudence helped her save for the future.

Publicity [pʌbˈlɪsɪti] (publicus "public")
(n.) Attention or notice given to someone or something by the media.
The event received widespread publicity in the press.

Q

Quantitatively [ˈkwɒntɪtətɪvli] (quantitas "amount" + -ively "in the manner of")
(adv.) In terms of quantity or measurable amounts.
The survey measured the impact quantitatively.

Question [ˈkwɛstʃən] (quaerere "to seek, ask")
(n.) A sentence or phrase used to find out information; (v.) to ask something or express doubt.
He asked a question about the new policy.
The validity of the report was questioned.

Questionable [ˈkwɛstʃənəbl] (quaerere "to seek, ask" + -able "capable of")
(adj.) Doubtful as regards truth or quality.
His explanation of the events was highly questionable.

Questioned [ˈkwɛstʃənd] (quaerere "to seek, ask")
(v.) Asked someone about something; expressed doubts or raised issues.
The investigator questioned the suspect for hours.

R

Random [ˈrændəm] (rand "impulse, surge")
(adj.) Made or done without method or conscious decision.
The numbers were chosen at random from a hat.

Rapid [ˈræpɪd] (rapidus "swift, tearing away")
(adj.) Happening in a short amount of time; quick.
The team's rapid response prevented further damage.

Rarely [ˈrɛəli] (rarus "thin, scattered")
(adv.) Not often; infrequently.
She rarely visits the museum, even though it's nearby.

Realize [ˈrɪəlaɪz] (realis "actual" + -ize "to make")
(v.) To become aware of something; to achieve or make something happen.
She realized the importance of her role in the project.

Reasonable [ˈriːznəbl] (rationem "reason" + -able "capable of")
(adj.) Fair, sensible, and moderate.
The price for the service was reasonable and affordable.

Recalcitrant [rɪˈkælsɪtrənt] (re- "back" + calcitrare "to kick back")
(adj.) Stubbornly disobedient or resistant to authority.
The recalcitrant student refused to follow the teacher's instructions.

Received [rɪˈsiːvd] (re- "back" + capere "to take")
(v.) To have been given, presented with, or paid; (adj.) generally accepted as true.
She received a package from her friend.
His ideas were well received by the committee.

Reciprocate [rɪˈsɪprəkeɪt] (re- "back" + procare "to move back and forth")
(v.) To respond to a gesture or action by doing something similar.
He reciprocated her kindness by helping her with her work.

Recognition [ˌrɛkəgˈnɪʃən] (re- "again" + cognoscere "to know")
(n.) The act of identifying someone or something; acknowledgment of achievement.
Her contributions to the project earned her well-deserved recognition.

Recognizable [ˈrɛkəgnaɪzəbl] (re- "again" + cognoscere "to know" + -able "capable of")
(adj.) Easily identified or known.
The landmark is recognizable from a great distance.

Recognize [ˈrɛkəgnaɪz] (re- "again" + cognoscere "to know")
(v.) To identify someone or something as already known; to acknowledge formally.
I immediately recognized her voice on the phone.

Recommended [ˌrɛkəˈmɛndɪd] (re- "again" + commendare "to entrust")
(v.) Suggested as the best course of action; endorsed.
The book was highly recommended by several critics.

Reconstitute [ˌriːˈkɒnstɪtjuːt] (re- "again" + constituere "to set up")
(v.) To build or form something again after it has been damaged or destroyed.
The soup can be reconstituted by adding hot water.

Rectify [ˈrɛktɪfaɪ] (rectus "straight" + -ify "to make")
(v.) To correct or make something right.
The company promised to rectify the billing error immediately.

Recurrent [rɪˈkʌrənt] (re- "again" + currere "to run")
(adj.) Happening repeatedly or periodically.
Recurrent headaches led her to seek medical advice.

Reduce [rɪˈdjuːs] (re- "back" + ducere "to lead")
(v.) To make something smaller in size, amount, or importance.
They aim to reduce waste by recycling more efficiently.

Refute [rɪˈfjuːt] (refutare "to repel, rebut")
(v.) To prove something to be wrong or false.
She refuted the claims made against her with solid evidence.

Regard [rɪˈgɑːd] (re- "back" + guarder "to guard, look at")
(v.) To consider or think of someone or something in a particular way; (n.) attention or concern for something.
He is highly regarded in his field.
Please send my regards to your family.

Register [ˈrɛdʒɪstə] (registra "a list, record")
(v.) To record or enroll officially; (n.) an official list or record.
She registered for the upcoming conference.
The register contains the names of all participants.

Regrettable [rɪˈgrɛtəbl] (re- "back" + greter "to lament")
(adj.) Causing sadness or disappointment; unfortunate.
The decision to cancel the program was regrettable but necessary.

Reject [rɪˈdʒɛkt] (re- "back" + jacere "to throw")
(v.) To refuse to accept, agree to, or consider something.
The proposal was rejected by the board.

Rejuvenate [rɪˈdʒuːvəneɪt] (re- "again" + juvenis "young")
(v.) To make someone or something look or feel younger, fresher, or more lively.
The spa treatments rejuvenated her after a stressful week.

Relatively [ˈrɛlətɪvli] (relativus "having relation")
(adv.) In comparison to something else; to a certain extent.
The task was relatively simple compared to the others.

Release [rɪ'liːs] (re- "back" + laxare "to loosen")
(v.) To set something or someone free; (n.) the act of freeing or making available.
The prisoner was released after serving ten years.
The release of the new album was highly anticipated.

Reliably [rɪ'laɪəbli] (re- "again" + ligare "to bind")
(adv.) In a trustworthy or dependable manner.
The machine has been performing reliably for years.

Reluctantly [rɪ'lʌktəntli] (re- "against" + luctari "to struggle")
(adv.) In an unwilling or hesitant way.
She reluctantly agreed to attend the meeting.

Renounce [rɪ'naʊns] (re- "back" + nuntiare "to announce")
(v.) To formally declare one's abandonment of something.
He renounced his claim to the inheritance.

Replace [rɪ'pleɪs] (re- "back" + placere "to place")
(v.) To put something in the place of another.
She replaced the old batteries with new ones.

Representative [ˌrɛprɪ'zɛntətɪv] (re- "again" + praesentare "to present")
(n.) A person chosen or appointed to act on behalf of others; (adj.) typical of a group or class.
The representative spoke on behalf of the workers.
The sample was representative of the entire population.

Reprieve [rɪ'priːv] (re- "back" + prehendere "to take hold of")
(n.) A temporary relief or delay; (v.) to grant a postponement.
The student was granted a reprieve from the exam deadline.

Reproduction [ˌriːprə'dʌkʃən] (re- "again" + producere "to lead forth")
(n.) The process of producing offspring or making a copy of something.
The reproduction of the painting was nearly indistinguishable from the original.

Repudiate [rɪ'pjuːdɪeɪt] (repudium "divorce, rejection")
(v.) To reject the validity of or refuse to accept.
She repudiated the accusations against her.

Repudiation [rɪˌpjuːdɪ'eɪʃən] (repudium "divorce, rejection")
(n.) The act of rejecting or disowning something.
His repudiation of the deal caused controversy.

Reputation [ˌrɛpjʊ'teɪʃən] (re- "again" + putare "to think")
(n.) The beliefs or opinions held about someone or something.
She has a stellar reputation as a dedicated teacher.

Require [rɪ'kwaɪə] (re- "again" + quaerere "to seek")
(v.) To need something or make something necessary.
This project requires a lot of time and effort.

Requirement [rɪˈkwaɪəmənt] (re- "again" + quaerere "to seek")
(n.) Something that is needed or demanded.
Meeting the educational requirements is essential for the job.

Resolve [rɪˈzɒlv] (re- "again" + solvere "to loosen")
(v.) To settle or find a solution to a problem; (n.) firm determination to do something.
They resolved the issue through negotiation.
Her resolve to succeed was unshakable.

Retain [rɪˈteɪn] (re- "back" + tenere "to hold")
(v.) To keep possession of something.
The company decided to retain its most experienced employees.

Retired [rɪˈtaɪəd] (re- "back" + tirer "to pull, draw")
(adj.) Having stopped working, typically due to age; (v.) to stop working.
He is a retired professor living a peaceful life.

Retroactively [ˌrɛtrəʊˈæktɪvli] (retro- "backward" + activus "active")
(adv.) In a way that applies to a period before enactment.
The law was applied retroactively, affecting earlier cases.

Revealed [rɪˈviːld] (re- "back" + velare "to cover")
(v.) Made known or shown something that was hidden.
The investigation revealed significant new information.

Revealing [rɪˈviːlɪŋ] (re- "back" + velare "to cover")
(adj.) Making something known; showing more than usual.
The revealing article shed light on the company's practices.

Revelation [ˌrɛvəˈleɪʃən] (re- "back" + velare "to cover")
(n.) A surprising and previously unknown fact that is made known.
The revelation about the scandal shocked everyone.

Reverence [ˈrɛvərəns] (revereri "to stand in awe of")
(n.) Deep respect for someone or something; (v.) to regard with great respect.
The community showed reverence for their leader.
He reverenced the traditions of his ancestors.

Revolted [rɪˈvəʊltɪd] (revolvere "to roll back")
(v.) Rose in rebellion against authority; (adj.) filled with disgust.
The citizens revolted against the unfair laws.
She was revolted by the graphic images in the film.

Rewards [rɪˈwɔːdz] (re- "again" + ward "guard, watch")
(n.) Benefits or compensations for effort or achievement; (v.) to give something as a reward.
The rewards for their hard work were well-deserved.
The company rewarded its employees with bonuses.

Rigorously [ˈrɪgərəsli] (rigor "stiffness, strictness")
(adv.) In a strict, thorough, or demanding way.
The new policy was rigorously enforced.

S

Sanction ['sæŋkʃən] (sanctio "decree, ratification")
(n.) Official permission or approval; a penalty for disobeying a rule; (v.) to approve or punish.
The government imposed sanctions on the violating companies.
The proposal was sanctioned by the board.

Sanguine ['sæŋgwɪn] (sanguineus "of blood, bloody")
(adj.) Optimistic or positive, especially in a difficult situation.
She remained sanguine about her chances of success despite the challenges.

Satiate ['seɪʃɪeɪt] (satiare "to fill, satisfy")
(v.) To fully satisfy a desire or appetite.
The meal was enough to satiate their hunger.

Satirize ['sætɪraɪz] (satura "poetic medley, dish of mixed ingredients")
(v.) To mock or criticize someone or something using satire.
The play satirized the corruption in politics.

Scheme [skiːm] (schema "form, outline")
(n.) A plan or arrangement; (v.) to make secret plans.
The government unveiled a new housing scheme.
He schemed to gain control of the company.

Scrutinize ['skruːtɪnaɪz] (scrutari "to search, examine")
(v.) To examine something closely and thoroughly.
The auditors scrutinized every financial detail.

Seamlessly ['siːmləsli] (seam "a line where two things join" + -less "without")
(adv.) Smoothly and continuously, without noticeable gaps or changes.
The two systems integrated seamlessly.

Selective [sɪ'lɛktɪv] (se- "apart" + ligere "to choose")
(adj.) Involving a careful choice of what to include or focus on.
She was very selective about the projects she took on.

Self-contradictory [ˌsɛlfˌkɒntrə'dɪktəri] (self "oneself" + contradicere "to speak against")
(adj.) Containing opposing or conflicting statements or ideas.
His argument was self-contradictory and lacked coherence.

Self-servingly [ˌsɛlf'sɜːvɪŋli] (self "oneself" + serving "acting to benefit")
(adv.) In a way that benefits oneself, often at the expense of others.
He self-servingly manipulated the data to support his claim.

Sensitive ['sɛnsɪtɪv] (sentire "to feel")
(adj.) Quick to detect or respond to slight changes; easily hurt emotionally.
The equipment is highly sensitive to temperature changes.
She is very sensitive to criticism.

Share [ʃɛə] (scearu "division, portion")
(v.) To give a portion of something to others; (n.) a part or portion of something.
They shared the profits equally among the team.
She owns a significant share of the company.

Shows [ʃəʊz] (sceawian "to look, see")
(v.) Displays or makes visible; (n.) performances or exhibitions.
The graph shows the trend over the past year.
The play was one of the best shows I've seen.

Shrewd [ʃruːd] (schreawa "wicked, cunning")
(adj.) Having sharp powers of judgment; astute.
She made a shrewd investment decision.

Significant [sɪɡˈnɪfɪkənt] (significare "to signify")
(adj.) Having meaning, importance, or influence.
The discovery was significant for the field of medicine.

Similar [ˈsɪmɪlər] (similis "like, resembling")
(adj.) Having a resemblance in appearance, character, or quantity, without being identical.
The two paintings are similar in style and composition.

Similarly [ˈsɪmɪlərli] (similis "like, resembling")
(adv.) In a way that shows resemblance or similarity.
The two proposals were similarly structured.

Simplification [ˌsɪmplɪfɪˈkeɪʃən] (simplex "simple" + -ficare "to make")
(n.) The process of making something easier to understand or do.
The new system is a simplification of the old one.

Sincerity [sɪnˈsɛrɪti] (sincerus "clean, pure")
(n.) The quality of being free from pretense, deceit, or hypocrisy.
Her sincerity in the apology was evident to everyone.

Situated [ˈsɪtjʊeɪtɪd] (situare "to place, position")
(adj.) Located or positioned in a particular place.
The hotel is conveniently situated near the airport.

Skeptically [ˈskɛptɪkli] (skeptikos "inquirer, doubter")
(adv.) In a way that shows doubt or disbelief.
He skeptically reviewed the plan, questioning its feasibility.

Skepticism [ˈskɛptɪsɪzəm] (skeptikos "inquirer, doubter")
(n.) An attitude of doubt or a tendency to question accepted opinions.
There was widespread skepticism about the government's new policy.

Slowly [ˈsləʊli] (slow "not quick" + -ly "in a manner of")
(adv.) At a low speed; not quickly.
The car moved slowly through the heavy traffic.

Solidified [səˈlɪdɪfaɪd] (solidus "firm, whole" + -ify "to make")
(v.) Made solid or more firmly established.
The agreement solidified their partnership.

Solidify [səˈlɪdɪfaɪ] (solidus "firm, whole" + -ify "to make")
(v.) To make or become solid or more definite.
The negotiations helped to solidify their understanding.

Soothed [suːðd] (soðian "to verify, prove to be true")
(v.) Calmed or comforted someone or something.
She soothed the crying baby with a lullaby.

Sophistication [səˌfɪstɪˈkeɪʃən] (sophisticare "tamper with, adulterate")
(n.) The quality of being refined, cultured, or complex.
The sophistication of the design impressed everyone at the exhibit.

Source [sɔːs] (surgere "to rise, spring forth")
(n.) The origin or starting point of something; (v.) to obtain from a specific place.
The river's source is high in the mountains.
The parts were sourced from local suppliers.

Specifically [spəˈsɪfɪkli] (specere "to look, observe")
(adv.) In a way that is clear, exact, or particular.
She asked for the details specifically related to the project.

Spectacle [ˈspɛktəkl] (spectaculum "a show, sight")
(n.) A visually striking performance or display.
The fireworks display was a breathtaking spectacle.

Speculate [ˈspɛkjʊleɪt] (specere "to look at")
(v.) To form a theory or conjecture without firm evidence.
The media speculated about the reasons behind the resignation.

Split [splɪt] (Dutch splitten "to split, divide")
(v.) To divide or separate into parts; (n.) a division or rift.
The group split into smaller teams to work on the project.
There was a split between the two factions of the organization.

Sporadic [spəˈrædɪk] (sporadikos "scattered, dispersed")
(adj.) Occurring at irregular intervals or only in a few places.
Sporadic power outages affected the town during the storm.

Sporadically [spəˈrædɪkli] (sporadikos "scattered, dispersed")
(adv.) Occasionally or at irregular intervals.
The machine worked sporadically, causing delays in production.

Spurious [ˈspjʊəriəs] (spurius "illegitimate, false")
(adj.) False or not genuine; not being what it purports to be.
The claims made in the advertisement were spurious and misleading.

Stabilizing [ˈsteɪbəlaɪzɪŋ] (stabilis "firm, steadfast" + -ize "to make")
(v.) Making or becoming steady or stable.
The measures were aimed at stabilizing the economy during the crisis.

Startle [ˈstɑːtl] (Old English styrtan "to leap up")
(v.) To surprise or frighten someone suddenly.
The loud noise startled everyone in the room.

State [steɪt] (status "condition, position")
(n.) A condition or situation; (v.) to express something in speech or writing.
The house was in a poor state of repair.
He stated his opinion clearly during the meeting.

Steadily [ˈstɛdɪli] (stead "place, position" + -ly "in a manner of")
(adv.) In a consistent or continuous way.
The company has been growing steadily over the past five years.

Steady [ˈstɛdi] (Old English stæðig "firm, fixed")
(adj.) Firmly fixed or stable; (v.) to make or become steady.
He kept a steady pace during the race.
She steadied herself before making the announcement.

Steering [ˈstɪərɪŋ] (Old English stieran "to guide")
(v.) Guiding or directing something, such as a vehicle or process.
He was steering the ship through rough waters.

Straightforward [ˌstreɪtˈfɔːwəd] (straight "direct" + forward "ahead")
(adj.) Simple, honest, and easy to understand.
The instructions were straightforward and easy to follow.

Strangely [ˈstreɪndʒli] (strange "foreign, unfamiliar" + -ly "in a manner of")
(adv.) In an unusual or unexpected way.
She behaved strangely after receiving the news.

Strikingly [ˈstraɪkɪŋli] (strike "to hit" + -ly "in a manner of")
(adv.) In a way that attracts attention or is remarkable.
The painting was strikingly beautiful and captivated everyone.

Stymie [ˈstaɪmi] (origin uncertain)
(v.) To prevent or hinder the progress of something.
The lack of funding stymied their efforts to complete the project.

Subdue [səbˈdjuː] (sub- "under" + ducere "to lead")
(v.) To overcome, quieten, or bring under control.
The firefighters managed to subdue the flames quickly.

Subordinate [səˈbɔːdɪnɪt] (sub- "under" + ordinare "to arrange")
(adj.) Lower in rank or position; (v.) to place in a lower rank; (n.) a person under someone else's authority.
He is a subordinate employee in the organization.
She subordinated her personal interests to those of the team.

Subside [səbˈsaɪd] (sub- "under" + sidere "to sit, settle")
(v.) To become less intense, violent, or severe.
The storm began to subside after several hours.

Substantial [səbˈstænʃəl] (substantia "essence, substance")
(adj.) Of considerable importance, size, or worth.
She received a substantial bonus for her excellent work.

Substantially [səbˈstænʃəli] (substantia "essence, substance")
(adv.) To a great or significant extent.
The policy has been substantially revised to meet new standards.

Subtlety [ˈsʌtlti] (subtilis "fine, delicate")
(n.) The quality of being delicate or difficult to detect; a fine distinction.
The subtlety of her performance was appreciated by critics.

Subvert [səbˈvɜːt] (sub- "under" + vertere "to turn")
(v.) To undermine or overthrow an established authority or system.
The propaganda was intended to subvert public trust in the government.

Successfully [səkˈsɛsfəli] (successus "an advance, achievement" + -ly "in a manner of")
(adv.) In a way that accomplishes a desired aim or result.
She successfully completed the project on time.

Successively [səkˈsɛsɪvli] (successus "to follow after" + -ively "in a manner of")
(adv.) One after another in sequence.
The team won successively for three years in a row.

Summations [sʌˈmeɪʃənz] (summa "sum, total" + -tion "action or process")
(n.) The process of adding things together; a concluding summary.
The lawyer's summation emphasized the key points of the case.

Superficial [ˌsuːpəˈfɪʃəl] (super- "above" + facies "face, surface")
(adj.) Existing on or near the surface; not thorough or deep.
His analysis of the problem was superficial and lacked depth.

Superfluous [suːˈpɜːfluəs] (super- "over, above" + fluere "to flow")
(adj.) Unnecessary, especially through being more than enough.
The report contained superfluous details that distracted from the main points.

Superior [suːˈpɪərɪə] (super- "above" + ior "comparative suffix")
(adj.) Higher in rank, quality, or importance; (n.) a person of higher rank.
She received superior ratings in her performance review.
He reported directly to his superior.

Supplant [səˈplɑːnt] (sub- "under" + plantare "to plant")
(v.) To take the place of something, often through force or strategy.
New technology has supplanted older methods of communication.

Supportive [səˈpɔːtɪv] (supportare "to carry, sustain")
(adj.) Providing encouragement or assistance.
Her family was very supportive during her recovery.

Supposition [ˌsʌpəˈzɪʃən] (supponere "to suppose" + -tion "action or process")
(n.) An uncertain belief or assumption.
The theory is based on supposition rather than concrete evidence.

Surprising [səˈpraɪzɪŋ] (surprendre "to overtake")
(adj.) Causing wonder or astonishment.
It was surprising to see such a large turnout at the event.

Surrender [səˈrɛndə] (sur- "over" + render "to give back")
(v.) To give up or yield to an authority or opponent; (n.) the act of giving up.
The soldiers surrendered after a long battle.
The terms of the surrender were discussed in detail.

Sustainable [səˈsteɪnəbl] (sustinere "to hold up, support")
(adj.) Able to be maintained or continued over the long term.
The company is committed to sustainable practices to protect the environment.

Symbolize [ˈsɪmbəlaɪz] (symbolum "a sign, mark, token")
(v.) To represent or stand for something, especially abstract ideas.
The dove symbolizes peace and harmony.

Sympathy [ˈsɪmpəθi] (syn- "together" + pathos "feeling")
(n.) Feelings of pity and compassion for someone else's misfortune.
She expressed her sympathy to the grieving family.

Synopsis [sɪˈnɒpsɪs] (syn- "together" + opsis "view")
(n.) A brief summary or general overview of something.
The synopsis of the book intrigued potential readers.

Systematically [ˌsɪstɪˈmætɪkli] (systema "organized whole" + -ally "in a manner of")
(adv.) In an organized, methodical way.
The tasks were systematically arranged to ensure efficiency.

T

Tally [ˈtæli] (talea "cutting, stick")
(n.) A record of scores or amounts; (v.) to count or record.
The tally of votes was announced after the polls closed.
They tallied the total sales for the month.

Teach [tiːtʃ] (tæcan "to show, instruct")
(v.) To impart knowledge or skill to someone.
She teaches mathematics at the local high school.

Tenuous [ˈtɛnjʊəs] (tenuis "thin, slight")
(adj.) Very weak or slight; lacking a strong basis.
The connection between the two events is tenuous at best.

Theoretically [ˌθɪəˈrɛtɪkli] (theoria "contemplation, speculation")
(adv.) In a way that relates to abstract reasoning or theory.
Theoretically, the plan should work if all conditions are met.

Thoroughly ['θʌrəli] (through "complete" + -ly "in a manner of")
(adv.) Completely and with great attention to detail.
She thoroughly checked every document before submitting it.

Thoughtfulness ['θɔːtfʊlnəs] (thought "idea, consideration" + -ful "full of")
(n.) Consideration for others; careful and reflective thinking.
His thoughtfulness was evident in the care he showed for others.

Thrive [θraɪv] (Old Norse þrifa "to grasp, get hold of")
(v.) To grow or develop well; to prosper.
The business continued to thrive despite economic challenges.

Timeworn ['taɪmwɔːn] (time + worn "damaged by use")
(adj.) Worn out or old-fashioned due to age or overuse.
The timeworn building was a historic landmark.

Tolerance ['tɒlərəns] (tolerare "to bear, endure")
(n.) The ability to accept or endure something unpleasant or different.
The team showed great tolerance for cultural differences.

Tough [tʌf] (tuk "strong, solid")
(adj.) Strong, durable, or difficult to deal with.
The material is tough enough to withstand harsh conditions.

Traced [treɪst] (tractare "to handle, draw out")
(v.) Found or discovered by investigation; (adj.) marked or outlined.
The detective traced the origin of the mysterious letter.

Traditional [trəˈdɪʃənl] (traditio "a handing down")
(adj.) Based on long-established customs or beliefs.
They celebrated the holiday in a traditional manner.

Tranquil ['træŋkwɪl] (tranquillus "quiet, calm")
(adj.) Calm and peaceful, free from disturbance.
The tranquil garden was the perfect place for meditation.

Transpose [trænsˈpəʊz] (trans- "across" + ponere "to place")
(v.) To change the order or position of something.
She transposed the numbers in the equation by mistake.

Triggered ['trɪgəd] (trigger "a mechanism that starts a process")
(v.) Caused something to happen or occur; (adj.) set off by a specific action or event.
The announcement triggered a wave of protests.

Trivial ['trɪvɪəl] (trivialis "commonplace")
(adj.) Of little importance or value.
He dismissed the issue as trivial and unworthy of attention.

U

Ubiquitous [juːˈbɪkwɪtəs] (ubique "everywhere")
(adj.) Present, appearing, or found everywhere.
Smartphones have become ubiquitous in modern society.

Unalterable [ʌnˈɔːltərəbl] (un- "not" + alterare "to change")
(adj.) Not capable of being changed.
The terms of the agreement were unalterable.

Unambiguously [ˌʌnæmˈbɪgjʊəsli] (un- "not" + ambiguus "doubtful")
(adv.) Clearly and without confusion.
The instructions were stated unambiguously to avoid misunderstandings.

Unassailable [ˌʌnəˈseɪləbl] (un- "not" + assail "to attack")
(adj.) Impossible to dispute or attack.
Her logic was unassailable, leaving no room for argument.

Unassuming [ˌʌnəˈsjuːmɪŋ] (un- "not" + assume "to take for oneself")
(adj.) Modest and not drawing attention to oneself.
Despite his success, he remained unassuming and humble.

Unattainable [ˌʌnəˈteɪnəbl] (un- "not" + attain "to reach")
(adj.) Not able to be achieved or reached.
For many, owning a home in the city feels unattainable.

Unavoidable [ˌʌnəˈvɔɪdəbl] (un- "not" + avoid "to evade")
(adj.) Impossible to prevent or evade.
The delays were unavoidable due to severe weather conditions.

Uncertain [ʌnˈsɜːtən] (un- "not" + certus "sure")
(adj.) Not known or definite.
The outcome of the election remains uncertain.

Unclassifiable [ˌʌnˈklæsɪfaɪəbl] (un- "not" + classificare "to classify")
(adj.) Not able to be categorized or placed into a clear group.
The strange object was unclassifiable and puzzled scientists.

Uncontroversial [ˌʌnkɒntrəˈvɜːʃəl] (un- "not" + controversial "likely to cause debate")
(adj.) Not likely to provoke disagreement or debate.
The proposal was uncontroversial and easily approved.

Uncovered [ʌnˈkʌvəd] (un- "not" + cover "to conceal")
(adj.) Revealed or exposed; (v.) to make visible or known.
The investigation uncovered crucial evidence.

Underestimate [ˌʌndərˈɛstɪmeɪt] (under- "below" + estimate "to value")
(v.) To assess something as less than its actual value; (n.) an undervaluation.
Don't underestimate her ability to handle the situation.

Undermine [ˌʌndəˈmaɪn] (under- "below" + mine "to dig")
(v.) To weaken or damage something, especially gradually.
The scandal undermined the public's trust in the administration.

Understand [ˌʌndəˈstænd] (under- "below" + standan "to stand")
(v.) To grasp the meaning, significance, or nature of something.
It's important to understand the implications of your decisions.

Undoubtedly [ʌnˈdaʊtɪdli] (un- "not" + dubitare "to doubt")
(adv.) Without a doubt; certainly.
She is undoubtedly one of the best athletes in the world.

Unequivocal [ˌʌnɪˈkwɪvəkl] (un- "not" + aequivocus "ambiguous")
(adj.) Clear and leaving no doubt.
His unequivocal support for the policy won widespread approval.

Unfailingly [ʌnˈfeɪlɪŋli] (un- "not" + fail "to fall short")
(adv.) In a reliable or constant way.
She unfailingly offered her help whenever it was needed.

Unflattering [ʌnˈflætərɪŋ] (un- "not" + flatter "to praise excessively")
(adj.) Not flattering; not showing something in a favorable way.
The review was unflattering and highlighted the film's flaws.

Uniformly [ˈjuːnɪfɔːmli] (uni- "one" + forma "form, shape")
(adv.) In a consistent or identical way across all instances.
The rules were uniformly applied to all participants.

Unintended [ˌʌnɪnˈtɛndɪd] (un- "not" + intend "to plan")
(adj.) Not planned or meant.
The policy had unintended consequences for small businesses.

Unknown [ˌʌnˈnəʊn] (un- "not" + known "understood, recognized")
(adj.) Not known or familiar; (n.) something that is not known.
The origins of the artifact remain unknown.
Explorers ventured into the unknown.

Unmistakable [ˌʌnmɪˈsteɪkəbl] (un- "not" + mistake "to error")
(adj.) Clearly recognizable; impossible to confuse with anything else.
The singer's unmistakable voice captivated the audience.

Unnecessary [ʌnˈnɛsəsəri] (un- "not" + necessarius "needful")
(adj.) Not needed or required.
The extra details were unnecessary and confused the argument.

Unnoticed [ʌnˈnəʊtɪst] (un- "not" + notice "to observe")
(adj.) Not seen or observed.
Her contributions to the project went unnoticed by her superiors.

Unparalleled [ˌʌnˈpærəleld] (un- "not" + parallel "equal, comparable")
(adj.) Having no equal; exceptional.
Her skill in negotiation is unparalleled in the industry.

Unprecedented [ʌnˈprɛsɪdəntɪd] (un- "not" + praecedere "to go before")
(adj.) Never done or known before.
The event was an unprecedented success, breaking all attendance records.

Unreliable [ˌʌnrɪˈlaɪəbl] (un- "not" + reliable "trustworthy")
(adj.) Not able to be depended on.
The old equipment was unreliable and frequently broke down.

Unrivaled [ˌʌnˈraɪvəld] (un- "not" + rival "competitor")
(adj.) Without competition; better than everyone or everything else.
The artist's talent is unrivaled in the contemporary art world.

Unspecified [ˌʌnˈspɛsɪfaɪd] (un- "not" + specify "to mention explicitly")
(adj.) Not stated or identified.
The contract included unspecified terms that were unclear.

Unsurprising [ˌʌnsəˈpraɪzɪŋ] (un- "not" + surprising "causing wonder")
(adj.) Not causing surprise or amazement.
Given the circumstances, their decision was unsurprising.

Unyielding [ʌnˈjiːldɪŋ] (un- "not" + yield "to give way")
(adj.) Not giving way to pressure; inflexible.
Her unyielding determination led her to overcome every obstacle.

Utilize [ˈjuːtɪlaɪz] (utilis "useful")
(v.) To make practical or effective use of something.
The team utilized the latest technology to improve efficiency.

V

Vacillating [ˈvæsɪleɪtɪŋ] (vacillare "to sway, waver")
(adj.) Indecisive; wavering between different opinions or actions.
His vacillating stance on the issue frustrated his colleagues.

Validate [ˈvælɪdeɪt] (validus "strong, well-founded")
(v.) To confirm or prove the truth or accuracy of something.
The results of the experiment validated the scientist's hypothesis.

Valued [ˈvæljuːd] (valere "to be strong, be worth")
(adj.) Considered to be important or beneficial; cherished.
She is a highly valued member of the team.

Vary [ˈveəri] (variare "to change, alter")
(v.) To differ in size, amount, or degree; to change or alter.
The colors of the fabric vary from light blue to dark green.

Venerate [ˈvɛnəreɪt] (venerari "to worship, revere")
(v.) To regard with great respect or reverence.
The community venerates its cultural traditions.

Veritable [ˈvɛrɪtəbl] (veritas "truth")
(adj.) Used as an intensifier, often to qualify a metaphor; true or genuine.
The garden was a veritable paradise.

Viable [ˈvaɪəbl] (vita "life" + -able "capable of")
(adj.) Capable of working successfully; feasible.
The plan is viable with the resources we currently have.

Vindicate [ˈvɪndɪkeɪt] (vindicare "to claim, defend")
(v.) To clear someone of blame or suspicion; to justify.
The new evidence vindicated her actions during the incident.

Visible [ˈvɪzəbl] (visibilis "that may be seen")
(adj.) Able to be seen or perceived.
The mountains were visible in the distance despite the fog.

Visually [ˈvɪʒuəli] (visualis "of sight")
(adv.) In a way that relates to sight or vision.
The presentation was visually appealing and well-organized.

Vividly [ˈvɪvɪdli] (vivere "to live")
(adv.) In a way that produces powerful or clear images in the mind.
She vividly remembered the day she first met him.

W

Warrant [ˈwɒrənt] (warantir "to guarantee")
(v.) To justify or necessitate something; (n.) authorization or guarantee.
His behavior warranted immediate action.
The police had a warrant to search the premises.

Withdrawing [wɪðˈdrɔːɪŋ] (with- "away" + draw "to pull")
(v.) Removing or taking back; retreating or moving away.
She is withdrawing from the race due to health reasons.

Y

Yield [jiːld] (gieldan "to pay, give")
(v.) To produce or provide; to give way under pressure; (n.) the amount produced.
The farm yielded an abundant harvest this year.
The material yielded under extreme pressure.

SAT Must-Know Poetry Words

Archaic Pronouns and Determiners

- **Thee:** You (objective case).
- **Thou:** You (subjective case).
- **Thy:** Your (possessive, before a consonant sound).
- **Thine:** Your (possessive, before a vowel sound or used as a possessive pronoun).
- **Ye:** You (plural or formal singular).

Common Archaic Words

- **Art:** Are (e.g., "Thou art" means "You are").
- **Hath:** Has (e.g., "He hath" means "He has").
- **Hast:** Have (e.g., "Thou hast" means "You have").
- **Dost:** Do (e.g., "Dost thou" means "Do you").
- **Doth:** Does (e.g., "He doth" means "He does").
- **Wilt:** Will (e.g., "Thou wilt" means "You will").
- **Shalt:** Shall (e.g., "Thou shalt" means "You shall").
- **O'er:** Over.
- **Ere:** Before.
- **Ne'er:** Never.
- **Whence:** From where.
- **Hence:** From here.
- **Thence:** From there.

- **Hither:** To here.
- **Thither:** To there.
- **Whither:** To where.
- **Oft:** Often.
- **Anon:** Soon.
- **Betwixt:** Between.
- **Fain:** Gladly.
- **Foe:** Enemy.
- **Mirth:** Joy or amusement.
- **Woe:** Sorrow or distress.
- **Quoth:** Said (e.g., "Quoth the raven" means "Said the raven").
- **Yonder:** Over there

CHAPTER 13

Answers

1.1 Sentence Completion Answers

▶ **QUESTION 1**: <u>Choice B is the best answer</u> because it most logically completes the text's discussion of the honeybees' "waggle dance". The phrase "advanced communication system" suggests a level of intricacy or development, which aligns with the meaning of "sophisticated". The fact that the dance provides "detailed information" about food sources also supports this conclusion.

Choice A is incorrect because "theatrical" refers to something being dramatic or showy, which doesn't necessarily relate to the advanced nature of the communication system. Choice C is incorrect because "confusing" contradicts the idea that the dance provides clear, detailed information. Choice D is incorrect because the text doesn't provide any context to suggest that the dance is more "time-consuming" than previously believed.

▶ **QUESTION 2**: <u>Choice C is the best answer</u> because the context implies a rapid or very fast pace of technological advancement which is making businesses adapt or risk irrelevance. The term "breakneck" connotes a very high speed or pace, aligning with the urgency in Mark Rogers' statement.

Choice A is incorrect because "stagnant" means lacking progression or development, which is the opposite of the text's implication about technological advancement. Choice B, "haphazard," suggests a lack of order or planning, which doesn't fit the context about the pace of technological advancement. Choice D is incorrect because "trivial" means of little value or importance, which doesn't align with the emphasized need for businesses to adapt.

▶ **QUESTION 3**: <u>Choice B is the best answer</u> because "oscillates" means to move or swing back and forth, especially between two points, which fits the context of a novel that switches between two time periods. The text highlights a transition between Ancient Rome and present day, suggesting a back-and-forth narrative structure.

Choice A, "fluctuates," generally refers to varying or changing irregularly, but doesn't specifically imply a back-and-forth motion between two points like "oscillates" does. Choice C, "stagnates," means to cease developing or to become inactive, which doesn't fit with the description of the novel moving between time periods. Choice D, "dives," suggests a deep exploration or a sudden drop, but doesn't convey the idea of moving between two distinct points as the context suggests.

▶ **QUESTION 4**: <u>Choice B is the best answer</u> because it most logically completes the text's discussion of why invasive species often thrive in new environments. The absence of "predators" would mean that there are no natural enemies to control the population of the invasive species, allowing them to flourish unchecked. This context is supported by the statement that the lack of these would "keep their populations in check."

Choice A is incorrect because "allies" would typically refer to species or organisms that cooperate or have mutualistic relationships. The absence of allies wouldn't necessarily lead to the unchecked growth of an invasive species. Choice C is incorrect because the term "habitats" is redundant in this context; the sentence already mentions "new environments." Choice D is incorrect because the lack of "nutrients" would likely hinder the growth of an invasive species, not promote it.

▶ **QUESTION 5**: <u>Choice B is the best answer</u> because it most logically completes the text's discussion of Jane's deep immersion in her writing. To "envelop" oneself means to completely surround or engross oneself in something, which aligns with the context of Jane being deeply immersed in her stories.

Choice A is incorrect because to "entrust" oneself typically means to place trust or responsibility in someone or something, which doesn't align with the context of being immersed in writing. Choice C is incorrect because "enclose" generally refers to being surrounded by physical barriers, which doesn't fit the context of being engrossed in writing. Choice D is incorrect because "ensnare" has a negative connotation of being trapped or caught, which doesn't align with the positive portrayal of Jane's passion and talent for writing.

▶ **QUESTION 6**: <u>Choice B is the best answer</u> because it most logically completes the text's portrayal of the desert ecosystem. The text describes the ecosystem as appearing simple but then hints at a deeper complexity. "Complex" means made up of many different parts or elements, which aligns with the described intricacy of the desert ecosystem.

Choice A, "fragile," suggests vulnerability, which doesn't match the mentioned resilience of the desert ecosystem. Choice C, "static," implies unchanging, which doesn't capture the intricate functionality of the ecosystem as suggested by the text. Choice D, "mundane," means lacking interest or excitement, which is not in line with the described intricacy and adaptability of the desert ecosystem.

▶ **QUESTION 7**: <u>Choice B is the best answer</u> as it completes the text in a way that logically connects to the context. If a deep-sea fish produces light in an otherwise dark environment, it would most likely "startle" or surprise potential predators with its sudden appearance of light, potentially deterring an attack.

Choice A, "luring," would imply that the fish is trying to attract predators, which would not be beneficial for its survival. Choice C, "entertaining," is too anthropomorphic and doesn't align with the survival mechanisms of deep-sea creatures. Choice D, "guiding," would suggest helping the predators, which is not a likely adaptation for prey.

▶ **QUESTION 8**: <u>Choice D is the best answer</u> as it aligns with the context and tone of mystery surrounding the transportation methods of the Moai statues. "Enigmatic" means mysterious or puzzling, which accurately describes the unclear methods by which the statues were transported.

Choice A, "celebrated," would suggest widespread recognition or commendation, but doesn't capture the mystery surrounding the transportation methods. Choice B, "mundane," means ordinary or dull, which contradicts the text's implication of a significant mystery. Choice C, "insignificant," doesn't fit as the transportation of such massive structures would be a significant endeavor.

▶ **QUESTION 9**: <u>Choice B is the best answer</u> as it completes the text in a way that logically connects to the context. If bioluminescent fungi emit a gentle green glow, it's most likely to "captivate" or attract attention, and in the context, this would be the attention of insects for pollination or spore distribution.

Choice A, "repelling," would suggest driving insects away, which would not be beneficial for pollination or spore distribution. Choice C, "camouflaging," contradicts the idea of emitting a noticeable glow. Choice D, "overpowering," suggests an intense or overwhelming force, which doesn't align with the description of a "gentle" glow.

▶ **QUESTION 10**: Choice B is the best answer as it logically completes the text's narrative. Given that fellow ornithologists believe certain external factors were not adequately considered in Dr. Claire Montgomery's conclusions, they would likely approach her findings with "skepticism" or doubt.

Choice A, "applause," suggests full agreement or commendation, which contrasts the context of disagreement provided. Choice C, "indifference," would mean that the ornithologists did not care one way or the other about her findings, which doesn't align with the active critique suggested. Choice D, "enthusiasm," would imply a positive reception, which again contrasts with the disagreement context.

▶ **QUESTION 11**: <u>Choice B is the best answer</u> because it most logically completes the text's discussion of the importance of understanding cultural subtleties in the context of international collaboration. "Nuances" refer to subtle differences or distinctions in meaning, expression, or response, which would be crucial for effective communication across different cultures.

Choice A is incorrect because "anomalies" refer to something that deviates from what is standard, normal, or expected, which doesn't necessarily capture the subtle cultural differences important for collaboration. Choice C is incorrect because "trivialities" refer to things of little value or importance, which doesn't align with the text's emphasis on the importance of understanding cultural aspects. Choice D is incorrect because "monotony" refers to a lack of variety and interest, which doesn't fit the context of understanding diverse cultural elements.

▶ **QUESTION 12**: <u>Choice B is the best answer</u> because it most logically completes the text's discussion of the decline of the ancient city of Petra. The context suggests that the city was no longer in use, which aligns with the term "abandoned."

Choice A is incorrect because "fortified" means to strengthen or secure, which doesn't align with the context of the city's decline. Choice C is incorrect because "expanded" suggests growth or enlargement, which contradicts the context of the city's decline and eventual obscurity. Choice D is incorrect because "prohibited" means to formally forbid something, which doesn't fit the context of the city being forgotten or no longer in use.

► **QUESTION 13:** <u>Choice B is the best answer</u> because it most logically completes the text's description of dance as a form of self-expression and cultural identity. In this context, a "medium" refers to an instrument or means of communicating something, which aligns with the idea that dance can convey messages or stories.

Choice A, "genre," refers more to a category or type, which doesn't capture the idea of conveying messages or stories. Choice C, "spectacle," suggests something visually impressive but doesn't necessarily convey the idea of communication or storytelling inherent in dance. Choice D, "pastime," refers to an activity people do for enjoyment rather than its potential for conveying deep cultural messages.

► **QUESTION 14:** <u>Choice C is the best answer</u> because it most logically completes the text's discussion of spider silk's potential applications in the industrial sector. Given its strength and elasticity, spider silk being seen as a "substitute" means it could replace or be used in place of other materials, such as steel, for certain applications.

Choice A is incorrect because "anomaly" refers to something that deviates from what is standard, normal, or expected, which doesn't fit the context of spider silk's potential uses. Choice B is incorrect because "detriment" refers to something that causes harm or damage, which contradicts the positive portrayal of spider silk's properties. Choice D is incorrect because "hindrance" means a thing that provides resistance or obstruction, which doesn't align with the idea of spider silk being beneficial for industrial applications.

► **QUESTION 15:** <u>Choice A is the best answer</u> because it logically completes the text's discussion about Mars and its past relationship with water. "Inundated with" means overwhelmed or flooded, suggesting that Mars was once filled or covered with water.

Choice B, "isolated from" suggests being separated from others or being solitary, which doesn't align with the context of Mars being filled with water. Choice C, "deprived of" implies a lack or denial of something necessary, which is the opposite of the context suggesting Mars might have had abundant water. Choice D, "polarized by" in general terms, refers to divisions or opposites, and doesn't fit the context of water presence on Mars.

► **QUESTION 16:** <u>Choice B is the best answer</u> as it logically completes the text's discussion of the differing opinions on using bamboo in sustainable architecture. "Resist" means to oppose or stand against something, which fits the context of traditionalists' stance against the use of bamboo in favor of more conventional materials.

Choice A, "endorse," means to support or approve of something, which contradicts the context suggesting a preference for traditional materials over bamboo. Choice C, "explore," means to investigate or study, which doesn't convey opposition or preference. Choice D, "magnify," means to make something appear larger or more important, which doesn't fit the context of traditionalists' stance on bamboo.

► **QUESTION 17:** <u>Choice B is the best answer</u> because it most logically completes the text's discussion of the connection between Beethoven's symphonies and his personal life. To say that his compositions "mirror" the turbulence and passion of his life means that they reflect or represent those emotions and experiences.

Choice A is incorrect because "negate" means to nullify or invalidate, which doesn't fit the context of Beethoven's compositions representing his personal experiences. Choice C is incorrect because "dilute" means to make something weaker in force, content, or value, which doesn't align with the text's portrayal of the profound emotion in Beethoven's symphonies. Choice D is incorrect because "abandon" means to give up or discontinue, which doesn't fit the context of Beethoven's compositions reflecting his personal life.

► **QUESTION 18:** <u>Choice C is the best answer</u> as it logically completes the text's description of the deep-sea's mysterious nature. Given that the depths of the sea are being described as strange and diverse, the term "alien" (which refers to something foreign or unfamiliar) best captures the sentiment.

Choice A, "terrestrial," pertains to the Earth or land, which does not emphasize the unfamiliarity of the deep sea. Choice B, "ordinary," suggests that something is usual or common, which contrasts with the context of the deep-sea's unique nature. Choice D, "transparent," typically refers to something clear or see-through, which does not emphasize the otherworldly or unfamiliar nature of the deep sea.

► **QUESTION 19:** <u>Choice A is the best answer</u> because it most logically completes the text's discussion of the challenges in book distribution across library branches. If popular titles "cluster" in certain branches, it means that many copies of those titles accumulate or gather in specific locations, leaving other branches with fewer copies of those sought-after books.

Choice B is incorrect because "vanish" implies a complete disappearance, which is too extreme for the context of book distribution. Choice C is incorrect because "replicate" means to make an exact copy of something, which doesn't fit the context of book distribution challenges. Choice D is incorrect because "decrease" would suggest that the number of popular titles is reducing, but the context suggests an uneven distribution, not a reduction.

1.2 Meaning in Context Answer

1> The following text is from Herman Melville's 1851 novel *Moby Dick*.

The passage emphasizes the minimalism of the captain's action—he did nothing more than point. The phrases "no grand gesture" and "no long speech" highlight that he only pointed.
A) only: Fits well, indicating he did just that and nothing more.

A
only

2> The following text is from Mark Twain's 1884 novel *The Adventures of Huckleberry Finn*.

Huck seeks solitude and quietness. The word "simply" underscores his desire for a peaceful activity amid chaos.
C) quietly: Accurately reflects his need for calm and silence.

C
quietly

3> The following text is from Henry David Thoreau's 1854 work *Walden*.

Thoreau openly shares his innermost thoughts with the reader.
D) openly: Conveys that he shared his thoughts candidly without reservation.

D
openly

4> The following text is from Emily Bronte's 1847 novel *Wuthering Heights*.

Her feelings for him were complex, interwoven with a history of joy, sorrow, and regret. But in this moment, she "simply" loved him, without conditions or reservations. Nothing else mattered but this raw emotion, this profound connection between their hearts.
B) purely: Fits perfectly, emphasizing the unadulterated and unconditional nature of her love.

B
purely

1> This passage is from Lewis Carroll's 1865 novel *Alice's Adventures in Wonderland*.

Alice is trying to understand her strange journey as she falls down the rabbit hole. She is curious and full of questions, which aligns best with D) wondering about.

D
wondering
about

2> The following text is from Mary Shelley's 1818 novel *Frankenstein*.

Dr. Frankenstein's feelings are described as awe mixed with dread. He is impressed—even amazed—by his creation, making the sense of "puzzling over" closest to C) marveling at.

C
marveling
at

3> The following text is from Bram Stoker's 1897 novel *Dracula*.
Jonathan Harker is uneasy and disturbed by the strange events with the Count. There's an underlying sense of anxiety and unease, which fits best with B) worrying about.

B
worrying
about

4> The following text is from Charles Dickens's 1861 novel *Great Expectations*.

Pip is unsettled and can't stop thinking about his odd encounter with the convict. He seems confused and off-balance, which can be captured by A) dazed by.

A
dazed by

1> The following text is from Jules Verne's 1870 novel Twenty Thousand Leagues Under the Sea.

The passage describes mechanical parts in the submarine's engine room. The "connections" are physical components that link parts of the machinery together, ensuring proper operation.

A
physical link

2> The following text is from Alexander Graham Bell's 1876 notes on the creation of the telephone.

Here, "connection" refers to the ability to communicate over long distances via the telephone—a means that links people for communication purposes.

B
means of communi-cation

3> The following text is from Emily Bronte's 1847 novel Wuthering Heights.

The "connection" between Catherine and Heathcliff is an emotional and relational bond. It signifies a profound relationship recognized by both.

D
recognized relationship

4> The following text is from Alexandre Dumas's 1844 novel The Count of Monte Cristo.

Edmond leverages his acquaintances to achieve his goals. In this context, "connection" refers to influential people he knows who can assist him.

C
influential person

1> The following text is from Arthur Conan Doyle's 1892 collection The Adventures of Sherlock Holmes.

Sherlock's reasoning is reliable and based on logic and facts. "Sound" here means his reasoning is valid and accurate

C
accurate

2> The following text is from Louisa May Alcott's 1868 novel Little Women.

Amy's attitude is hopeful, encouraging, and forward-looking.
"Sound" here means her attitude is optimistic and positive.

B
positive

3> The following text is from Charles Dickens's 1859 novel A Tale of Two Cities.

Mr. Lorry's management is reliable and thorough. His careful and comprehensive approach indicates that "sound" means thorough.

A
thorough

4> The following text is from Charles Dickens's 1843 novel A Christmas Carol.

Elizabeth Bennet's regard for Mr. Darcy is steady, unwavering, and rooted in genuine understanding.
"Sound" here means her feelings remain stable and firm.

D
firm

▶ **QUESTION 1:**
Read the question and sentence.
Identify the word, in this case, "sin."
Understand the context: Atticus is telling his son about the morality of killing birds, especially mockingbirds.
Paraphrase the sentence: "Remember it's a 'wrongdoing' to kill a mockingbird."
Evaluate the options: "Immorality" seems to fit well into the paraphrased context.
Eliminate wrong answers: "Mistake", "Crime", and "Disobedience" do not fit as well in the context as "Immorality" does.
Make an educated guess: Based on the process, it seems like "D) Immorality" is the best fit.
So the answer should be "D) Immorality".

▶ **QUESTION 2:**
Read the question and sentence.
Identify the word, in this case, "signs."
Understand the context: Jim, a character in the book, is said to know various signs in relation to the behavior of bees.
Paraphrase the sentence: "Jim knew all kinds of 'indications/omens'."
Evaluate the options: "Omens" seems to fit well into the paraphrased context.
Eliminate wrong answers: "Warnings", "Symbols", and "Directions" do not fit as well in the context as "Omens" does.
Make an educated guess: Based on the process, it seems like "D) Omens" is the best fit.
So the answer should be "D) Omens".

▶ **QUESTION 3:**
Read the question and sentence.
Identify the word, in this case, "depends."
Understand the context: The Cat is responding to Alice's question about which direction she should take.
Paraphrase the sentence: "That 'relies' a good deal on where you want to get to," said the Cat.
Evaluate the options: "Relies" seems to fit well into the paraphrased context.
Eliminate wrong answers: "Hinges", "Descends", and "Pertains" do not fit as well in the context as "Relies" does.
Make an educated guess: Based on the process, it seems like "B) Relies" is the best fit.
So the answer should be "B) Relies".

▶ **QUESTION 4:**
Read the question and sentence.
Identify the word, in this case, "productive."
Understand the context: Their visits to Mrs. Phillips resulted in interesting information, thus were 'productive.'
Paraphrase the sentence: "Their visits to Mrs. Phillips were now 'yielding' the most interesting intelligence."
Evaluate the options: "Yielding" seems to fit well into the paraphrased context.
Eliminate wrong answers: "Industrious", "Fertile", and "Effective" do not fit as well in the context as "Yielding" does.
Make an educated guess: Based on the process, it seems like "C) Yielding" is the best fit.
So the answer should be "C) Yielding".

▶ **QUESTION 5:**
Read the question and sentence.
Identify the word, in this case, "actuate."
Understand the context: The word "actuate" is used to describe the reasons that motivate or cause a particular action.
Paraphrase the sentence: "Mr. Heathcliff may have entirely dissimilar reasons for keeping his hand out of the way when he meets a would-be-acquaintance, to those which 'drive' me."
Evaluate the options: "Drive" seems to fit well into the paraphrased context.
Eliminate wrong answers: "Perform", "Begin", and "Design" do not fit as well in the context as "Drive" does.
Make an educated guess: Based on the process, it seems like "B) Drive" is the best fit.
So the answer should be "B) Drive".

▶ **QUESTION 6:**
Read the question and sentence.
Identify the word, in this case, "constituted."
Understand the context: The word "constituted" is used to explain how every human being is inherently a profound secret and mystery to others.
Paraphrase the sentence: "A wonderful fact to reflect upon, that every human creature is 'formed' to be that profound secret and mystery to every other."
Evaluate the options: "Formed" seems to fit well into the paraphrased context.
Eliminate wrong answers: "Authorized", "Composed", and "Elected" do not fit as well in the context as "Formed" does.
Make an educated guess: Based on the process, it seems like "A) Formed" is the best fit.
So the answer should be "A) Formed".

▶ **QUESTION 7:**
Read the question and sentence.
Identify the word, in this case, "want."
Understand the context: The word "want" is used to express the lack of justice and basic necessities in the lives of the Parisian commoners.
Paraphrase the sentence: "Every cobblestone seemed to echo with the 'need' of justice."
Evaluate the options: "Need" seems to fit well into the paraphrased context.
Eliminate wrong answers: "Absence", "Ambition", and "Greed" do not fit as well in the context as "Need" does.
Make an educated guess: Based on the process, it seems like "A) Need" is the best fit.
<u>So the answer should be "A) Need".</u>

▶ **QUESTION 8:**
Read the question and sentence.
Identify the word, in this case, "curiosity."
Understand the context: Phantom vibrations are described as a "curiosity" – a strange, unusual phenomenon that has become part of our daily lives.
Paraphrase the sentence: "Phantom vibrations can sometimes be a mere 'oddity'."
Evaluate the options: "Oddity" seems to fit well into the paraphrased context.
Eliminate wrong answers: "Concern", "Question", and "Wonder" do not fit as well in the context as "Oddity" does.
Make an educated guess: Based on the process, it seems like "C) Oddity" is the best fit.
<u>So the answer should be "C) Oddity".</u>

▶ **QUESTION 9:**
Read the question and sentence.
Identify the word, in this case, "exact."
Understand the context: The conductor in the orchestra is particularly focused on the precise timing of each instrument.
Paraphrase the sentence: "He had a keen ear and could discern if the violin was even slightly out of 'precise' timing."
Evaluate the options: "Precise" seems to fit well into the paraphrased context.
Eliminate wrong answers: "Rigorous", "Honest", and "Distinct" do not fit as well in the context as "Precise" does.
Make an educated guess: Based on the process, it seems like "A) Precise" is the best fit.
<u>So the answer should be "A) Precise".</u>

▶ **QUESTION 10:**
Read the question and sentence.
Identify the word, in this case, "control."
Understand the context: The park authorities implement a "control" on the number of tourists to limit human impact on the ancient forest.
Paraphrase the sentence: "They implemented a 'restrictive mechanism' on the number of tourists who could visit each day."
Evaluate the options: "Restrictive mechanism" seems to fit well into the paraphrased context.
Eliminate wrong answers: "Regulating force", "Comparative element", and "Supervising factor" do not fit as well in the context as "Restrictive mechanism" does.
Make an educated guess: Based on the process, it seems like "B) Restrictive mechanism" is the best fit.
<u>So the answer should be "B) Restrictive mechanism".</u>

▶ **QUESTION 11:**
Read the question and sentence.
Identify the word, in this case, "practically."
Understand the context: The word "practically" is used to describe how closely an athlete's routine resembles the life of a monk.
Paraphrase the sentence: "When an athlete adheres to such a routine, he or she is 'effectively' living the life of a monk, with little room for deviation."
Evaluate the options: "Effectively" seems to fit well into the paraphrased context.
Eliminate wrong answers: "Reasonably", "Cleverly", and "Partially" do not fit as well in the context as "Effectively" does.
Make an educated guess: Based on the process, it seems like "A) Effectively" is the best fit.
<u>So the answer should be "A) Effectively".</u>

▶ **QUESTION 12:**
Read the question and sentence.
Identify the word, in this case, "disposition."
Understand the context: "Disposition" is used here to describe a general attitude or inclination, in this case towards change, equality, and freedom.
Paraphrase the sentence: "The terrorists are trying to stop us, but the 'attitude' towards change, towards equality, and towards freedom is stronger than ever."
Evaluate the options: "Attitude" seems to fit well into the paraphrased context.
Eliminate wrong answers: "Habit", "Placement", and "Settlement" do not fit as well in the context as "Attitude" does.

Make an educated guess: Based on the process, it seems like "D) Attitude" is the best fit.
So the answer should be "D) Attitude".

▶ **QUESTION 13:**
Read the question and sentence.
Identify the word, in this case, "want."
Understand the context: Oliver is in a sad and lonely place, surrounded by misery and "want."
Paraphrase the sentence: Oliver was surrounded by misery and "lack."
Evaluate the options: "Absence" seems to fit well into the paraphrased context.
Eliminate wrong answers: "Need", "Ambition", and "Greed" do not fit as well in the context as "Absence" does.
Make an educated guess: Based on the process, it seems like "B) Absence" is the best fit.
So the answer should be "B) Absence".

▶ **QUESTION 14:**
Read the question and sentence.
Identify the word, in this case, "excels."
Understand the context: Lady Capulet is comparing Romeo to Paris and suggesting that Paris is superior.
Paraphrase the sentence: Paris "surpasses" your first match, Romeo.
Evaluate the options: "Surpasses" seems to fit well into the paraphrased context.
Eliminate wrong answers: "Shines", "Extinguishes", and "Masters" do not fit as well in the context as "Surpasses" does.
Make an educated guess: Based on the process, it seems like "B) Surpasses" is the best fit.
So the answer should be "B) Surpasses".

▶ **QUESTION 15:**
Read the question and sentence.
Identify the word, in this case, "pure."
Understand the context: Hedda said something without any ulterior motive or hidden intention.
Paraphrase the sentence: I said that in "complete" thoughtlessness.
Evaluate the options: "Complete" seems to fit well into the paraphrased context.
Eliminate wrong answers: "Clean", "Simple", and "Innocent" do not fit as well in the context as "Complete" does.
Make an educated guess: Based on the process, it seems like "C) Complete" is the best fit.
So the answer should be "C) Complete".

▶ **QUESTION 16:**
Read the question and sentence.
Identify the word, in this case, "settled."
Understand the context: Orgon has made a decision about Mariane's future husband and is firm in his choice.
Paraphrase the sentence: I've "decided" it.
Evaluate the options: "Resolved" seems to fit well into the paraphrased context.
Eliminate wrong answers: "Stabilized", "Paid", and "Compromised" do not fit as well in the context as "Resolved" does.
Make an educated guess: Based on the process, it seems like "C) Resolved" is the best fit.
So the answer should be "C) Resolved".

▶ **QUESTION 17:**
Read the question and sentence.
Identify the word, in this case, "common."
Understand the context: The vendor's stall had typical fruits and vegetables that are usually seen.
Paraphrase the sentence: The vendor's stall was filled with "usual" fruits and vegetables.
Evaluate the options: "Usual" seems to fit well into the paraphrased context.
Eliminate wrong answers: "Shared", "Inferior", and "Widespread" do not fit as well in the context as "Usual" does.
Make an educated guess: Based on the process, it seems like "A) Usual" is the best fit.
So the answer should be "A) Usual".

▶ **QUESTION 18:**
Read the question and sentence.
Identify the word, in this case, "artificial."
Understand the context: Higgins is pointing out that the airs and manners of the person are not genuine.
Paraphrase the sentence: Your airs, your voice, your demeanor—they're all "not genuine" as your manners.
Evaluate the options: "Fabricated" seems to fit well into the paraphrased context.
Eliminate wrong answers: "Exaggerated", "Misleading", and "Forced" do not fit as well in the context as "Fabricated" does.
Make an educated guess: Based on the process, it seems like "D) Fabricated" is the best fit.
So the answer should be "D) Fabricated".

▶ **QUESTION 19:**

Read the question and sentence.

Identify the word, in this case, "produce."

Understand the context: Lyubov is emphasizing the need to come up with a plan before making any decisions about the estate.

Paraphrase the sentence: But before any of that, we must "come up with" a plan.

Evaluate the options: "Devise" seems to fit well into the paraphrased context.

Eliminate wrong answers: "Provoke", "Fund", and "Disclose" do not fit as well in the context as "Devise" does.

Make an educated guess: Based on the process, it seems like "B) Devise" is the best fit.

So the answer should be "B) Devise".

▶ **QUESTION 20:**

Read the question and sentence.

Identify the word, in this case, "curiously."

Understand the context: Jack is making a witty remark about Algernon's potential forgetfulness regarding marriage.

Paraphrase the sentence: The Divorce Court was specially invented for people whose memories are "oddly" constituted.

Evaluate the options: "Strangely" seems to fit well into the paraphrased context.

Eliminate wrong answers: "Eagerly", "Suspiciously", and "Frequently" do not fit as well in the context as "Strangely" does.

Make an educated guess: Based on the process, it seems like "A) Strangely" is the best fit.

So the answer should be "A) Strangely".

2. Factual Question Answer

▶ **QUESTION 1:**

Read the Main Instruction:

The main instruction asks about one potential drawback of Dr. Elston's method.

Carefully Read the Text:

The text discusses Dr. Elston's computational model for analyzing themes in 19th-century novels, noting that the dataset mainly includes works by prominent authors while underrepresenting lesser-known regional authors.

Analyze Each Statement:

    A) This statement suggests that the algorithms used might misinterpret themes, but the text does not mention any issues with algorithm accuracy or misinterpretation. This statement is not supported by the text.

    B) This statement claims that the method focuses on themes less relevant to modern readers. However, the text does not mention anything about the relevance of the themes to modern readers. This statement is not supported by the text.

    C) This statement accurately reflects a drawback mentioned in the text: that the dataset is limited to well-preserved works from prominent authors, which leads to underrepresentation of lesser-known regional authors. This is supported by the text.

    D) This statement suggests that the method assumes thematic uniformity among all 19th-century authors. The text does not mention such an assumption. This statement is not supported by the text.

Confirm Your Answer: The correct answer is C) It excludes works by lesser-known authors, potentially skewing the results, as this accurately represents the drawback described in the text.

▶ **QUESTION 2:**

Read the Main Instruction: The main instruction asks why Ishmael goes to sea.

Carefully Read the Text: The text provides information about Ishmael's reasons for going to sea, related to his mood and mental state.

Analyze Each Statement:

    A) The text doesn't mention leisure and relaxation as Ishmael's reason for going to sea. This statement is not relevant.

    B) The text mentions Ishmael's thoughts about funeral processions and melancholy, which are related to his decision to go to sea. This statement is relevant.

    C) The text doesn't mention escaping strong moral principles of society as Ishmael's reason for going to sea. This statement is not relevant.

    D) The text explicitly states that Ishmael goes to sea to alleviate his periods of melancholy and restlessness. This statement is relevant.

Confirm Your Answer: The text supports statement D) Ishmael goes to sea to alleviate his periods of melancholy and restlessness.

Thus, the correct answer is D) Ishmael goes to sea to alleviate his periods of melancholy and restlessness.

▶ **QUESTION 3:**

Read the Main Instruction: The main instruction is asking what is the primary reason for the threat to the rich biodiversity of the Amazon Rainforest based on the provided text.

Carefully Read the Text: The text mentions that the rich biodiversity of the Amazon Rainforest is under threat due to extensive deforestation primarily driven by agriculture, livestock farming, and illegal logging.

Analyze Each Statement:

    (A) The text does not mention shifts in climatic conditions and global temperature as the primary reason for the threat. The emphasis is on deforestation caused by human actions.

    (B) The text does not attribute the threat to unforeseen calamities and uncontrolled blazes. It specifies that the primary driver is extensive deforestation caused by specific human activities.

    (C) This statement accurately reflects the information in the text. The text states that the threat to the rich biodiversity of the Amazon Rainforest is primarily due to extensive deforestation propelled by agriculture, livestock farming, and illegal logging.

    (D) The text does not mention intrusive species and diseases caused by deforestation as the primary reason for the threat. The primary focus is on the direct impact of human activities such as agriculture, livestock farming, and illegal logging.

Confirm Your Answer: <u>Among the options, (C)</u> is the most accurate statement based on the text. The primary reason for the threat to the rich biodiversity of the Amazon Rainforest is extensive deforestation propelled by human actions. Therefore, the correct answer is (C) Widespread clearing of forests propelled by human actions.

▶ **QUESTION 4:**

Read the Main Instruction: The main instruction is asking what can be said about Jane's feelings towards the man she describes.

Carefully Read the Text: The text describes the man's appearance and Jane's feelings and reactions toward him.

Analyze Each Statement:

    A) The text does not indicate that Jane is deeply afraid of the man. It actually states, "I felt no fear of him." This statement is not true.

    B) The text does not suggest that Jane finds the man attractive or is eager to assist him. It says she "should not have dared to stand thus questioning him against his will," which indicates reluctance. This statement is not true.

    C) The text does not imply indifference. It mentions that she "felt no fear of him, and but little shyness." She does have some emotions, but they are not strongly negative or positive. This statement is partially true.

    D) The text suggests that Jane has reservations about approaching the man and offering her help when it says, "offering my services unasked." This statement is true.

Confirm Your Answer: <u>The text supports statement D)</u> She has no reservations about approaching him and offering her help. Thus, the correct answer is D) She has no reservations about approaching him and offering her help.

▶ **QUESTION 5:**

Read the Main Instruction: The question asks how public parks in cities are similar to other community elements.

Carefully Read the Text: The text discusses the role of public parks in enhancing mental and physical health, providing a natural environment, and contributing to environmental conservation in urban areas.

Analyze Each Statement:

    A) Compares parks to libraries as resource hubs, but the text focuses more on health and environmental benefits rather than resource provision.

    B) Likens parks to hospitals, emphasizing their contribution to health and well-being, which aligns with the text's focus on mental and physical health benefits.

    C) Equates parks with museums in preserving artifacts, which is not a focus of the text.

    D) Similar to schools in providing education, but the text emphasizes health and environmental benefits more.

Confirm Your Answer: <u>The correct answer is B)</u> hospitals, as essential services that contribute to the health and well-being of the community, aligning with the text's emphasis on health and environmental benefits.

▶ **QUESTION 6:**

Read the Main Instruction: The question asks "what is true about the narrator's feelings?" based on the given text.

Carefully Read the Text: The text describes the narrator's feelings about leaving places without acknowledging the departure.

Analyze Each Statement:

    A) The narrator expresses a dislike for leaving places without realizing it, contradicting this statement.

    B) The narrator mentions feeling worse when he doesn't acknowledge his departures, which supports this statement.

    C) The text doesn't specify that the narrator always ensures a cheerful farewell.

    D) The narrator's feelings suggest that he finds good-byes important, contradicting this statement.

Confirm Your Answer: Option B is directly supported by the text and accurately describes the narrator's feelings. <u>So, the answer is B.</u>

► **QUESTION 7:**
Read the Main Instruction: The question asks "what is true about the International Space Station (ISS)?" according to the given text.
Carefully Read the Text: The text describes the International Space Station, its launch and occupation, its segments, and the conditions required for research conducted on the station.
Analyze Each Statement:
  A) The text states that the station has been continuously occupied since November 2000, not unoccupied.
  B) The ISS is described as being in low Earth orbit, not high.
  C) The United States Orbital Segment (USOS) is shared by many nations, and does not say whether it is operated solely by the United States.
  D) The text does confirm that research on the ISS often requires conditions present in low Earth orbit.

Confirm Your Answer: After analyzing each statement, it's clear that option D is the only one that is directly supported by the text. Therefore, the answer is D.

► **QUESTION 8:**
Read the Main Instruction: The question asks "what is true about the speaker's feelings?" based on the given text.
Carefully Read the Text: The text describes the speaker's deep emotional connection and feelings towards another person.
Analyze Each Statement:
  A) The speaker says, "I cannot imagine a world without him," which contradicts this statement.
  B) The depth of emotion expressed in the text goes beyond a "casual fondness."
  C) The speaker mentions that the person's presence is as essential as the air she breathes, indicating a deep bond and its importance to her existence.
  D) The speaker emphasizes the unique connection she has with him, suggesting he's not like everyone else in her life.

Confirm Your Answer: Option C is directly supported by the text and accurately describes the speaker's feelings. So, the answer is C.

► **QUESTION 9:**
Read the Main Instruction: The question asks why public awareness campaigns are important for environmental conservation.
Carefully Read the Text: The text highlights the role of these campaigns in educating the public about preserving natural resources and the negative effects of pollution.
Analyze Each Statement:
  A) Discusses financial support for research, which is not mentioned in the text.
  B) Focuses on encouraging eco-friendly practices, directly aligning with the text's mention of adopting environmentally friendly behaviors.
  C) Talks about offering technological solutions, which is not covered in the text.
  D) Mentions job creation in environmental science, not discussed in the text.

Confirm Your Answer: The correct answer is B) encourage individuals to adopt eco-friendly practices, as it directly reflects the text's emphasis on the impact of public awareness in fostering environmentally friendly behavior.

► **QUESTION 10:**
Read the Main Instruction: The question asks, "According to the text, what is true about the Amazon Rainforest?"
Carefully Read the Text: The text describes the Amazon Rainforest as the world's largest tropical rainforest, spanning eight countries. It is known for its biodiversity. The forest is so dense that sunlight takes about ten minutes to reach the ground. The rainforest is under threat due to deforestation and illegal logging.
Analyze Each Statement:
  A) The Amazon Rainforest only spans across one country. This statement is incorrect as the text mentions the rainforest spans across eight countries.
  B) Sunlight reaches the ground instantaneously in the Amazon Rainforest. This statement is incorrect. The text specifically mentions that sunlight can take as long as ten minutes to reach the ground due to the forest's density.
  C) The Amazon Rainforest is currently under threat due to deforestation and illegal logging. This statement is directly supported by the text.
  D) The Amazon Rainforest is not known for its biodiversity. This statement contradicts the text, which states that the rainforest is famous for its biodiversity.

Confirm Your Answer: From the above analysis, option C) The Amazon Rainforest is currently under threat due to deforestation and illegal logging is the only statement that is supported by the text.
Therefore, the answer is C) The Amazon Rainforest is currently under threat due to deforestation and illegal logging.

► **QUESTION 11:**

Read the Main Instruction: The question asks "what is true about Jane Eyre?" based on the given text.
Carefully Read the Text: The text describes Jane's reading habits and her specific interests in a book about British Birds.
Analyze Each Statement:

A) The text doesn't mention Jane reading a novel about a family.
B) Jane expresses a particular interest in the parts of the book that discuss the haunts of sea-fowl.
C) The text mentions that Jane cared little for the letterpress in general, contradicting this statement.
D) The book discusses the coast of Norway, not France.

Confirm Your Answer: Option B is directly supported by the text and accurately describes Jane Eyre's interest. So, the answer is B.

► **QUESTION 12:**

Read the Main Instruction: The main instruction is asking what can be logically inferred about the rainfall predictions.
Carefully Read the Text: The passage discusses predictions of expected rainfall for three coastal towns by eight weather forecasting agencies. Two towns have consistent rainfall patterns, and predictions for them show minimal variation. The third town, prone to sudden weather changes, has significantly varied rainfall predictions across agencies.
Analyze Each Statement:

(A) The passage does not provide information about the difficulty of predicting rainfall for inland towns. It specifically focuses on variations in predictions for coastal towns.
(B) This statement is not supported by the passage. The text mentions that predictions for towns with consistent weather patterns show minimal variation, indicating reliability.
(C) The passage does not provide information about the rate of change in rainfall patterns for coastal towns with sudden weather changes. It focuses on the significant variations in predictions for the third town.
(D) This statement is logically inferred from the passage. The text mentions that predictions for towns with consistent rainfall patterns showed minimal variation across agencies, suggesting that these agencies are likely to be equally reliable in predicting rainfall for such towns.

Confirm Your Answer: Among the options, (D) is the most logically inferred statement based on the passage. The passage indicates that predictions for towns with consistent weather patterns are generally reliable, as minimal variation is observed. Therefore, the correct answer is (D) The agencies are likely to be equally reliable in predicting rainfall for towns with consistent weather patterns.

► **QUESTION 13:**

Read the Main Instruction: The question asks "how does Prince Andrew feel about the Council of State's opening?" based on the given text.
Carefully Read the Text: The text describes Prince Andrew's feelings and reactions to the account of the opening of the Council of State.
Analyze Each Statement:

A) The text mentions that the event seemed quite insignificant to Prince Andrew, contradicting this statement.
B) Prince Andrew reflects that the event did not affect him and seemed insignificant, supporting this statement.
C) The text doesn't mention Prince Andrew eagerly waiting for the next Council meeting.
D) The text doesn't mention Prince Andrew being upset about not being present at the Council.

Confirm Your Answer: Option B is directly supported by the text and accurately describes Prince Andrew's feelings. So, the answer is B.

► **QUESTION 14:**

Read the Main Instruction: The question asks for a similarity between investing in renewable energy and another action.
Carefully Read the Text: The text discusses the significance of renewable energy for a sustainable future and environmental preservation.
Analyze Each Statement:

A) Compares it to saving money, focusing on future security but missing the environmental aspect.
B) Equates it with planting trees, which is akin to contributing to environmental health and sustainability, as mentioned in the text.
C) Talks about educating children, a future-focused action, but not directly related to environmental impact.
D) Discusses building infrastructure, more economic in focus rather than environmental.

Confirm Your Answer: The correct answer is B) planting trees to contribute to a greener environment, as it parallels the text's emphasis on renewable energy's role in environmental sustainability.

► **QUESTION 15:**

Read the Main Instruction: The main instruction is asking what the speaker (Van Helsing) believes about Dr. John Seward based on the provided text.

Carefully Read the Text: In the text, Van Helsing is expressing his beliefs about Dr. John Seward's attitude and approach.

Analyze Each Statement:

  A) The text does not suggest that the speaker believes that Dr. John Seward should always trust science to explain everything. This is not mentioned in the text.

  B) This revised choice suggests that Dr. John Seward is too hasty in accepting the unknown, which is not in line with Van Helsing's actual beliefs in the text. This statement is not supported by the text.

  C) The text does not explicitly state that Dr. John Seward should not contemplate things he doesn't understand. This statement is not explicitly true.

  D) The text suggests that the speaker (Van Helsing) believes Dr. John Seward is too closed-minded to see beyond what he encounters in his daily life. Van Helsing mentions that Seward does not let his eyes see nor his ears hear what is outside his daily life, which aligns with this statement. This is supported by the text.

Confirm Your Answer: The text supports statement D) They are too closed-minded to see beyond what they encounter in their daily life. Thus, the correct answer is D) They are too closed-minded to see beyond what they encounter in their daily life.

► **QUESTION 16:**

Read the Main Instruction: The main instruction is asking what is true about LED bulbs based on the provided text.

Carefully Read the Text: The text discusses the transition from traditional incandescent light bulbs to energy-efficient LED bulbs driven by the growing awareness of energy conservation. However, once LED bulbs became widely adopted, some consumers reported experiencing increased eye strain and discomfort.

Analyze Each Statement:

  (A) This statement is supported by the text. The passage mentions that once LED bulbs became widely adopted, some consumers reported experiencing increased eye strain and discomfort, suggesting that LED bulbs may emit a different type of light compared to traditional incandescent bulbs.

  (B) The text mentions that governments began promoting the use of energy-efficient LED bulbs because they claimed to significantly reduce electricity consumption. This implies that traditional incandescent bulbs are less energy-efficient than LED bulbs.

  (C) The text does not suggest that the government's promotion of LED bulbs was based on misinformation about their energy-saving benefits. It attributes the promotion to the growing awareness of energy conservation.

  (D) This statement is contradicted by the text. Some consumers reported increased eye strain and discomfort after the widespread adoption of LED bulbs, indicating that LED bulbs do have an impact on eye comfort compared to traditional incandescent bulbs.

Confirm Your Answer: Among the options, (A) is the most accurate statement based on the text. The passage suggests that LED bulbs may emit a different type of light, leading to increased eye strain and discomfort for some consumers. Therefore, the correct answer is (A) LED bulbs emit a different type of light that can cause eye strain compared to traditional incandescent bulbs.

► **QUESTION 17:**

Read the Main Instruction: The main instruction is asking what the rising wind caused based on the provided text.

Carefully Read the Text: The text mentions a rising wind and its effects as Dorian and Basil ascend the stairs. It states, "A rising wind made some of the windows rattle."

Analyze Each Statement:

  (A) The text does not suggest that the rising wind caused the lamp to cast fantastic shadows. The casting of shadows is attributed to the lamp itself.

  (B) The text does mention that they walked softly, but it does not specify that the rising wind caused them to walk more quietly.

  (C) This statement accurately reflects the information in the text. The rising wind made some of the windows rattle.

  (D) The text states, "When they reached the top landing, Dorian took out the key and turned it in the lock." It does not suggest that the rising wind directly caused Dorian to take out the key.

Confirm Your Answer: Among the options, (C) is the most accurate statement based on the text. The rising wind made some of the windows rattle. Therefore, the correct answer is (C) Some of the windows not to stay still.

► **QUESTION 18:**

Read the Main Instruction: The question asks, "According to the text, why is marine biodiversity declining?"

Carefully Read the Text: The text describes a project conducted by a group of scientists led by Dr. Maria Alverez in 2022, which studied the impact of climate change on marine biodiversity. After comparing the current number of species in a particular marine ecosystem with past records, they found a significant reduction in the number of species. They attributed this loss of biodiversity to the effects of climate change, specifically warmer ocean temperatures and acidification.

Analyze Each Statement:

   A) Because the marine ecosystem is naturally evolving over time. This statement is not supported by the text, which attributes the decline in biodiversity to climate change, not natural evolution.

   B) Because of the overfishing practices carried out by humans. Overfishing is not mentioned as a cause for the decline in marine biodiversity in the text.

   C) Because marine animals are moving to different habitats. The text does not mention any migration of marine animals to other habitats.

   D) Because of rising ocean temperatures and acidification. This statement aligns directly with the information provided in the text.

Confirm Your Answer: From the analysis, option D) Because of rising ocean temperatures and acidification is the only statement that is directly supported by the text.

Therefore, the answer to the question "According to the text, why is marine biodiversity declining?" is D) Because of rising ocean temperatures and acidification.

► **QUESTION 19:**

Read the Main Instruction: The main instruction is asking why Dr. Mitchell's quantum computer is significant, based on the information in the text.

Carefully Read the Text: The text describes the groundbreaking discovery made by Dr. Lisa Mitchell and her team in the field of quantum computing.

Analyze Each Statement:

   A) The text does not mention that Dr. Mitchell's quantum computer is the first quantum computer ever developed. It focuses on the significance of its processing power compared to classical computers. This statement is not supported by the text.

   B) The text does not mention the size of the quantum computer in relation to existing classical computers. It emphasizes its processing power. This statement is not supported by the text.

   C) The text states that Dr. Mitchell's quantum computer has significantly greater processing power than any existing classical computer. This statement is supported by the text and accurately reflects the significance of the computer.

   D) The text mentions the potential impact of the quantum computer on fields like cryptography, machine learning, and drug discovery, but it does not state that these are its primary aims. This statement is not explicitly supported by the text.

Confirm Your Answer: The text clearly supports statement C, which accurately reflects the significance of Dr. Mitchell's quantum computer. Thus, the correct answer is C) It boasts a substantially superior computational capacity compared to its classical counterparts.

► **QUESTION 20:**

Read the Main Instruction: The question asks, "According to the text, why is the discovery of Proxima Centauri c significant?"

Carefully Read the Text: The text explains that in 2030, Astrophysicist Dr. Elena Rodriguez and her team discovered signs of a potential exoplanet in the Proxima Centauri system, the closest star system to Earth. The exoplanet, named Proxima Centauri c, is in the star's habitable zone, indicating the possibility of life-sustaining conditions. It is 1.5 times the size of Earth, and further research is ongoing to study its atmosphere and potential for water.

Analyze Each Statement:

   A) It is the first exoplanet ever discovered. The text does not say that this is the first exoplanet discovered.

   B) It is the largest planet discovered in the Proxima Centauri system. The text doesn't compare the size of this planet to others in the Proxima Centauri system.

   C) It is the closest planet to Earth. The text doesn't claim that this exoplanet is the closest to Earth, only that it is in the Proxima Centauri system, the closest star system to our own.

   D) It could potentially have conditions suitable for life. This is directly mentioned in the text, as the planet is within the star's habitable zone.

Confirm Your Answer: From the analysis, option D) It could potentially have conditions suitable for life is the only statement that is directly supported by the text.

Therefore, the answer to the question is D) It could potentially have conditions suitable for life.

▶ **QUESTION 21:**
Read the Main Instruction: The question asks, "According to the text, why is the discovery of the ancient city significant?"
Carefully Read the Text: The text explains that in 2031, Dr. Matthew Hopkins and his team of archaeologists discovered an ancient city buried beneath the Sahara desert. The artifacts indicated that the city had a complex social structure and advanced architecture, and it was a thriving metropolis around 2000 BC.
Analyze Each Statement:

    A) The city was once the capital of a powerful African empire. The text does not mention anything about the city being the capital of an empire.

    B) The city was built with advanced architectural techniques that were not known to have existed in 2000 BC. The text doesn't say that the architectural techniques used in the city were not known to have existed in 2000 BC.

    C) The city was discovered in the Sahara desert, which is unusual for an urban settlement. While the city was discovered in the Sahara, the text does not state that this is unusual for an urban settlement.

    D) The city is estimated to be one of the earliest known urban settlements in Africa. This statement aligns with the information in the text which states that the city was at its peak around 2000 BC, making it one of the oldest known urban settlements in Africa.

Confirm Your Answer: From the analysis, option D) The city is estimated to be one of the earliest known urban settlements in Africa is the only statement that is directly supported by the text.
Therefore, the answer to the question "According to the text, why is the discovery of the ancient city significant?" is D) The city is estimated to be one of the earliest known urban settlements in Africa.

3. Main Idea Answer

▶ **QUESTION 1:**
Read the Passage Carefully: The text talks about the potential impact of autonomous vehicles on society, highlighting both positive aspects (reduced accidents, alleviated congestion, and lower carbon emissions) and potential drawbacks (job losses and safety risks).
Identify Key Points: Autonomous vehicles could transform cities and lives. They have potential benefits, like reducing traffic accidents, congestion, and carbon emissions. However, there are concerns about job losses and safety risks.
Summarize in Your Own Words: The adoption of autonomous vehicles will have significant effects on society. While they could offer benefits such as fewer traffic accidents and less congestion, they could also lead to job losses in the transportation sector and create unforeseen safety issues. The balance of these potential benefits and drawbacks will shape their impact.
Analyze the Options:

    A) Autonomous vehicles are the future of transportation and will have many benefits - This statement overlooks the potential drawbacks mentioned in the text.

    B) Autonomous vehicles are controversial due to potential job losses and safety risks - This choice only focuses on the drawbacks and ignores the potential benefits.

    C) The impact of autonomous vehicles on society will depend on the balance between their potential benefits and drawbacks - This choice encapsulates all the key points mentioned in the text.

    D) Critics believe autonomous vehicles pose more risks than benefits to society - This statement only captures the critics' viewpoint and does not take into account the potential benefits.

Eliminate Incorrect Options: Options A, B, and D can be eliminated as they do not fully capture the main idea of the text.

Choose the Best Fit: Option C, "The impact of autonomous vehicles on society will depend on the balance between their potential benefits and drawbacks," best encapsulates the main idea.
Review: Upon revisiting the text with Option C in mind, it aligns well with the main idea, which talks about the potential benefits and drawbacks of autonomous vehicles, and how their impact will depend on how these aspects balance out.

▶ **QUESTION 2:**
Read the Passage Carefully: The text introduces a new species of bird, the Flame Crest, discovered in the Amazon rainforest. It also highlights the threat posed to its habitat by deforestation.
Identify Key Points: The Flame Crest is a new species, characterized by its bright red crest and loud call. The bird's habitat is threatened due to deforestation.
Summarize in Your Own Words: A new bird species called the Flame Crest has been discovered in the Amazon, but it's under threat due to rampant deforestation.
Analyze the Options:

    A) The Flame Crest is a newly discovered species in the Amazon rainforest that is under threat due to deforestation - This option encapsulates the key points of the passage.

    B) Scientists discovered the Flame Crest bird due to its distinctive loud vocalizations - This doesn't cover the entire idea of the text, particularly the deforestation threat.

C) Deforestation in the Amazon rainforest is the primary reason for the decline in bird species - While this is part of the main idea, it neglects to mention the new discovery of the Flame Crest.

D) The Flame Crest is the only bird in the Amazon rainforest with a bright red crest - This is not stated in the passage and misses the main point about the threat to its habitat.

Eliminate Incorrect Options: B, C, and D don't fully reflect the main idea of the passage.

Choose the Best Fit: Option A, "The Flame Crest is a newly discovered species in the Amazon rainforest that is under threat due to deforestation," is the best choice as it encapsulates the key points in the text.

Review: Reading the text again with Option A in mind confirms that this selection accurately reflects the main idea of the passage, capturing both the discovery of the Flame Crest and the threat to its habitat.

▶ **QUESTION 3:**

Read the Passage Carefully: The text provides information about the bicycle culture in Copenhagen, Denmark, explaining how many residents commute by bike, the extent of bike lanes in the city, and the benefits of this culture.

Identify Key Points: Copenhagen promotes bicycle use for commuting, has an extensive network of bike lanes, and the city's focus on cycling infrastructure reduces congestion, pollution and contributes to the physical health of citizens.

Summarize in Your Own Words: Copenhagen is a city that prioritizes cycling as a major form of transport, supporting it through a comprehensive network of bike lanes and emphasizing its benefits for the environment and citizens' health.

Analyze the Options:

A) Copenhagen, Denmark is a city that highly values and promotes cycling as a primary mode of transport - This captures all the key points from the text.

B) Cycling in Copenhagen, Denmark is primarily for commuting to work or school - While true, this option doesn't address the extent of the city's cycling infrastructure or the benefits mentioned.

C) The citizens of Copenhagen, Denmark are exceptionally physically healthy due to cycling - This only addresses a portion of the benefits mentioned and omits the discussion of the city's infrastructure and commitment to cycling.

D) The city of Copenhagen, Denmark has over 400 kilometers of bike lanes - This fact is part of the text, but it's just one aspect of the city's commitment to cycling and doesn't encompass the overall main idea.

Eliminate Incorrect Options: Options B, C, and D can be eliminated because they don't fully represent the main idea of the passage.

Choose the Best Fit: Option A, "Copenhagen, Denmark is a city that highly values and promotes cycling as a primary mode of transport," best captures the main idea of the text.

Review: Reading the text again with Option A in mind confirms that this choice correctly reflects the main idea, capturing the city's commitment to cycling, its extensive infrastructure, and the benefits of this approach.

▶ **QUESTION 4:**

Read the Passage Carefully: The text describes Elizabeth's reflections on her relationship with Mr. Darcy, noting the contradictions and complexities in their interactions. She seems to experience some regret over the changes in her feelings, which once would have celebrated the end of their acquaintance but now wish for its continuance.

Identify Key Points: Elizabeth's relationship with Mr. Darcy is full of contradictions and varieties, and her feelings have changed from wanting their relationship to end to wanting it to continue.

Summarize in Your Own Words: Elizabeth is reflecting on her complex and contradictory relationship with Mr. Darcy, expressing some regret about the shift in her feelings, which now lean towards maintaining their relationship instead of ending it.

Analyze the Options:

A) Elizabeth Bennet is thrilled by Mr. Darcy's proposal and can't wait to see him again - This does not capture the conflicted and complex nature of Elizabeth's feelings.

B) Elizabeth Bennet is confused about her feelings toward Mr. Darcy and their complicated relationship - This matches well with the text's description of the relationship being "full of contradictions and varieties".

C) Elizabeth Bennet strongly regrets ever meeting Mr. Darcy - This is not reflected in the text. Elizabeth's regret seems to be over her changing feelings, not over meeting Mr. Darcy.

D) Elizabeth Bennet is indifferent to Mr. Darcy and his proposal - Indifference is not the sentiment expressed in the text. - Elizabeth is seen to experience complex and changing feelings.

Eliminate Incorrect Options: Options A, C, and D can be eliminated because they do not accurately reflect the content of the passage.

Choose the Best Fit: Option B, "Elizabeth Bennet is confused about her feelings toward Mr. Darcy and their complicated relationship," is the best fit as it captures the essence of the passage.

Review: Revisiting the text with Option B in mind, it's clear that this choice correctly reflects the main idea of the passage - the complexity and contradiction in Elizabeth's feelings towards Mr. Darcy.

▶ **QUESTION 5:**

Read the Passage Carefully: The passage is a vivid description of the town of Maycomb, highlighting its age, tiredness, and the hot, uncomfortable weather conditions.

Identify Key Points: Maycomb is an old and tired town. It becomes particularly uncomfortable during hot weather when streets turn into "red slop," and the heat affects both people and animals.

Summarize in Your Own Words: Maycomb is characterized as an old and weary town. The intense heat affects the town's inhabitants and animals, painting a picture of a place that's both tired and uncomfortable.

Analyze the Options:

    A) Maycomb is a bustling town full of activity throughout the day - This contradicts the description of Maycomb as a "tired old town."

    B) The people of Maycomb are unhappy due to the hot and uncomfortable weather - The text doesn't state that the people are unhappy, just that the weather conditions are uncomfortable.

    C) Scout dislikes living in Maycomb due to its old age and hot weather - The passage doesn't indicate Scout's personal feelings about living in Maycomb.

    D) The town of Maycomb is described as old and weary, with a hot and uncomfortable climate - This statement covers the main points about Maycomb's age, its tiredness, and its hot weather.

Eliminate Incorrect Options: Options A, B, and C do not accurately reflect the main points of the passage.

Choose the Best Fit: Option D, "The town of Maycomb is described as old and weary, with a hot and uncomfortable climate," best states the main idea of the text.

Review: Upon revisiting the text with Option D in mind, it aligns well with the main idea, which is a descriptive portrayal of Maycomb as an old, weary town with a hot and uncomfortable climate.

▶ **QUESTION 6:**

Read the Passage Carefully: The poem emphasizes the power of will and determination, suggesting that they can overcome any obstacle or challenge.

Identify Key Points: The power of a determined soul can overcome any external factors like chance, destiny, or fate. The will is described as a mighty force.

Summarize in Your Own Words: The poem underscores the idea that determination and willpower are paramount, and they can surmount any external challenges or obstacles.

Analyze the Options:

    A) The poem suggests the opposite, that destiny and fate cannot control a determined soul.

    B) This statement captures the essence of the poem's message about the power of will.

    C) The poem doesn't focus on the unpredictability of the natural world; it uses natural imagery to emphasize the power of will.

    D) The poem explicitly states that "Gifts count for nothing; will alone is great."

Eliminate Incorrect Options: Options A, C, and D do not capture the main idea of the text.

Choose the Best Fit: Option B, "The power of will and determination can overcome any obstacle or challenge," best encapsulates the main idea.

▶ **QUESTION 7:**

Read the Passage Carefully: The text delves into Raskolnikov's emotional state after committing a crime, emphasizing his feelings of enduring misery and guilt.

Identify Key Points: Raskolnikov feels a deep, lasting misery that feels eternal. His guilt is so profound that even the environment around him seems to reflect his desolation.

Summarize in Your Own Words: Raskolnikov is consumed by a sense of unending guilt and misery, with his surroundings seemingly echoing his internal torment.

Analyze the Options:

    A) The text does not mention Raskolnikov enjoying the sunset.

    B) Raskolnikov's sadness is described as having a feeling of permanence, not temporary.

    C) The text describes Raskolnikov's feelings as a "foretaste of hopeless years" and mentions his guilt, supporting this statement.

    D) The text does not discuss Raskolnikov contemplating the vastness of the universe.

Eliminate Incorrect Options: Options A, B, and D can be eliminated as they do not capture the main idea of the text.

Choose the Best Fit: Option C, "The weight of his actions led Raskolnikov to feel an enduring, inescapable misery," best encapsulates the main idea.

Review: Upon revisiting the text with Option C in mind, it aligns well with the main idea, which portrays Raskolnikov's profound guilt and enduring misery.

▶ **QUESTION 8:**

Read the Passage Carefully: The passage provides a basic explanation of quantum computing and how it differs from classical computing.

Identify Key Points: Quantum computing uses quantum bits or "qubits," which can be both 0 and 1 at the same time, due to the principle of superposition. This capacity allows quantum computers to process complex computations faster than classical computers.

Summarize in Your Own Words: Quantum computing utilizes the concept of superposition in quantum bits to process information, potentially offering faster computations than classical computers.

Analyze the Options:

A) The state of superposition is the main advantage of quantum computing - This statement is partly correct but doesn't fully encapsulate the main idea, as the advantage discussed is not the state of superposition itself, but the faster computation it enables.

B) Quantum computing is a complex field that only experts can truly understand - This statement isn't supported by the passage, which doesn't touch on the complexity of understanding the field.

C) Quantum computing, with its use of qubits, has the potential to perform computations faster than classical computers - This statement accurately summarizes the main point of the passage.

D) Classical computers are becoming obsolete due to the development of quantum computing - This is not stated or implied in the passage.

Eliminate Incorrect Options: Options A, B, and D can be eliminated because they either do not fully capture the main idea or are not supported by the passage.

Choose the Best Fit: Option C, "Quantum computing, with its use of qubits, has the potential to perform computations faster than classical computers," best states the main idea of the text.

Review: Upon revisiting the text with Option C in mind, it aligns well with the main idea, which is the potential for faster computations offered by quantum computing due to the use of qubits.

▶ **QUESTION 9:**

Read the Passage Carefully: Alice is falling down a rabbit hole and she's thinking about the distance she has fallen.

Identify Key Points: Alice is considering the distance she's fallen and applies some of her schoolroom lessons to estimate that she might be nearing the center of the earth.

Summarize in Your Own Words: While falling down a rabbit hole, Alice tries to calculate how far she has fallen, using what she's learned in school to hypothesize that she might be nearing the center of the earth.

Analyze the Options:

A) Alice is reflecting on her lessons from school while falling down a rabbit hole - This is partially true, but it leaves out Alice's application of her school knowledge to estimate how far she's fallen, which is a key point.

B) Alice believes that she has fallen to the center of the earth - This isn't entirely accurate. Alice is wondering if she's nearing the center of the earth, not believing she's already there.

C) Alice is growing bored and frustrated with her seemingly endless fall - This isn't mentioned or implied in the passage.

D) Alice is estimating the distance she has fallen down the rabbit hole - This correctly summarizes the passage, as Alice is trying to calculate the distance she's fallen.

Eliminate Incorrect Options: Options A, B, and C can be eliminated based on the analysis above.

Choose the Best Fit: Option D, "Alice is estimating the distance she has fallen down the rabbit hole," best states the main idea of the text.

Review: Upon revisiting the text with Option D in mind, it aligns well with the main idea, which is Alice's estimation of the distance she's fallen.

▶ **QUESTION 10:**

Read the Passage Carefully: The passage discusses the impact of Artificial Intelligence (AI) on various sectors and highlights the benefits and challenges it presents.

Identify Key Points: AI has improved several sectors by enhancing decision-making and efficiency. However, it also poses ethical challenges, such as job displacement, privacy concerns, and potential misuse.

Summarize in Your Own Words: While AI has significantly benefited various sectors due to its ability to process vast data and enhance decision-making, it also brings up several ethical issues, including job loss, privacy threats, and possible misuse.

Analyze the Options:

A) Artificial Intelligence has significantly improved several sectors but also presents ethical challenges and concerns - This captures both the benefits and drawbacks of AI mentioned in the passage.

B) AI's ability to process vast amounts of data is transforming various sectors, despite the potential for job displacement - This option focuses more on the positive aspect of AI and only addresses one of the challenges, ignoring privacy concerns and potential misuse.

C) The most significant impact of AI has been in healthcare, finance, transportation, and education - This option only highlights the positive impact of AI and fails to address the challenges it poses.

D) The rapid development of AI technologies is causing significant concern about job displacement and privacy - This option emphasizes the challenges and doesn't consider the benefits of AI.

Eliminate Incorrect Options: Options B, C, and D can be eliminated based on the analysis above.

Choose the Best Fit: Option A, "Artificial Intelligence has significantly improved several sectors but also presents ethical challenges and concerns," best states the main idea of the text.

Review: Upon revisiting the text with Option A in mind, it aligns well with the main idea, which discusses both the benefits and challenges of AI.

► **QUESTION 11:**

Read the Passage Carefully: The Time Traveller observes a seemingly desolate future world, noting the absence of visible life and the stillness of the environment.

Identify Key Points: The world appears devoid of animal life, with only green slime indicating the presence of life. The environment is silent and still.

Summarize in Your Own Words: In this future world, signs of life are scarce, with the environment characterized by stillness and silence.

Analyze the Options:

    A) The text does not describe the world as vibrant or the Time Traveller as eager to explore.

    B) The text mentions the absence of visible life and the presence of green slime, supporting this statement.

    C) The Time Traveller does not observe a variety of animals and plants.

    D) The text does not describe the green slime as harmful or dangerous.

Eliminate Incorrect Options: Options A, C, and D do not accurately reflect the main points of the passage.

Choose the Best Fit: Option B, "Life seemed almost extinct, with only subtle signs indicating its presence," best states the main idea of the text.

Review: Upon revisiting the text with Option B in mind, it aligns well with the main idea, which highlights the scarcity of life in the observed future world.

► **QUESTION 12:**

Read the Passage Carefully: The passage discusses the serious issue of global warming, its effects, and the urgent need for action.

Identify Key Points: The main points include the serious impacts of global warming (melting ice caps, rising sea levels, extreme weather events, impact on human lives, wildlife habitats, and the global economy) and the urgent need for action (reducing greenhouse gas emissions, protecting and restoring forests, and transitioning to renewable energy).

Summarize in Your Own Words: Global warming is causing severe problems that require immediate action, such as reducing emissions and shifting to renewable energy.

Analyze the Options:

    A) Melting ice caps and rising sea levels are among the most concerning effects of global warming - This only captures part of the text regarding the effects of global warming and ignores the call to action.

    B) The impacts of global warming are severe, requiring immediate measures like reducing greenhouse gas emissions and transitioning to renewable energy - This option accurately summarizes the main points in the passage.

    C) Global warming is negatively affecting wildlife habitats, human lives, and the global economy - This option focuses on the impacts of global warming but does not mention the urgent need for action.

    D) The primary solution to global warming is transitioning to renewable energy sources - This option focuses on one potential solution, ignoring the broader range of impacts and solutions discussed in the text.

Eliminate Incorrect Options: Based on the analysis above, options A, C, and D can be eliminated as they don't encompass all the main points of the text.

Choose the Best Fit: Option B, "The impacts of global warming are severe, requiring immediate measures like reducing greenhouse gas emissions and transitioning to renewable energy," best states the main idea of the text.

Review: Upon revisiting the text with Option B in mind, it aligns well with the main idea, encompassing both the severe impacts of global warming and the need for immediate action.

► **QUESTION 13:**

Read the Passage Carefully: The text describes Phileas Fogg's routine and solitary lifestyle.

Identify Key Points: Fogg lives alone, has a fixed routine, dines alone at the club, and does not socialize or bring guests.

Summarize in Your Own Words: Phileas Fogg is a solitary individual who adheres to a strict routine and avoids social interactions.

Analyze the Options:

    A) The text describes Fogg as not bringing guests to his home, contradicting this statement.

    B) The text emphasizes Fogg's strict routine and solitude, supporting this statement.

    C) The text does not focus on the club's atmosphere or Fogg's interactions there.

    D) The text describes Fogg's life as methodical and predictable, not chaotic.

Eliminate Incorrect Options: Options A, C, and D do not capture the main idea of the text.

Choose the Best Fit: Option B, "Fogg is a creature of habit, living a life of strict routine and solitude," best encapsulates the main idea.

Review: Upon revisiting the text with Option B in mind, it aligns well with the main idea, which portrays Fogg's regimented and solitary lifestyle.

► **QUESTION 14:**

Read the Passage Carefully: Captain Nemo speaks about the vastness and wonder of the sea, describing it as a living entity full of life and movement.

Identify Key Points: The sea covers a significant portion of the earth, and it is full of life and wonder. It is described as the "living infinite."

Summarize in Your Own Words: Captain Nemo views the sea as a vast, living expanse full of wonder and life, representing the infinite possibilities of the underwater world.

Analyze the Options:

A) The text doesn't describe the sea as dangerous or unpredictable.

B) This statement captures Captain Nemo's reverence and wonder for the sea.

C) The text doesn't warn humans to avoid the sea; rather, it speaks of the wonders within.

D) The text focuses on the wonder of the sea, not comparing it to the terrestrial world.

Eliminate Incorrect Options: Options A, C, and D do not capture the main idea of the text.

Choose the Best Fit: Option B, "The sea, for Captain Nemo, represents a vast, living entity full of wonder," best encapsulates the main idea.

▶ **QUESTION 15:**

Read the Passage Carefully: The text describes the aftermath of the revolution on the farm, focusing on the pigs' leadership and the disparity in equality among the animals.

Identify Key Points: The pigs, who led the revolution, started making decisions for the farm. Over time, their leadership appeared to deviate from the initial ideals of equality.

Summarize in Your Own Words: After the revolution, the pigs took charge, and though they claimed to be working for the farm's betterment, their actions began to betray the principles of the revolt.

Analyze the Options:

A) The text describes the pigs as the "brains of the revolution," contradicting this statement.

B) The statement "some animals are more equal than others" and the pigs' actions suggest that not all animals lived in equality.

C) The text indicates that the pigs' leadership was not as selfless as it initially seemed, supporting this statement.

D) The text suggests that there were negative consequences to the revolution, particularly in the pigs' leadership.

Eliminate Incorrect Options: Options A, B, and D do not capture the main idea of the text.

Choose the Best Fit: Option C, "The pigs began to exert dominance and betray the ideals of the revolution," best encapsulates the main idea.

Review: Upon revisiting the text with Option C in mind, it aligns well with the main idea, which portrays the pigs' increasing dominance and deviation from the revolution's ideals.

▶ **QUESTION 16:**

Read the Passage Carefully: The passage discusses the issue of plastic pollution, its impacts, and potential solutions.

Identify Key Points: Plastic pollution is a serious problem, affecting wildlife and human health. The plastic waste takes a long time to decompose and eventually becomes microplastics. Solutions include reducing plastic consumption, improving waste management, and finding eco-friendly alternatives.

Summarize in Your Own Words: Plastic pollution is a significant environmental issue, affecting both wildlife and human health. Solutions include reducing plastic usage, better waste management, and the development of environmentally friendly alternatives.

Analyze the Options:

A) Plastic pollution is a grave environmental issue that requires efforts to reduce plastic consumption, improve waste management, and develop eco-friendly alternatives - This statement encompasses the major points made in the passage.

B) The danger of plastic waste lies in its slow decomposition and its eventual breakdown into microplastics - While this is true, it doesn't fully encapsulate the main idea of the passage, which also includes the negative effects of plastic pollution and potential solutions.

C) The massive amounts of plastic waste discarded annually are severely damaging wildlife and human health - This statement focuses only on the problem and its impacts but neglects to mention the proposed solutions.

D) Efforts to combat plastic pollution must prioritize the development and investment in eco-friendly alternatives to plastic - This option highlights one of the potential solutions but doesn't fully cover the main idea, which also includes the problem and its impacts.

Eliminate Incorrect Options: Options B, C, and D can be eliminated because they do not fully cover all the key points of the passage.

Choose the Best Fit: Option A, "Plastic pollution is a grave environmental issue that requires efforts to reduce plastic consumption, improve waste management, and develop eco-friendly alternatives," best states the main idea of the text.

Review: Upon revisiting the text with Option A in mind, it aligns well with the main idea that plastic pollution is a significant problem requiring efforts to reduce plastic use, improve waste handling, and find environmentally friendly alternatives.

▶ **QUESTION 17:**

Read the Passage Carefully: The text describes Silas Marner's life of solitude and repetitive tasks, drawing a parallel between his life and that of wiser men who might have faced similar feelings of purposelessness.

Identify Key Points: Silas's life is reduced to weaving and hoarding, without a clear purpose or end goal.

Summarize in Your Own Words: Silas lives a life centered around repetitive tasks, devoid of a larger purpose, similar to wiser men who might have found solace in erudite pursuits.

Analyze the Options:
  A) The text doesn't mention Silas's life being centered around academic pursuits.
  B) This statement captures the essence of Silas's life as described in the text.
  C) The text doesn't focus on wealth and possessions as primary concerns for most men.
  D) Silas doesn't compare his life; the narrator does.
Eliminate Incorrect Options: Options A, C, and D do not capture the main idea of the text.

Choose the Best Fit: Option B, "Silas's life was devoid of purpose, focused only on repetitive tasks," best encapsulates the main idea.

▶ **QUESTION 18:**
Read the Passage Carefully: The text describes the influence of classical art, science, and literature from ancient Greece and Rome on the Renaissance.
Identify Key Points: The Renaissance was marked by a revival of classical influences, which impacted art and introduced new techniques.
Summarize in Your Own Words: The Renaissance was influenced by classical works, leading to iconic art and new techniques.
Analyze the Options:
  A) The text mentions multiple artists, not just these two.
  B) This statement captures the essence of the Renaissance's classical revival.
  C) The text mentions the introduction of new techniques.
  D) The text contradicts this statement.
Eliminate Incorrect Options: Options A, C, and D do not capture the main idea of the text.

Choose the Best Fit: Option B, "The Renaissance was marked by the revival of classical influences, profoundly affecting the arts and sciences," best encapsulates the main idea.

▶ **QUESTION 19:**
Read the Passage Carefully: The text discusses the significance of the Library of Alexandria and its symbolic representation of the value of knowledge.
Identify Key Points: The library was a beacon of knowledge, and its legacy symbolizes the importance of preserving knowledge.
Summarize in Your Own Words: The Library of Alexandria stands as a symbol of the enduring human value of collecting and preserving knowledge.
Analyze the Options:
  A) The text mentions the library's fate as a mystery but doesn't focus on the date.
  B) The text mentions more than just the scrolls in the library.
  C) This statement captures the symbolic significance of the library.
  D) The text doesn't focus on ancient records as primary sources.
Eliminate Incorrect Options: Options A, B, and D do not capture the main idea of the text.

Choose the Best Fit: Option C, "The Library of Alexandria represents the enduring human desire to store and cherish knowledge," best encapsulates the main idea.

▶ **QUESTION 20:**
Read the Passage Carefully: The text highlights the intelligence and adaptability of octopuses, contrasting these traits with their short lifespan.
Identify Key Points: Octopuses are intelligent and adaptable, but they have a surprisingly short lifespan.
Summarize in Your Own Words: Octopuses, despite their remarkable abilities, live only for a short duration.
Analyze the Options:
  A) The text mentions their lifespan, but this isn't the main focus.
  B) This statement only captures part of the text's focus.
  C) This statement captures the contrast between their abilities and lifespan.
  D) The text mentions more than just their soft bodies.
Eliminate Incorrect Options: Options A, B, and D do not capture the main idea of the text.

Choose the Best Fit: Option C, "Despite their impressive intelligence and adaptability, octopuses live only a short time," best encapsulates the main idea.

▶ **QUESTION 21:**
Read the Passage Carefully: The poem reflects on the challenges, disappointments, and struggles of life, with the speaker questioning the purpose and meaning amid these difficulties.
Identify Key Points: The speaker mentions the recurring questions of life, the faithless, the foolish, and the struggle that seems to be ever-present.

Summarize in Your Own Words: The poem delves into the existential questions of life, highlighting the challenges, disappointments, and the continuous search for purpose.
Analyze the Options:
  A) The poem doesn't celebrate life in cities.
  B) The speaker is not content; he's questioning the purpose of life.
  C) This statement captures the essence of the poem's reflection on life's challenges.
  D) The poem doesn't focus on positive outcomes.
Eliminate Incorrect Options: Options A, B, and D do not capture the main idea of the text.

Choose the Best Fit: Option C, "The poem reflects on the challenges and disappointments of life," best encapsulates the main idea.

▶ **QUESTION 22:**
Read the Passage Carefully: The text discusses the rise of plastic as a versatile material in the 20th century and its subsequent environmental impact due to its non-biodegradability.
Identify Key Points: Plastic's durability made it popular, but this same longevity led to environmental issues as it accumulated in landfills and oceans.
Summarize in Your Own Words: While plastic became a revolutionary material in the 20th century due to its durability, this same quality has contributed to environmental problems.
Analyze the Options:
  A) The text mentions multiple industries, not just automotive.
  B) This statement captures the dual nature of plastic's benefits and drawbacks.
  C) The text mentions threats to the broader ecosystem, not just marine life.
  D) The text doesn't state that industries have stopped using plastic.
Eliminate Incorrect Options: Options A, C, and D do not capture the main idea of the text.

Choose the Best Fit: Option B, "The durability of plastic has led to an environmental crisis due to its non-biodegradability," best encapsulates the main idea.

▶ **QUESTION 23:**
Read the Passage Carefully: The text paints a vivid picture of the Italian countryside, focusing on the beauty of violets covering the hillside.
Identify Key Points: The hillside is covered with violets, creating a breathtaking view.
Summarize in Your Own Words: The beauty of the Italian landscape, especially the violets, leaves a profound impression.
Analyze the Options:
  A) This statement captures the essence of Lucy's experience with the Italian landscape.
  B) The hillside is described as being covered with violets, not devoid of vegetation.
  C) The text doesn't mention Lucy searching for an answer.
  D) The violets are the focus, but the text doesn't say they're the only plants.
Eliminate Incorrect Options: Options B, C, and D do not capture the main idea of the text.

Choose the Best Fit: Option A, "Lucy was overwhelmed by the beauty of the Italian landscape," best encapsulates the main idea.

▶ **QUESTION 24:**
Read the Passage Carefully: The passage talks about Robotic Process Automation (RPA), highlighting its benefits of improving efficiency and accuracy by automating routine tasks and its drawbacks such as potential job displacement and data security concerns.
Identify Key Points: RPA is a technology that uses software robots to automate routine tasks, improving efficiency and accuracy. However, it raises concerns about job displacement and data security.
Summarize in Your Own Words: The passage describes RPA as a technology that has the potential to enhance work efficiency and accuracy through automation but also mentions its potential downsides, like job loss and data security issues.
Analyze the Options:
  A) RPA is a promising technology that is likely to replace human workers in routine tasks - This option only partially reflects the passage; while it discusses the automation of routine tasks, it doesn't mention the potential concerns.
  B) RPA is a technology that improves efficiency and accuracy but raises concerns about job displacement and data security - This statement captures the benefits of RPA as well as its potential drawbacks, which aligns with the main idea in the passage.
  C) RPA bots mimic human actions and are primarily used to improve accuracy in tasks - This statement is also incomplete as it only addresses one aspect of RPA's benefits and doesn't mention the potential drawbacks.
  D) Concerns about job displacement and data security are hindering the widespread adoption of RPA - This statement is skewed towards the concerns and does not accurately capture the benefits of RPA discussed in the passage.
Eliminate Incorrect Options: Options A, C, and D do not fully represent the main idea of the passage.

<u>Choose the Best Fit: Option B,</u> "RPA is a technology that improves efficiency and accuracy but raises concerns about job displacement and data security," best states the main idea of the text.

Review: Upon revisiting the text with Option B in mind, it aligns well with the main idea, encapsulating both the advantages of RPA and the potential concerns it raises.

4. Main Purpose Answer

▶ **QUESTION 1:**

Read the passage carefully: This passage provides a brief description of the 3D printing process, from the initial design stage through to the final product. It mentions the tools used in creating a design, the printers that turn the design into a physical object, and the types of materials typically used.

Identify the central idea: The core of this text revolves around explaining the process of 3D printing, including how designs are created and the types of materials that might be employed in the printing process.

Look for the author's intent: The intention of the author seems to be to give readers a basic understanding of how 3D printing works, from the start of creating a design to the final printed product. The author does not seem to be pushing a particular viewpoint or heavily promoting one aspect of 3D printing over another.

Eliminate incorrect options:

    A) "To highlight the aesthetic artifacts that can be produced through 3D printing" can be ruled out as the passage mentions both useful and aesthetic products but does not particularly focus on aesthetic artifacts.

    B) "To emphasize the importance of CAD applications in the 3D printing industry" can be eliminated because, although CAD applications are mentioned, they're only a part of the whole process being described.

    C) "To differentiate between the materials used in home and commercial 3D printers" can be disregarded since the main focus isn't on differentiating the materials, but on explaining the overall process.

<u>Choose the best answer:</u> Based on the remaining options, "D) To provide an overview of the 3D printing process" best represents the author's main objective and the central idea of the passage. The narrative provides a concise introduction to how 3D printing works, making this the best choice.

▶ **QUESTION 2:**

Read the passage carefully: This passage is about research studies on the note patterns in crow calls.

Identify the central idea: The main theme is the function of note patterns in crow calls and how they vary across different crow populations.

Look for the author's intent: The author appears to be informing readers about the purpose of note patterns in crow calls, as revealed by several studies.

Eliminate incorrect options:

    B) "To summarize that crows are the most intelligent bird species" can be eliminated because the passage doesn't make a claim about the intelligence of crows relative to other birds.

    C) "To account for a discrepancy between the results of several studies that analyzed note patterns" can be eliminated because the passage doesn't mention any discrepancies between the studies.

    D) "To compare crow communication patterns with those of other birds" can be eliminated because the passage focuses on crows, without comparing their communication patterns to those of other birds.

<u>Choose the best answer:</u> The remaining option, "A) To describe studies that identified the function of particular note patterns in crow calls," best matches the author's intent and the central idea of the text. The passage primarily describes the purpose and variability of note patterns in crow calls, making this the best answer.

▶ **QUESTION 3:**

Read the passage carefully: This passage is about the moral opposition to slavery and how it contradicts American values.

Identify the central idea: The main theme is the immorality of slavery and its contrast to American ideals such as liberty, justice, and the pursuit of happiness.

Look for the author's intent: The author appears to be persuading the reader that slavery is fundamentally against American values.

Eliminate incorrect options:

    A) "To argue that the founding fathers were against slavery" can be eliminated because the passage does not specifically argue about the founding fathers' views on slavery.

    C) "To discuss the history of slavery in America" can be eliminated because the passage doesn't delve into the historical aspect of slavery, but rather its moral implications.

    D) "To debate the effects of slavery on modern society" can be eliminated because the passage doesn't discuss the modern effects of slavery.

Choose the best answer: The remaining option, "B) To convince the audience that slavery opposes American values," best matches the author's intent and the central idea of the text. The passage primarily aims to convince the reader that slavery is in direct opposition to American values, making this the best answer.

▶ **QUESTION 4:**

Read the Passage Carefully: The passage discusses the unique properties of stem cells, their potential in medical treatments, and the controversies surrounding their research.

Identify the Central Idea: The main theme is the potential of stem cell research, its promise in treating diseases, and the ethical concerns associated with it.

Look for the Author's Intent: The author aims to provide an overview of stem cell research, highlighting its potential benefits and the controversies it has sparked.

Eliminate Incorrect Options:

    A) While the passage touches upon the characteristics of stem cells, it doesn't delve into their biological functions in detail.

    B) The ethical dilemmas and regulatory challenges are mentioned, but they aren't the sole focus of the passage.

    D) The future prospects of regenerative medicine are implied, but the passage doesn't analyze them in depth.

Choose the Best Answer: The remaining option, "C) To provide an overview of stem cell research, its potential, and associated controversies," best aligns with the author's intent and the central idea of the text.

▶ **QUESTION 5:**

Read the passage carefully: Huck reflects on the beauty and peace of life on the raft, especially at night as they gaze at the stars. He recalls a discussion with Jim about the origin of the stars and mentions the comforting sounds from the shore.

Identify the central idea: The passage primarily captures the serenity of raft-life at night and Huck's feelings of closeness and safety.

Look for the author's intent: Twain is depicting a quiet, introspective moment in Huck's adventures where the beauty of nature and the depth of human connection come to the fore.

Eliminate incorrect options:

    A) While the wonder Huck feels at the stars is touched upon, it's not the main thrust of the passage.

    B) The disagreement about the stars is a minor detail in the passage, and doesn't represent the overarching theme.

    D) While Huck expresses an opinion on the origin of the stars, the passage doesn't primarily focus on his skepticism about universal creation.

Choose the best answer: The best answer is "C) To describe the peaceful nature of life on the raft and the intimacy of the river at night." The narrative is centered on the tranquility and intimacy Huck feels during these moments.

▶ **QUESTION 6:**

Read the Passage Carefully: The passage discusses Martin Luther's "95 Theses," its symbolic act, and the profound impact it had on European religious dynamics.

Identify the Central Idea: The main theme is the significance of Luther's "95 Theses" and its role in sparking the Protestant Reformation.

Look for the Author's Intent: The author aims to emphasize the transformative impact of Luther's actions on European religious structures.

Eliminate Incorrect Options:

    A) The architectural significance of the Wittenberg Castle Church isn't the main focus of the passage.

    C) While the Protestant Reformation is mentioned, the passage doesn't outline its entirety.

    D) The passage doesn't analyze the economic implications of the sale of indulgences in detail.

Choose the Best Answer: The remaining option, "B) To emphasize the impact of Luther's 95 Theses on European religious dynamics," best captures the author's intent and the central idea of the text.

▶ **QUESTION 7:**

Read the passage carefully: The text provides a series of juxtapositions and contrasts to describe the state of the times.

Identify the central idea: Dickens paints the era as simultaneously embodying a range of extremes—from wisdom to foolishness, hope to despair.

Look for the author's intent: Dickens intends to convey the intricate duality and paradoxes of the times, setting the tone for the complex narrative that unfolds in the novel.

Eliminate incorrect options:

    A) There's no mention of geographical distinctions between two cities.

    C) Dickens presents both positive and negative aspects, neither is particularly emphasized over the other.

    D) This line doesn't delve into a historical account; rather, it offers a thematic introduction.

Choose the best answer: Based on the contrasts provided, "B) To contrast the stark differences and paradoxes of the era described in the novel" emerges as the most fitting choice. This famous opening line is meant to highlight the tumultuous and contradictory nature of the period in which "A Tale of Two Cities" is set.

▶ **QUESTION 8:**

Read the Passage Carefully: The passage focuses on Mikhail Gorbachev's leadership of the Soviet Union, his policies, and their unintended consequences.

Identify the Central Idea: The main theme is Gorbachev's reforms and how they inadvertently led to the collapse of the Soviet Union.

Look for the Author's Intent: The author aims to inform readers about Gorbachev's policies and their significant implications.

Eliminate Incorrect Options:

    A) The passage doesn't discuss the entire history of the Soviet Union.

    B) While the geopolitical changes are mentioned, they are not the main focus of the passage.

    D) The passage doesn't analyze the economic structure of the Soviet Union in detail.

Choose the Best Answer: The remaining option, "C) To outline Mikhail Gorbachev's reforms and their global implications," best captures the author's intent and the central idea of the text.

▶ **QUESTION 9:**

Read the passage carefully: The passage gives a set of conditions or characteristics that, if met, the author claims will result in the listener becoming a 'Man'.

Identify the central idea: The central idea seems to be the characteristics or attributes that the author considers to be the ideal or marks of a 'Man'.

Look for the author's intent: The author's intent appears to be to convey his conception of what an ideal man should be like.

Eliminate incorrect options:

    B) "To outline the political issues of the late 19th century" can be eliminated because there's no mention or implication of political issues in the passage.

    C) "To detail the process of running a successful business" can be eliminated because there's no focus on business practices or operations in the passage.

    D) "To explain the workings of the natural world" can be eliminated because the passage is not about nature or natural phenomena, but about human characteristics.

Choose the best answer: The remaining option, "A) To describe the characteristics of an ideal man," is the one that best encapsulates the entire passage, which lays out a vision of what the author sees as the ideal man.

▶ **QUESTION 10:**

Read the Passage Carefully: The passage discusses the introduction of the World Wide Web by Tim Berners-Lee and how it transformed the use of the internet from a tool for researchers and the military to a global platform for the general public.

Identify the Central Idea: The main theme is the introduction of the World Wide Web and its impact on making the internet accessible and useful to the general public.

Look for the Author's Intent: The author aims to inform readers about the significance of the World Wide Web and its transformative effect on the internet's usage.

Eliminate Incorrect Options:

    A) The military use of the early internet is a minor detail and not the main focus.

    C) The passage does not delve into the technical details of hypertext.

    D) The passage does not focus on showcasing the achievements of British computer scientists in general but specifically mentions Tim Berners-Lee.

Choose the Best Answer: The remaining option, "B) To discuss the global impact of the World Wide Web," best aligns with the author's intent and the central idea of the text.

▶ **QUESTION 11:**

Read the passage carefully: The passage speaks about the ongoing fight against slavery and the need for collective action to end it.

Identify the central idea: The central idea is the call to action against the continuation of slavery in parts of the world.

Look for the author's intent: The author's intent seems to be motivating the reader to continue fighting against slavery.

Eliminate incorrect options:

    A) "To discuss the history of slavery and its abolition" can be eliminated as the passage does not focus on the history of slavery.

    B) "To analyze the socio-economic factors contributing to modern slavery" can be eliminated because the passage doesn't delve into socio-economic factors of slavery.

    D) "To criticize governments for their inaction against slavery") can be eliminated as the passage does not criticize governments but is a call to action for everyone.

Choose the best answer: The remaining option, "C) To rally a sympathetic audience to continue working against slavery," best aligns with the author's intent and the central idea of the text. The passage mainly aims to motivate the audience to continue their efforts against slavery, making this the best answer.

▶ **QUESTION 12:**

Read the Passage Carefully: The passage discusses the phenomenon of "latchkey kids" who return to empty homes due to their parents working. It touches upon the responsibilities these children often have and the concerns surrounding their situation.

Identify the Central Idea: The main theme is the rise of the "latchkey kid" phenomenon, its implications, and the concerns it raised.

Look for the Author's Intent: The author aims to inform readers about the challenges and responsibilities faced by latchkey kids and the societal concerns about their well-being.

Eliminate Incorrect Options:

    A) While the term "latchkey kid" is explained, the passage delves deeper into the implications of the phenomenon.

    B) The rise of dual-income households is mentioned as a cause but is not the main focus of the passage.

    C) The responsibilities of latchkey kids are mentioned but are not the sole focus of the passage.

Choose the Best Answer: The remaining option, "D) To address the pros and cons of children being left unsupervised," best aligns with the author's intent and the central idea of the text.

▶ **QUESTION 13:**

Read the Passage Carefully: The passage discusses The Great Leap Forward, its objectives, and the consequences it had on China, including the widespread famine and its eventual abandonment.

Identify the Central Idea: The main theme is the introduction, execution, and aftermath of The Great Leap Forward in China.

Look for the Author's Intent: The author aims to inform readers about the intentions behind The Great Leap Forward and the severe consequences that followed.

Eliminate Incorrect Options:

    A) The passage doesn't focus on agricultural practices in China before 1958.

    B) While Mao Zedong's role is mentioned, the passage doesn't delve into his leadership style in detail.

    D) The passage doesn't primarily analyze the political landscape of China post-1962.

Choose the Best Answer: The remaining option, "C) To outline the intentions and consequences of The Great Leap Forward," best aligns with the author's intent and the central idea of the text.

▶ **QUESTION 14:**

Read the passage carefully: The passage involves a fairy inviting a human child to come away with it, suggesting that the world is full of sorrow beyond the child's comprehension.

Identify the central idea: The central idea is the fairy's attempt to lure the child away from the human world.

Look for the author's intent: The author's intent seems to be portraying the fairy's persuasive attempts to attract the child into its world by highlighting the sorrow in the human world.

Eliminate incorrect options:

    A) "To argue that the child should reject all human relationships" can be eliminated because the fairy is not arguing against human relationships but suggesting a departure from the human world.

    B) "To detail the wonders of the natural world around the child" can be eliminated as the main focus is not on detailing the wonders of nature, but on persuading the child to escape the human world.

    C) "To express the fairy's contempt for the human world" can be eliminated as the fairy's focus is not to express contempt but to lure the child away.

Choose the best answer: The remaining option, "D) To persuade the child to escape the sorrows of the human world and join the fairy world," best aligns with the author's intent and the central idea of the text. The passage mainly aims to depict the fairy's persuasion, making this the best answer.

▶ **QUESTION 15:**

Read the Passage Carefully: The passage describes the role of "muckrakers" during the Progressive Era, their objectives, and the impact they had on society.

Identify the Central Idea: The main theme is the emergence of muckrakers, their investigative work, and the societal changes they influenced.

Look for the Author's Intent: The author aims to inform readers about the muckrakers' role in exposing societal issues and pushing for reforms.

Eliminate Incorrect Options:

    A) The passage doesn't provide a detailed history of all the social movements of the Progressive Era.

    B) The passage doesn't delve into the literary techniques and styles used by muckrakers.

    D) The economic implications of the reforms are not the primary focus of the passage.

Choose the Best Answer: The remaining option, "C) To highlight the impact and objectives of the muckrakers during the Progressive Era," best aligns with the author's intent and the central idea of the text.

QUESTION 16:

Read the Passage Carefully: The passage provides an overview of Vincent Van Gogh's artistic contributions, his struggles, and the posthumous recognition of his works.

Identify the Central Idea: The main theme is Van Gogh's artistic legacy, his unique style, and the lasting influence he has had on the art world.

Look for the Author's Intent: The author aims to highlight Van Gogh's significance in the realm of art and his enduring influence.

Eliminate Incorrect Options:

B) The passage doesn't delve into the post-impressionist movement in detail.

C) While the passage touches upon aspects of Van Gogh's life, it doesn't provide a comprehensive biography.

D) The economic value of art is mentioned but isn't the primary focus of the passage.

Choose the Best Answer: The remaining option, "A) To highlight Vincent Van Gogh's artistic legacy and influence," best aligns with the author's intent and the central idea of the text.

▶ **QUESTION 17:**

Read the passage carefully: Ishmael discusses his reasons for heading to the sea, particularly when he feels overwhelmed or despondent.

Identify the central idea: The passage depicts the sea as a refuge for Ishmael, especially when he's in a dark frame of mind.

Look for the author's intent: Melville is portraying the sea as a therapeutic escape for Ishmael from his internal struggles.

Eliminate incorrect options:

A) There is no mention of specific preparations for a sea journey.

C) While city dangers might be implied, the focus isn't on the city's threats but on Ishmael's internal struggles.

D) The antagonist of the novel isn't introduced or even referred to in this passage.

Choose the best answer: The most fitting answer is "B) To illustrate Ishmael's deep need for the sea as a way to combat his internal turmoil." Ishmael's connection to the sea as a way to handle his emotional distress is the primary theme of this excerpt.

▶ **QUESTION 18:**

Read the Passage Carefully: The passage describes the 1989 Tiananmen Square protests, their origins, and the Chinese government's response.

Identify the Central Idea: The main theme is the events and significance of the 1989 Tiananmen Square protests.

Look for the Author's Intent: The author aims to outline the events leading up to and during the Tiananmen Square protests and the subsequent government crackdown.

Eliminate Incorrect Options:

B) While Hu Yaobang's death is mentioned, the passage doesn't focus on his life and legacy.

C) The passage doesn't provide a comprehensive history of Beijing's landmarks.

D) The current political climate in China isn't the main focus of the passage.

Choose the Best Answer: The remaining option, "A) To outline the events and significance of the 1989 Tiananmen Square protests," best aligns with the author's intent and the central idea of the text.

5. Overall Structure Answer

▶ **QUESTION 1:**

Read the Text Carefully: The text begins by describing a falcon losing its connection to its falconer, which is then used as a metaphor to describe the chaos and disorder in the world.
Identify Key Themes and Ideas: The main theme in this text is the state of chaos and disorder. The author uses the imagery of a falcon losing its connection with the falconer to symbolize the loss of control and order in the world.
Understand the Progression of Ideas: The text starts with a metaphor of a falcon and falconer, and progressively expands this metaphor to discuss the state of the world - highlighting anarchy, a blood-dimmed tide, the loss of innocence, and the lack of conviction in the good.
Analyze the Options:

    A) The speaker does not describe a festive ceremony or the mood of the attendees. This option does not align with the text's content.
    B) The text doesn't discuss a lost relationship or predict emotional aftermath of a separation. This option is not representative of the text's content.
    C) Although the speaker describes chaotic events, they are metaphorical rather than natural disasters, and human behavior's role is not explicitly considered.
    D) This option accurately describes the text. The speaker begins by observing the behavior of a falcon and uses this observation to comment on the state of the world.

Therefore, the best choice is D) "The speaker observes the behavior of a falcon, then extrapolates this to comment on the state of the world." This option accurately describes the overall structure of the text. The initial observation of the falcon is used as a metaphor to comment on larger societal and global issues.

▶ **QUESTION 2:**

Read the Text Carefully: The text describes Gulliver's realization that he is in an unfamiliar wilderness, surrounded by tall trees and unknown terrain. He moves cautiously, fearing potential threats, and tries to make sense of a large object in the distance.
Identify Key Themes and Ideas: The main themes are Gulliver's sense of disorientation in an unfamiliar land and his cautious exploration of the environment.
Understand the Progression of Ideas: The text starts with Gulliver's realization of being in a vast wilderness, describes his cautious movements, and ends with his attempt to understand a large object in the distance.
Analyze the Options:

    A) This option accurately captures the essence of the text. It describes Gulliver's initial confusion and then focuses on his cautious exploration.
    B) While Gulliver does mention the stars, the text does not primarily focus on his fascination with the night sky.
    C) The text does emphasize Gulliver's isolation, but it doesn't contrast it with the vastness of the unknown world; instead, it focuses on his cautious exploration.
    D) The text does set the scene of a dense forest, but the primary focus is on Gulliver's attempts to understand his surroundings, not just the forest.

Therefore, the best choice is A) "It describes Gulliver's initial confusion in a new land, and then focuses on his cautious exploration of the unfamiliar terrain." This option accurately describes the overall structure of the text.

▶ **QUESTION 3:**

Read the Text Carefully: The text discusses how Shakespeare's writing style evolved over time, from his early plays to his later works, and gives examples to illustrate this.
Identify Key Themes and Ideas: The main theme of the text is the evolution of Shakespeare's writing style throughout his career.
Understand the Progression of Ideas: The text starts with a general statement about the evolution of Shakespeare's writing style and then provides specific examples from his early, middle, and later periods to support this idea.
Analyze the Options:

    A) While the text does provide a chronological analysis of Shakespeare's plays, it does not discuss the impact of his work on contemporary playwrights.
    B) The text does not debate the literary value of Shakespeare's work nor does it examine the varying public reception of his plays.
    C) This option aligns with the text. It traces the evolution of Shakespeare's writing style throughout his career, highlighting examples from different periods.
    D) While the text does outline the characteristics of Shakespeare's early plays and compare them to his later works, it also discusses his middle period, which this option doesn't mention.

Therefore, the best choice is C) "It traces the evolution of Shakespeare's writing style throughout his career, highlighting examples from different periods." This option accurately captures the overall structure of the text, which traces the evolution of Shakespeare's writing style from his early plays to his later works, providing examples along the way.

▶ **QUESTION 4:**

Read the Text Carefully: The poem describes the speaker's experience of stumbling upon a field of daffodils while wandering alone. This unexpected sight of blooming flowers brings him joy and lifts his spirits.

Identify Key Themes and Ideas: The key themes in this poem are solitude, nature, and joy. The speaker initially describes himself as "lonely as a cloud," but his solitude is transformed into a joyful experience through his encounter with the daffodils.

Understand the Progression of Ideas: The poem begins with the speaker's state of solitude as he wanders alone. This solitude is interrupted by the sight of a vibrant field of daffodils, which brings a shift in his mood from loneliness to joy.

Analyze the Options:

    A) This option aligns well with the poem. The speaker recalls wandering alone and then vividly describes his encounter with a field of daffodils, causing a shift in his mood.

    B) The poem does not shift to a criticism of society's disconnection from nature. The focus remains on the speaker's personal experience and emotions.

    C) The speaker does not generalize about the natural world. Instead, he offers a specific and detailed account of his experience with the daffodils.

    D) The poem does not narrate a journey through diverse landscapes nor focuses on the significance of a particular location. It focuses on the speaker's experience and emotional response to the sight of the daffodils.

Therefore, the best choice is A) "The speaker recalls wandering alone, then vividly describes an encounter with a field of daffodils." This option accurately describes the overall structure of the poem.

▶ **QUESTION 5:**

Read the Text Carefully: The text describes Mrs. Manstey's apartment, the view she has, and her particular admiration for a golden cross on a church dome.

Identify Key Themes and Ideas: The main themes are Mrs. Manstey's living situation and her admiration for the golden cross.

Understand the Progression of Ideas: The text starts with a description of Mrs. Manstey's living situation and moves on to her admiration for the golden cross.

Analyze the Options:

    A) This option accurately captures the essence of the text. It describes Mrs. Manstey's living situation and then focuses on her admiration for the golden cross.

    B) The text does not primarily focus on the city's transformation across different times of the day.

    C) The text does not emphasize Mrs. Manstey's solitude.

    D) While the text does set the scene of an old New York house, it doesn't delve into the details of its surroundings.

Therefore, the best choice is A) "It describes Mrs. Manstey's living situation, and then focuses on her admiration for a golden cross on a church dome." This option accurately describes the overall structure of the text.

▶ **QUESTION 6:**

Read the Text Carefully: The poem speaks about the speaker asserting her resilience and strength, despite being belittled and oppressed. The speaker is confident, sassy, and not defeated by any form of degradation or negativity.

dentify Key Themes and Ideas: The key themes in this poem are resilience, strength, and self-confidence. The speaker, despite being written down in history with bitter, twisted lies, and being treaded in the dirt, maintains her strength and rises like dust.

Understand the Progression of Ideas: The poem begins with the speaker being put down or oppressed, but quickly shifts to her strong, defiant reaction. Throughout the text, the speaker continues to rise above her challenges with unwavering resilience and confidence.

Analyze the Options:

    A) The speaker does not recount a specific personal experience of betrayal and her subsequent recovery. The poem is more about overcoming general oppression and negativities.

    B) This option aligns well with the poem. The speaker reflects on the negative experiences and then expresses her unwavering resilience.

    C) The speaker does not condemn societal norms nor propose an alternative way of life. The main focus is on her personal resilience.

    D) The speaker does not articulate a universal truth nor illustrate it with personal anecdotes. The text is more about her personal experience of resilience and strength.

Therefore, the best choice is B) "The speaker reflects on historical injustices, then expresses her unwavering resilience." This option accurately captures the overall structure of the poem.

► **QUESTION 7:**

Read the Text Carefully: The text discusses how J.K. Rowling has used names in her Harry Potter series, noting that the names often reflect the characters' personalities or roles. Specific examples are provided to support this observation.

Identify Key Themes and Ideas: The main theme of the text is the purposeful use of names in the Harry Potter series, with an emphasis on how names can hint at character traits or roles in the story.

Understand the Progression of Ideas: The text starts with a general statement about Rowling's use of names, then offers specific examples from the series to illustrate this point.

Analyze the Options:

    A) This option aligns with the text. The text introduces a general observation about Rowling's naming strategy and then provides specific examples to illustrate this point.

    B) The text does not provide a chronological overview of how names were chosen throughout the series, nor does it speculate about future naming patterns.

    C) The text does not discuss the importance of names in literature in general, nor does it criticize Rowling's approach to character naming.

    D) The text does not primarily describe the characteristics of various Harry Potter characters with their names revealed as an afterthought. Instead, it discusses how the names chosen by Rowling reflect the characters' traits or roles.

Therefore, the best choice is A) "It first introduces a general observation about Rowling's naming strategy, then provides specific examples that illustrate this point." This option accurately captures the structure and progression of ideas in the text.

► **QUESTION 8:**

Read the Text Carefully: The poem discusses the condition of the speaker and their companions, describing them as 'hollow' and 'stuffed'. It includes various analogies to emphasize this state of emptiness and meaninglessness.

Identify Key Themes and Ideas: The key themes of the poem are emptiness and despair. Eliot paints a bleak picture of the "hollow men", emphasizing their voicelessness and lifelessness.

Understand the Progression of Ideas: The poem starts by declaring the state of the speakers as hollow and stuffed, and then progresses to further illustrate their condition through analogies, such as wind in dry grass or rats' feet over broken glass.

Analyze the Options:

    A) The speaker does describe a group living in despair, but there is no mention or imagination of potential redemption in the provided text.

    B) While the speaker does present their condition, there is no clear shift to describe personal alienation.

    C) The speaker indeed introduces the persona of "hollow men", but there is no contrasting with images of vitality and richness.

    D) This option accurately describes the progression in the poem. The speaker declares their empty state and uses unsettling analogies to emphasize this condition.

Therefore, the best choice is D) "The speaker first declares their empty state, then draws unsettling analogies to emphasize their condition." This choice accurately describes the overall structure of the poem, capturing the declaration of emptiness and the subsequent elaboration through unsettling comparisons.

► **QUESTION 9:**

Read the Text Carefully: The text describes Margaret Hale's activity in the drawing-room, the sounds she hears, and the eventual realization that her mother is in the room.

Identify Key Themes and Ideas: The main themes are Margaret's activity, the sounds in the house, and the realization of her mother's presence.

Understand the Progression of Ideas: The text starts with a description of Margaret's activity, moves on to the sounds she hears, and ends with the realization that her mother is present.

Analyze the Options:

    A) This option accurately captures the essence of the text. It describes Margaret's activity and setting, followed by the introduction of an unexpected visitor.

    B) The text does not focus on Margaret's longing for the countryside.

    C) The text does focus on the sounds and movements in the house, but the emphasis on revealing the identity of the person is minimal.

    D) The text does not set the scene of a quiet afternoon.

Therefore, the best choice is A) "It describes Margaret's activity and setting, and then introduces an unexpected visitor." This option accurately describes the overall structure of the text.

► **QUESTION 10:**

Read the Text Carefully:The poem illustrates the changing conditions in the sea with the rising sun, and the consequent experiences of the mariner, emphasizing the lack of life and activity around him.

Identify Key Themes and Ideas: The key themes in this poem are isolation and the juxtaposition of the natural environment and human conditions. The poet starts by painting a picture of the sea at sunrise, and then transitions to the desolation and loneliness of the mariner's experience.

Understand the Progression of Ideas: The poem begins with a description of a sunrise over the sea, and then moves to the experiences of the mariner in this setting, noting the absence of birds and the quietness of his surroundings.

Analyze the Options:

A) The speaker does not express a personal fascination with the sea nor reflect on its potential dangers.

B) The speaker does not present a day in the life of a mariner, nor does he highlight the contrast between the mariner's expectations and reality.

C) The speaker does start with a vivid description of natural phenomena (sunrise, sea, wind) and then transitions to the human condition (the mariner's isolation) in this setting.

D) This option accurately captures the progression of the poem. It starts with a serene ocean sunrise and then shifts to a description of its unsettling aftermath.

Therefore, the best choice is D) "The speaker depicts a serene ocean sunrise, then shifts to a description of its unsettling aftermath." This option accurately describes the overall structure of the poem. It captures the shift from the tranquil and picturesque sunrise to the isolation and desolation experienced by the mariner.

► **QUESTION 11:**

Read the Text Carefully: The text discusses the way Dickens selected names for his characters that often echoed their personalities or roles in his novels. The text gives specific examples from "A Tale of Two Cities," "A Christmas Carol," and "Great Expectations."

Identify Key Themes and Ideas: The main theme of the text is the correlation between names and character traits or roles in Dickens's novels.

Understand the Progression of Ideas: The text begins with a general observation about Dickens's naming strategy, then moves on to provide specific examples from different novels to back up this observation.

Analyze the Options:

A) The text does not discuss the significance of Dickens's personal history, nor does it apply these insights to his choice of character names.

B) The text does not present a theory about the symbolic meaning of names in literature, nor does it criticize Dickens's deviations from this theory.

C) The text does not start by focusing on one specific character's name and then broaden the discussion to include the whole array of Dickens's characters. Instead, it discusses various characters from different novels.

D) This option aligns with the text. The text describes the traits and roles of various characters in Dickens's novels and then reveals how their names reflect these aspects.

Therefore, the best choice is D) "It describes the traits and roles of various characters in Dickens's novels, then reveals how their names reflect these aspects." This option accurately describes the overall structure of the text. It captures the idea of describing character traits and roles and then discussing how their names align with these aspects.

► **QUESTION 12:**

Read the Text Carefully: The poem is a reflection on the concept of success, suggesting it's most appreciated by those who haven't succeeded. It uses the metaphor of a victorious army to illustrate the point, implying that the soldier who dies in defeat understands the value of victory better than those who have won.

Identify Key Themes and Ideas: The main themes in this poem are success and the differing perceptions of it, based on one's experiences.

Understand the Progression of Ideas: The poem starts with a general assertion about success, then moves on to illustrate this point with a vivid image of a soldier experiencing defeat in battle.

Analyze the Options:

A) This option partially describes the poem. The speaker does discuss the idea of success, and there is a transition to the image of an army, but this image is used to further explore the idea of success rather than being a separate point.

B) This option aligns well with the poem. It correctly identifies the initial definition of success and the subsequent contrast between the perceptions of those who succeed and those who don't.

C) The speaker doesn't start with a broad reflection on life nor narrows the focus to personal experiences. The poem revolves around a specific idea: success.

D) The speaker does explore the concept of victory, but not in various fields. The focus is solely on the idea of success and the perception of it based on experiences.

Therefore, the best choice is B) "The speaker defines success, then contrasts the perception of it between those who succeed and those who don't." This option accurately describes the overall structure of the poem.

► **QUESTION 13:**

Read the Text Carefully:The text discusses how the portrayal of superheroes in comic books has changed over different periods, aligning with societal changes, and gives examples to illustrate this.

Identify Key Themes and Ideas:The main theme of the text is the transformation of the depiction of superheroes in comic books, reflecting societal changes.

Understand the Progression of Ideas:The text begins with a general statement about the changing depiction of superheroes, and then provides specific examples from different periods (Golden Age, Silver Age, and Modern Age) to support this idea.

Analyze the Options:

A) While the text provides an overview of the superhero genre, it does not zoom in on a particular comic book for a detailed analysis.

B) The text does discuss the changes in the portrayal of superheroes, but it does not argue for a reevaluation of their role in society.

C) This option aligns with the text. It chronologically traces the transformation of superhero portrayal in comic books, providing examples from different periods.

D) The text does introduce the concept of superheroes and their changing portrayal, but it does not compare their depiction in comic books and movies.

Therefore, the best choice is C) "It chronologically traces the transformation of superhero portrayal in comic books, providing examples from different periods." This option accurately captures the overall structure of the text, which traces the transformation of the depiction of superheroes in comic books over time, providing examples along the way.

► **QUESTION 14:**

Read the Text Carefully: The text describes Elizabeth Bennet's journey to Pemberley, her reactions to the estate's beauty, and Mr. Darcy's occasional glances and smiles towards her.

Identify Key Themes and Ideas: The main themes are Elizabeth's anticipation and admiration of Pemberley, and the subtle interactions between her and Mr. Darcy.

Understand the Progression of Ideas: The text starts with Elizabeth's anticipation, moves on to describe the beauty of Pemberley, and ends with Mr. Darcy's subtle interactions with her.

Analyze the Options:

A) This option accurately captures the essence of the text. Elizabeth's anticipation is evident, followed by her admiration of Pemberley.

B) The text does not emphasize Mr. Darcy's pride or Elizabeth's reaction to it.

C) While the journey to Pemberley is described, the focus on interactions between Elizabeth and Mr. Darcy is minimal.

D) The text does not reveal Elizabeth's reservations about visiting Pemberley.

Therefore, the best choice is A) "It portrays Elizabeth's anticipation, followed by her admiration of Pemberley's beauty." This option accurately describes the overall structure of the text.

► **QUESTION 15:**

Read the Text Carefully: The text describes a stormy night, with Victor Frankenstein noticing the creature he created during a flash of lightning.

Identify Key Themes and Ideas: The main themes are the stormy setting and the sudden appearance of the creature.

Understand the Progression of Ideas: The text starts with a description of the stormy night and culminates in the sudden appearance of the creature during a flash of lightning.

Analyze the Options:

A) This option accurately captures the essence of the text. The stormy night is described, followed by the sudden appearance of the creature.

B) The text does not focus on Victor's fear, and the creature's actions during the storm aren't detailed.

C) While the natural elements are portrayed, the text doesn't emphasize the unnatural creation of Victor.

D) The creature's intentions are not revealed in the text.

Therefore, the best choice is A) "It describes a stormy night, and then reveals the sudden appearance of the creature." This option accurately describes the overall structure of the text.

Read the Text Carefully: The speaker in the poem is recounting an eerie event that occurred while he was alone at midnight. A tapping sound at his chamber door and the rustling of his purple curtains spark feelings of terror within him.

Identify Key Themes and Ideas: The poem features themes of mystery, fear, and suspense. The speaker describes a mysterious tapping sound, and his escalating fear is evoked by the mysterious visitor and the uncertain rustling of curtains.

Understand the Progression of Ideas: The poem starts by establishing a haunting atmosphere, with the speaker alone at midnight. The tension then escalates with the sudden tapping at the chamber door and the speaker's growing fear.

Analyze the Options:

A) The speaker does reflect on a mysterious event, but his emotional reaction is not a transition; it's part of the same event.

B) This option accurately describes the structure of the poem, starting with a haunting atmosphere and introducing a mysterious event that heightens tension.

C) The reminiscence the speaker begins with is not lighthearted but rather eerie and suspenseful.

D) The speaker does present a chilling tale, but does not question the reliability of his narrative in the given text.

Therefore, the best choice is B) "The speaker sets up a haunting atmosphere, then introduces a mysterious occurrence that increases tension." This choice accurately captures the establishment of a haunting atmosphere and the introduction of a mysterious event that amplifies the suspense.

▶ **QUESTION 17:**

Read the Text Carefully: The text describes the setting of a town during sunset, the sound of children playing, and a group of adults waiting outside Mother Danbury's house.

Identify Key Themes and Ideas: The main themes are the serene setting of the town and the revered role of Mother Danbury.

Understand the Progression of Ideas: The text starts with a description of the town during sunset and moves on to introduce the gathering outside Mother Danbury's house.

Analyze the Options:

A) This option accurately captures the essence of the text. It describes the setting sun and children playing, followed by the gathering at Mother Danbury's house.

B) While there is a contrast between the children's laughter and the adults' solemnity, the focus isn't solely on this contrast.

C) This option also aligns well with the text. It sets the scene of a village evening and then focuses on Mother Danbury's role.

D) The text does not delve into the daily activities of the village.

Therefore, the best choice is C) "It sets the scene of a village evening, and then focuses on the revered role of Mother Danbury." This option accurately describes the overall structure of the text.

▶ **QUESTION 18:**

Read the Text Carefully: The poem speaks about the speaker observing the bending of birch trees. The speaker discusses two possible causes of their bending - a boy swinging on them, and the weight of ice after a storm.

Identify Key Themes and Ideas: The key themes in this poem are nature, imagination, and reality. The speaker first offers a fanciful explanation for the birch trees' bending (a boy swinging on them), before acknowledging the actual, natural cause (ice storms).

Understand the Progression of Ideas: The poem begins with an observation of the birch trees and a whimsical interpretation. Then it shifts to a more realistic explanation of how the trees come to be bent - the weight of ice after a winter storm.

Analyze the Options:

A) This option aligns well with the poem. The speaker begins by describing the birch trees and then presents two possible explanations for their bending.

B) The speaker does not reminisce about a past experience. His current observations and explanations are based on what he sees and knows about nature.

C) The speaker does not question the validity of his initial, fanciful interpretation. Instead, he simply presents a more realistic cause for the bending of the trees.

D) The speaker does not make an environmental appeal. He describes the natural event of an ice storm but does not use this to argue for any environmental cause or issue.

Therefore, the best choice is A) "The speaker begins by describing birch trees, then elaborates on two possible reasons for their bending." This option accurately captures the overall structure of the poem.

Read the Text Carefully: The text describes the reaction of schoolboys to a public event, the minister's triumphant yet weak condition, and the reactions of Hester and Roger Chillingworth.

Identify Key Themes and Ideas: The main themes are the public event, the minister's condition, and the reactions of those around him.

Understand the Progression of Ideas: The text starts with the schoolboys' reaction and moves on to describe the minister's condition and the reactions of Hester and Roger Chillingworth.

Analyze the Options:

A) This option accurately captures the essence of the text. It describes the reaction of schoolboys and then shifts focus to the minister and those around him.

B) The text does not primarily focus on the public punishment of Hester Prynne.

C) While the text does focus on the minister's triumph and subsequent weakness, it also emphasizes the reactions of those around him.

D) The text does not primarily set the scene of a public gathering.

Therefore, the best choice is A) "It describes the reaction of schoolboys to a public event, and then shifts focus to the minister's condition and those around him." This option accurately describes the overall structure of the text.

► QUESTION 20:

Read the Text Carefully: The text presents hope as a bird that resides in the soul and never stops singing. This bird is resilient, enduring storms and hardship without asking anything in return.

Identify Key Themes and Ideas: The key theme in this poem is hope. The author uses the metaphor of a bird to depict hope as a constant, resilient, and selfless presence within us.

Understand the Progression of Ideas: The text begins with the metaphor of hope as a bird, then goes on to expand this metaphor by describing the characteristics of this "bird" in various challenging circumstances.

Analyze the Options:

A) While the metaphor of a bird singing is used, it is not compared to the singing of people around the world. Instead, it is used to symbolize hope.

B) The speaker does not describe a personal journey or recall specific sights and sounds.

C) This option accurately describes the poem. The speaker presents a metaphor for hope and then expands on its characteristics and resilience.

D) The speaker does not introduce a creature with the intent to capture it. The "creature" (bird) is a metaphor for hope, not an entity to be pursued.

Therefore, the best choice is C) "The speaker presents a metaphor for hope, then expands upon its characteristics and resilience in various circumstances." This option accurately describes the overall structure of the poem, which uses the metaphor of a bird to symbolize the concept of hope and its resilience.

6. The Function of a Sentence Answers

▶ **QUESTION 1:**

Read and Understand the Entire Passage: The passage discusses the roles of African American women during the Civil Rights Movement, particularly focusing on their influence as customers of local businesses. The context indicates that these women demanded equal service rights, leading to businesses changing their practices to avoid backlash.

Identify the Sentence's Role: The sentence in quotation marks is: "the customers demanded improved equal service rights, and business owners, eager to avoid public backlash and maintain their operations, complied." This sentence provides an example of the agency of African American women during the Civil Rights Movement.

Understand the Answer Choices:

A) It expands on a statement about customer-business interactions in a specific sector discussed earlier in the text.

B) It serves as an illustration of a societal shift during the Civil Rights Movement era mentioned earlier in the text.

C) It points out a potential deviation from the broader narrative of the Civil Rights Movement outlined earlier in the text.

D) It provides additional information about the identity of the customers referenced earlier in the text.

Eliminate Incorrect Answers:

A) The sentence does provide more details on the interaction between businesses and customers, but it does so in the context of the societal shift during the Civil Rights Movement, not a specific sector.

C) The sentence doesn't deviate from the broader narrative but aligns with it, showing how African American women asserted their influence.

D) While it indirectly talks about the identity of the customers, the primary focus is on their actions and the response from business owners.

Choose the Best Answer: B) This choice captures the essence of the sentence in quotation marks. It serves as an illustration of the societal shift during the Civil Rights Movement, wherein African American women exerted their influence. Thus, the correct answer is B) It serves as an illustration of a societal shift during the Civil Rights Movement era mentioned earlier in the text.

▶ **QUESTION 2:**

Read and Understand the Entire Passage: The passage discusses the potential impact of using biodegradable materials for art sculptures on the preservation of art history. It highlights the importance of sculptures as historical sources and the risk of losing them if they degrade over time.

Identify the Sentence's Role: The sentence in quotation marks is: "The increasing popularity of biodegradable materials for creating art sculptures will lead to the decline of art history preservation." This sentence presents the main argument or claim of the passage.

Understand the Answer Choices:

A) It provides a summary of the potential impact of a current trend in art.

B) It illustrates the materials used by artists in creating sculptures.

C) It offers a critique of modern art preservation techniques.

D) It argues for the preservation of historical artworks in controlled environments.

Eliminate Incorrect Answers:

B) The sentence doesn't specifically illustrate the materials.

C) The sentence doesn't critique modern art preservation techniques.

D) The sentence doesn't argue for preservation but states the potential impact of a trend.

Choose the Best Answer: A) This is the correct answer. The sentence summarizes the potential impact of a current trend in art. So, the correct answer is A) It provides a summary of the potential impact of a current trend in art.

▶ **QUESTION 3:**

Read and Understand the Entire Passage: The passage talks about the chestnut blight fungus that originated in Asia and was accidentally brought to North America. The fungus later appeared in European chestnut forests.

Identify the Sentence's Role: The sentence in question is: "But evolutionary connections between pathogens and their hosts can persist over time and geographical distance." This sentence explains the reason why the fungus was able to infect chestnut trees in different geographical locations.

Understand the Answer Choices:

A) It states the hypothesis that researchers had planned to test using chestnut trees and the blight fungus.

B) It presents a broad concept that is exemplified by the specific case of the chestnut trees and the blight fungus.

C) It proposes an alternate interpretation for the results of the researchers' observations.

D) It gives background information that explains why the species spread to new locations.

Eliminate Incorrect Answers:

    A) There's no mention in the text of researchers planning to test a hypothesis using chestnut trees and the blight fungus.

    C) The sentence doesn't propose an alternate interpretation; instead, it explains the reason why the fungus spread.

    D) The sentence doesn't directly give information on why the species spread to new locations; it talks more about the resilience of the pathogen-host relationship.

Choose the Best Answer: B) The sentence presents a broad concept (the enduring connections between pathogens and hosts) that is exemplified by the specific case of the chestnut trees and the blight fungus. So, the correct answer is B) It presents a broad concept that is exemplified by the specific case of the chestnut trees and the blight fungus.

▶ **QUESTION 4:**

Read and Understand the Entire Passage: The passage from "Moby Dick" depicts the narrator's feelings of desolation and his inclination to act out when those feelings become overwhelming. He then explains that his solution to these feelings is to head out to sea.

Identify the Sentence's Role: The sentence in question is: "This is my substitute for pistol and ball." This sentence highlights the narrator's method of coping – instead of resorting to violence ("pistol and ball"), he chooses to take to the sea.

Understand the Answer Choices:

    A) It introduces a new character to the story.

    B) It offers a detailed description of the protagonist's surroundings.

    C) It hints at the upcoming events of the story.

    D) It indicates the protagonist's coping mechanism.

Eliminate Incorrect Answers:

    A) It doesn't introduce a new character.

    B) The sentence does not describe the surroundings.

    C) It doesn't hint at specific events; rather, it's about the narrator's coping mechanism.

Choose the Best Answer: D) This is the correct answer. The sentence explains that the sea is the narrator's way of dealing with his overwhelming feelings – it's his coping mechanism. So, the correct answer is A) It indicates the protagonist's coping mechanism.

▶ **QUESTION 5:**

Read and Understand the Entire Passage: The passage from "Adventures of Huckleberry Finn" describes a morning canoe trip on the river, with the beauty of nature all around. Within this setting, Huck expresses a moment of longing for his home as they pass by it.

Identify the Sentence's Role: The sentence in question is: "When we went by our house, I wished I was there, but I weren't." This sentence reveals Huck's emotional connection and longing for his home.

Understand the Answer Choices:

    A) It highlights the protagonist's sense of adventure.

    B) It reveals the protagonist's longing and emotional connection to his home.

    C) It provides a vivid description of the river's scenery.

    D) It emphasizes the physical exertion of the canoe trip.

Eliminate Incorrect Answers:

    A) The sentence doesn't emphasize a sense of adventure.

    C) The sentence does not describe the scenery.

    D) The sentence does not focus on the physical exertion.

Choose the Best Answer: B) This is the correct answer. The sentence captures Huck's emotional connection to his home and his longing to be there. So, the correct answer is B) It reveals the protagonist's longing and emotional connection to his home.

▶ **QUESTION 6:**

Read and Understand the Entire Passage: The passage describes a journey through a forest, revealing the narrator's intent to visit the place where William had been killed. The surrounding environment and its relation to the protagonist are highlighted.

Identify the Sentence's Role: The sentence in question is: "No birds sang in these woods, for the presence of man, my unnatural self, had scared them away." This sentence speaks to the unnaturalness and isolation of the protagonist, suggesting that his very presence has altered the natural order of the forest.

Understand the Answer Choices:

    A) It emphasizes the peace and tranquility of the forest.

    B) It showcases the protagonist's ability to appreciate nature.

    C) It symbolizes the protagonist's isolation and the consequences of his actions.

    D) It highlights the protagonist's deep connection with William.

Eliminate Incorrect Answers
   A) The sentence indicates a lack of peace due to the protagonist's presence.
   B) The protagonist's appreciation for nature is not the focal point.
   D) It does not specifically connect to William.

Choose the Best Answer: C) The sentence reflects on the protagonist's effect on the environment, underlining his isolation and the implications of his unnatural actions. Therefore, the correct answer is C) It symbolizes the protagonist's isolation and the consequences of his actions.

▶ **QUESTION 7:**
Read and Understand the Entire Passage:The passage describes the red-room, focusing on its color and furnishings.
Identify the Sentence's Role:The sentence in question is: "The bed, too, had crimson curtains." This sentence continues the description of the room's dominant color theme.
Understand the Answer Choices:
   A) It contrasts with the overall mood and setting of the narrative.
   B) It introduces a shift in the narrative's focus.
   C) It emphasizes the luxuriousness of the room's furnishings.
   D) It underscores the dominant color theme of the room.
Eliminate Incorrect Answers:
   A) The sentence doesn't offer a contrast but adds to the established theme.
   B) There is no shift in narrative focus.
   C) The luxuriousness of the room's furnishings isn't the main emphasis.

Choose the Best Answer: D) This is the correct answer. The sentence adds another detail that emphasizes the red or crimson theme of the room. Therefore, the correct answer is D) It underscores the dominant color theme of the room.

▶ **QUESTION 8:**
Read and Understand the Entire Passage:The passage offers insight into Mrs. Bennet's character, particularly her self-perception and her tendency to misjudge others.
Identify the Sentence's Role:The sentence in question is: "Yet, for all her confidence, she frequently misjudged those around her." This sentence illustrates the contrast between Mrs. Bennet's self-perception and her actual ability to judge character.
Understand the Answer Choices:
   A) It provides background information on Mrs. Bennet's past decisions.
   B) It emphasizes the irony of Mrs. Bennet's self-perception versus reality.
   C) It portrays Elizabeth as the primary source of the narrative's humor.
   D) It introduces a new character to the narrative.
Eliminate Incorrect Answers:
   A) The sentence doesn't provide specifics about past decisions.
   C) Elizabeth's role as a source of humor isn't the main point of the sentence.
   D) No new character is introduced.

Choose the Best Answer: B) This is the correct answer. The sentence emphasizes the disconnect between Mrs. Bennet's confidence in her judgment and her frequent errors. So, the correct answer is B) It emphasizes the irony of Mrs. Bennet's self-perception versus reality.

▶ **QUESTION 9:**
Read and Understand the Entire Passage: The passage introduces the reader to Ishmael and reveals his propensity to take to the sea when feeling despondent.
Identify the Sentence's Role: The sentence in question is: "It is a way I have of driving off the spleen and regulating the circulation." This sentence offers insight into Ishmael's personal remedy for melancholy.
Understand the Answer Choices:
   A) It provides a detailed account of the protagonist's financial situation.
   B) It offers a humorous reflection on the protagonist's whims and decisions.
   C) It elucidates the personal remedy the protagonist employs when feeling melancholic.
   D) It serves as a transition between the protagonist's introduction and his maritime tales.
Eliminate Incorrect Answers:
   A) The sentence doesn't focus on his finances.
   B) While there might be a touch of humor, the primary function is not comedic.
   D) The sentence doesn't transition to maritime tales but rather explains his reasons for going to sea.

Choose the Best Answer: C) This is the correct answer. The sentence provides insight into Ishmael's method of coping with feelings of melancholy. Therefore, the correct answer is C) It elucidates the personal remedy the protagonist employs when feeling melancholic.

▶ **QUESTION 10:**

Read and Understand the Entire Passage: The passage discusses the discovery of pottery fragments in a region of South America and the implications of this discovery regarding the agricultural practices of the tribes that lived there.

Identify the Sentence's Role: The sentence in quotation marks is: "Unless they have advanced agricultural techniques, tribes are unlikely to settle in a region where there are no naturally fertile lands available to them." This sentence provides a general principle that supports the conclusion drawn in the text.

Understand the Answer Choices:

    A) It provides historical context about the agricultural practices of ancient tribes.

    B) It offers a general principle that supports the conclusion drawn in the text.

    C) It describes the physical characteristics of the pottery fragments found in the region.

    D) It highlights the challenges faced by the tribes in adapting to the region's conditions.

Eliminate Incorrect Answers:

    A) The sentence doesn't provide historical context.

    C) The sentence doesn't describe the pottery fragments.

    D) The sentence doesn't highlight challenges but provides a general principle.

Choose the Best Answer: B) This is the correct answer. The sentence offers a general principle that supports the conclusion drawn in the text. So, the correct answer is B) It offers a general principle that supports the conclusion drawn in the text.

▶ **QUESTION 11:**

Read and Understand the Entire Passage: The passage describes Alice's desire to explore a beautiful garden but faces the physical limitation of not fitting through the small door.

Identify the Sentence's Role: The sentence in question is: "And even if my head would go through," thought poor Alice, "it would be of very little use without my shoulders."

Understand the Answer Choices:

    A) It portrays Alice's determination to overcome the obstacles she encounters.

    B) It underscores Alice's realization of the impracticality of her situation.

    C) It emphasizes the physical challenges posed by the environment.

    D) It serves as a transition between her desire and her subsequent actions.

Eliminate Incorrect Answers:

    A) While determination is a theme in the story, this sentence does not highlight it.

    C) It's about Alice's realization more than the environment's physical challenges.

    D) The transition is there, but the main focus is on Alice's realization.

Choose the Best Answer: B) This is the correct answer. The sentence emphasizes Alice's realization of the impracticality of her situation. So, the correct answer is B) It underscores Alice's realization of the impracticality of her situation.

▶ **QUESTION 12:**

Read and Understand the Entire Passage: The passage discusses the vibrant colors of parrots and how these colors make them noticeable to predators. It then presents a behavior exhibited by parrots to counteract this vulnerability.

Identify the Sentence's Role: The sentence in quotation marks is: "When parrots fly in a flock, as they often do when sensing threats, their combined colors create a dazzling display, making it challenging for a predator to focus on a single bird." This sentence provides an explanation for how parrots counteract their vulnerability to predators.

Understand the Answer Choices:

    A) It provides an extended description of the habitat where parrots live.

    B) It offers an example of a defensive behavior exhibited by parrots.

    C) It explains the main reason why eagles target parrots.

    D) It highlights the individual beauty of each parrot within the flock.

Eliminate Incorrect Answers:

    A) The sentence doesn't describe the habitat.

    C) The sentence doesn't explain why eagles target parrots.

    D) The sentence doesn't highlight individual beauty but a collective behavior.

Choose the Best Answer: B) This is the correct answer. The sentence offers an example of a defensive behavior exhibited by parrots. So, the correct answer is B) It offers an example of a defensive behavior exhibited by parrots.

► **QUESTION 13:**

Read and Understand the Entire Passage: The passage centers on the return of Miss Cynthy and the impact it has on Mother Danbury and the community.

Identify the Sentence's Role: The sentence in question is: "It ain't so much dat she's been away," said Mother Danbury, "but it's de trouble dat she done gone th'ough."

Understand the Answer Choices:

    A) It highlights the community's lack of knowledge about Miss Cynthy's experiences.

    B) It illustrates Mother Danbury's concern about the time duration of Miss Cynthy's absence.

    C) It emphasizes the significance of Miss Cynthy's experiences while she was away.

    D) It portrays Mother Danbury as being out of touch with the town's gossip.

Eliminate Incorrect Answers:

    A) The community seems to know about the trouble, so this is not correct.

    B) The emphasis is on the trouble, not the time.

    D) There's no indication Mother Danbury is out of touch.

Choose the Best Answer: C) This is the correct answer. Mother Danbury's statement emphasizes that the reason for the community's interest in Miss Cynthy's return is not her absence but the troubles she experienced. The correct answer is C) It emphasizes the significance of Miss Cynthy's experiences while she was away.

► **QUESTION 14:**

Read and Understand the Entire Passage: The passage describes the simplicity and routine nature of life in Three Forks, yet emphasizes how the community still finds interest in their existence.

Identify the Sentence's Role" The sentence in question is: "Even the coming of a stranger was an event to be chronicled and discussed."

Understand the Answer Choices:

    A) It underscores the monotonous nature of life in Three Forks.

    B) It suggests the tight-knit and close community within Three Forks.

    C) It highlights the significance of minor occurrences in a tranquil environment.

    D) It portrays Three Forks as an unwelcoming community to outsiders.

Eliminate Incorrect Answers:

    A) The passage already states the routine nature of life, and this sentence doesn't further underscore it.

    B) This could be true, but the emphasis in the sentence is more on the significance of events.

    D) The sentence doesn't portray the community as unwelcoming, just that they take note of strangers.

Choose the Best Answer: C) This is the correct answer. The fact that the arrival of a stranger is an event of note highlights the significance of even minor occurrences in the environment of Three Forks. The correct answer is C) It highlights the significance of minor occurrences in a tranquil environment.

► **QUESTION 15:**

Read and Understand the Entire Passage

The passage describes Mrs. Manstey's residence and her particular interest in the view from her room's windows which look out over the backyards.

Identify the Sentence's Role

The sentence in question is: "The yard was a narrow pocket hemmed in by three tall brick walls." This sentence provides a specific description of the yard she overlooks.

Understand the Answer Choices

    A) Highlights the bustling nature of New York life.

    B) Contrasts the confined nature of Mrs. Manstey's environment with the city's expanse.

    C) Underscores Mrs. Manstey's preference for her specific city view.

    D) Introduces a new character into Mrs. Manstey's narrative.

Eliminate Incorrect Answers

    A) The sentence doesn't mention anything about the bustling nature of New York.

    C) The sentence provides a description and doesn't emphasize her preference.

    D) The sentence doesn't introduce any new character.

Choose the Best Answer: B) The sentence provides a vivid description of the yard's confined and isolated nature. Hence, B) Contrasts the confined nature of Mrs. Manstey's environment with the city's expanse is the correct answer.

▶ **QUESTION 16:**

Read and Understand the Entire Passage: The passage paints a vivid picture of Alexandra Bergson driving her sleigh on a bright winter morning, taking in the sights of the land.

Identify the Sentence's Role: The sentence in question is: "The fields and meadows were empty, with only the distant silhouette of a lone tree or a barn." This sentence provides a description of the landscape Alexandra observes.

Understand the Answer Choices:

    A) Evokes a sense of isolation and solitude in the landscape.

    B) Emphasizes the vibrant colors of the morning.

    C) Introduces a major event or turning point in Alexandra's journey.

    D) Highlights Alexandra's enthusiasm for her surroundings.

Eliminate Incorrect Answers:

    B) The sentence does not focus on colors.

    C) There's no indication of a major event or turning point.

    D) The sentence doesn't highlight Alexandra's enthusiasm.

Choose the Best Answer: A) The sentence creates an imagery of a vast, open landscape with little in sight, emphasizing a sense of isolation. So, the correct answer is A) It evokes a sense of isolation and solitude in the landscape.

▶ **QUESTION 17:**

Read and Understand the Entire Passage: The passage describes an artist walking in a corridor filled with pictures and his reaction to a specific portrait that isn't his own.

Identify the Sentence's Role: The sentence in question is: "'How wonderful!' he said, 'what power, what expression! I have never seen such a portrait. How living, how clearly defined against the dark background is that pale face, with its burning eyes.'" This sentence captures the artist's immediate and strong reaction to a particular painting.

Understand the Answer Choices:

    A) Indicates the artist's dissatisfaction with his own work.

    B) Highlights the artist's recognition of an unfamiliar style.

    C) Captures the artist's admiration and astonishment for the depicted art.

    D) Emphasizes the crowded nature of the exhibition.

Eliminate Incorrect Answers:

    A) The sentence doesn't reflect any dissatisfaction about his own work.

    B) While he recognizes the work of a "strange artist," the sentence emphasizes his admiration more.

    D) The crowded nature of the exhibition isn't the focus of this sentence.

Choose the Best Answer: C) The artist's words clearly reflect his admiration and astonishment for the portrait he's observing. Thus, the correct answer is C) It captures the artist's admiration and astonishment for the depicted art.

▶ **QUESTION 18:**

Read and Understand the Entire Passage: The passage comments on the trajectory of young girls after leaving their homes and introduces the character of Carrie Meeber, providing some insight into her personality.

Identify the Sentence's Role: The sentence in question is: "Of an intermediate balance, under the circumstances, there is no possibility." This sentence declares that there are only two possible outcomes for girls like Carrie once they leave home.

Understand the Answer Choices:

    A) Underscores the inevitability of Carrie's choices after leaving home.

    B) Suggests that Carrie's intellect played a major role in her decisions.

    C) Emphasizes the importance of home and family in determining character.

    D) Compares Carrie to other girls of her age and social standing.

Eliminate Incorrect Answers:

    B) The sentence doesn't comment specifically on Carrie's intellect in relation to her decisions.

    C) While the concept of home is crucial in the passage, the sentence doesn't emphasize the role of home and family.

    D) The sentence doesn't directly compare Carrie to other girls.

Choose the Best Answer: A) The sentence clarifies that for girls like Carrie, once they leave home, there are only two definite paths and no middle ground. This means the answer is A) It underscores the inevitability of Carrie's choices after leaving home.

▶ **QUESTION 19:**

Read and Understand the Entire Passage: The passage describes the beauty of Miss Brooke and how her plain dress accentuates her natural beauty. Her beauty is contrasted with provincial fashion.

Identify the Sentence's Role: The sentence in question is: "Her profile as well as her stature and bearing seemed to gain the more dignity from her plain garments, which by the side of provincial fashion gave her the impressiveness of a fine quotation from the Bible." This sentence compares Miss Brooke's dignified appearance in plain clothes to the impact of a biblical quotation.

Understand the Answer Choices:

    A) Emphasizes the contrast between Miss Brooke's natural beauty and the prevailing fashion trends.

    B) Illustrates Miss Brooke's religious devotion.

    C) Describes the societal norms regarding women's dress.

    D) Portrays Miss Brooke's preference for modesty over ostentation.

Eliminate Incorrect Answers:

    B) While the Bible is mentioned as a comparison, the sentence doesn't highlight Miss Brooke's religious devotion.

    C) The sentence isn't about societal norms but rather Miss Brooke's specific appearance.

    D) The sentence talks about the impact of her dress but doesn't explicitly convey her personal preference for modesty.

Choose the Best Answer: A) The focus of the sentence is on how Miss Brooke's natural beauty is enhanced and contrasted by her plain garments, especially when compared to provincial fashion. This leads to the answer being A) It emphasizes the contrast between Miss Brooke's natural beauty and the prevailing fashion trends.

▶ **QUESTION 20:**

Read and Understand the Entire Passage: The passage introduces Fanny Price, describing her physical appearance, demeanor, and the initial reception she receives from Sir Thomas and Lady Bertram.

Identify the Sentence's Role: The sentence in question describes Fanny's physical appearance and temperament, contrasting her lack of striking beauty with her sweet voice and pleasant countenance.

Understand the Answer Choices:

    A) Suggests that Fanny's physical appearance was the sole reason for her acceptance by her relatives.

    B) Contrasts Fanny's physical characteristics with her gentle nature and demeanor.

    C) Underscores Fanny's position as an outsider in the Bertram household.

    D) Highlights the superficial values of the society in which Fanny lives.

Eliminate Incorrect Answers:

    A) The sentence doesn't imply that her appearance was the "sole" reason for her acceptance.

    C) The sentence doesn't specifically address Fanny's position as an outsider.

    D) While the societal context is implied, the sentence focuses more on Fanny's personal attributes.

Choose the Best Answer: B) The sentence highlights how, despite not having striking beauty, Fanny's voice and countenance are pleasant. This description contrasts her simple physical features with her gentle and endearing qualities. Therefore, the correct answer is B) It contrasts Fanny's physical characteristics with her gentle nature and demeanor.

7. Illustrating a Claim Answer

▶ **QUESTION 1:**

Read the Claim Carefully: The claim is that startups provide immense learning opportunities but can also lead to high-stress levels due to the uncertainty and risk involved.

Identify Key Points: The key points are "immense learning opportunities" and "high-stress levels".

Evaluate the Options: We now read the options, looking for a quote that encapsulates both of these key points.

Compare Options to Claim:

    A) This quote touches on both key points - learning something new every day (learning opportunities) and the uncertainty of the future causing stress (high-stress levels).

    B) While this quote mentions a fulfilling experience and the ability to make impactful decisions, it does not address the stress aspect mentioned in the claim.

    C) This quote talks about the inspiration and excitement derived from working at a startup, but doesn't mention learning opportunities or stress levels.

    D) This quote highlights the variety of roles and the interesting aspect of working at a startup, but it doesn't specifically mention high-stress levels.

Check for Relevance: Among the options, Option A is the one that aligns directly with the claim about startups providing learning opportunities and potentially leading to high-stress levels.

Select the Best Option: Based on the analysis, Option A) "Building a startup from the ground up has been an incredibly enriching experience. Every day, I am learning something new, but the uncertainty of the future can be quite stressful." is the best choice. It clearly addresses both aspects of the claim - learning opportunities and high stress due to uncertainty.

▶ **QUESTION 2:**

Read the Claim Carefully: The claim is that collaboration in scientific research teams significantly influences the individual scientist's work, who might previously have been accustomed to conducting independent research.

Identify Key Points: The key points are "collaboration", "influence", and "individual scientist's work".

Evaluate the Options: We now read the options, looking for a quote that demonstrates how collaboration influences the work of an individual scientist.

Compare Options to Claim:

A) This quote talks about a research team disbanding due to disagreements on research credits and roles, but it does not explicitly show how collaboration influenced individual work.

B) While this quote acknowledges the collaborative nature of the work, it doesn't explicitly discuss the influence of this collaboration on individual work.

C) This quote directly addresses the claim, showing how working as part of a research team influences an individual scientist's work. It mentions that team collaboration fosters individual ideas, which is a clear example of influence.

D) This quote talks about outside scientists collaborating on projects, but it doesn't directly address how collaboration influences individual work.

Check for Relevance: Among the options, Option C is the one that aligns directly with the claim about collaboration significantly influencing the work of individual scientists.

Select the Best Option: Based on the analysis, Option C) "Having worked as part of a research team for several years, it's sometimes hard to recall what it was like to conduct research independently. The team's support doesn't stifle my individual ideas but actually fosters them." is the best choice. It clearly illustrates how the collaborative nature of scientific research teams influences individual scientists' work.

▶ **QUESTION 3:**

Read the Claim Carefully: The claim is that Melville depicts Captain Ahab as a man whose obsession with the great white whale, Moby Dick, consumes his entire existence.

Identify Key Points: The key points are "Captain Ahab", "obsession", and "consumes his entire existence".

Evaluate the Options: We now read the options, looking for a quote that shows Ahab's obsession with Moby Dick consuming his entire existence.

Compare Options to Claim:

A) This quote describes Ahab focusing all his rage and hate onto the whale, to the point of symbolically bursting his heart upon it. This effectively illustrates the claim of Ahab's obsession consuming him.

B) This quote doesn't directly refer to Ahab's obsession with Moby Dick.

C) This quote doesn't directly show Ahab's obsession consuming him.

D) This quote, while showing Ahab's intense state of mind, doesn't directly reference his obsession with Moby Dick.

Check for Relevance: Among the options, Option A is the most relevant to the claim.

Select the Best Option: Based on the analysis, Option A) "He piled upon the whale's white hump the sum of all the general rage and hate felt by his whole race from Adam down; and then, as if his chest had been a mortar, he burst his hot heart's shell upon it." is the best choice. It is the only option that directly illustrates Ahab's all-consuming obsession with Moby Dick.

▶ **QUESTION 4:**

Read the Claim Carefully: The claim is that Fitzgerald portrays Jay Gatsby as a character whose life and identity are deeply shaped by his unattainable dreams.

Identify Key Points: The key points are "Jay Gatsby", "life and identity", "deeply shaped", and "unattainable dreams".

Evaluate the Options: We now read the options, looking for a quote that shows Gatsby's life and identity being shaped by his unattainable dreams.

Compare Options to Claim:

A) This quote depicts Gatsby's dream as close and nearly within his grasp, which could indicate his life and identity are shaped by this pursuit.

B) This quote, while it could be interpreted to indirectly refer to Gatsby's situation, does not directly reflect on his personal dreams shaping his life and identity.

C) This quote doesn't directly address Gatsby or his unattainable dreams.

D) This quote uses a metaphor that could be interpreted as an embodiment of Gatsby's unattainable dreams, but it doesn't directly mention Gatsby.

Check for Relevance: Among the options, Option A is the most relevant to the claim.

Select the Best Option: Based on the analysis, Option A) "He had come a long way to this blue lawn, and his dream must have seemed so close that he could hardly fail to grasp it." is the best choice. It provides a direct illustration of how Gatsby's life and identity are shaped by his pursuit of an unattainable dream.

► **QUESTION 5:**
Read the Claim Carefully: The claim is that in the sonnets, Rilke muses on the power of art and its capacity to transform and transcend reality.
Identify Key Points: The key points are "power of art", "transform", and "transcend reality".
Evaluate the Options: We now read the options, looking for a quote that shows Rilke musing about the transformative and transcendent power of art.
Compare Options to Claim:
  A) This quote speaks to desire and change, but it doesn't directly connect to the power of art or its transformative/transcendent nature.
  B) This quote encourages to be ahead of parting, which could be interpreted metaphorically, but it doesn't directly speak to the power of art.
  C) This quote talks about being a "magic power" at the crossroad of the senses, which could be interpreted as an allusion to the transformative and transcendent power of art.
  D) This quote suggests that happiness comes from overcoming hardships, which might be interpreted metaphorically as the transformative power of experiences, but it does not directly relate to the power of art.
Check for Relevance: Among the options, Option C is the most relevant to the claim.

Select the Best Option: Based on the analysis, Option C) "Be, in this immensity of night, be magic power at your senses' crossroad, the meaning of their strange encounter." is the best choice. It is the option that comes closest to illustrating the idea of art's transformative and transcendent power.

► **QUESTION 6:**
Read the Claim Carefully: The claim is that in the story, Gilman provides a critique of the limitations imposed on women by a patriarchal society, through the deteriorating mental health of the female protagonist.
Identify Key Points: The key points are "limitations on women", "patriarchal society", and "deteriorating mental health".
Evaluate the Options: We now read the options, looking for a quote that shows the critique of societal limitations on women and their impact on the protagonist's mental health.
Compare Options to Claim:
  A) This quote speaks to a woman's actions, possibly hinting at her mental state, but does not directly reference societal limitations or critique them.
  B) This quote speaks to the protagonist's relationship with the wallpaper, possibly a metaphor for her mental state, but it doesn't directly critique societal limitations on women.
  C) This quote shows the protagonist's defiance and possibly the deterioration of her mental state. The mention of "you can't put me back" could be interpreted as a critique of societal limitations.
  D) This quote is a general statement about trust, not directly related to the societal critique or the protagonist's mental health.
Check for Relevance: Among the options, Option C is the most relevant to the claim.

Select the Best Option: Based on the analysis, Option C) "I've got out at last," said I, "in spite of you and Jane. And I've pulled off most of the paper, so you can't put me back!" is the best choice. It is the only option that directly illustrates the protagonist's deteriorating mental health and her defiance against the societal limitations imposed on her.

► **QUESTION 7:**
Read the Claim Carefully: The claim is that in the novel, Wharton describes Ethan Frome as a character deeply affected by his oppressive and isolated environment.
Identify Key Points: The key points are "Ethan Frome", "deeply affected", "oppressive and isolated environment".
Evaluate the Options: We now read the options, looking for a quote that shows how Ethan Frome is affected by his oppressive and isolated environment.
Compare Options to Claim:
  A) This quote describes Ethan's physical appearance and age, but it doesn't directly link to the environment's oppression or isolation.
  B) This quote gives a vivid description of the winter morning. It mentions the isolated and cold environment, but it doesn't directly connect it to Ethan's character.
  C) This quote describes Ethan as a part of the melancholy landscape and speaks to him being frozen in woe, which clearly illustrates the connection between Ethan and his oppressive, isolated environment.
  D) This quote presents Ethan's perception of his kitchen as a place for a man to die in, which could symbolize his oppressive and isolated existence, but it doesn't make the connection as directly as option C.
Check for Relevance: Among the options, Option C is the most relevant to the claim.

Select the Best Option: Based on the analysis, Option C) "He seemed a part of the mute melancholy landscape, an incarnation of its frozen woe, with all that was warm and sentient in him fast bound below the surface." is the best choice. It directly illustrates how Ethan Frome is affected by his oppressive and isolated environment.

▶ **QUESTION 8:**

Read the Claim Carefully: The claim is that in the biography, Forster details Dickens's profound sense of social justice, arguing that Dickens used his writing as a means of highlighting societal injustices.

Identify Key Points: The key points are "Dickens's profound sense of social justice", and "Dickens used his writing to highlight societal injustices".

Evaluate the Options: We now read the options, looking for a quote that shows how Dickens used his writing to highlight societal injustices.

Compare Options to Claim:

    A) This quote does refer to Dickens's novels as showing a world full of injustice and suffering, but it doesn't speak to his purpose of highlighting societal injustices.

    B) This quote talks about Dickens's perception of the greatest evil as poverty and degradation, but it doesn't clearly show how Dickens used his writing to combat this.

    C) This quote refers to Dickens's faculty for description and his sense of the ludicrous and the pathetic, but it doesn't directly connect to the claim of using writing to highlight injustices.

    D) This quote mentions the suffering caused by the world's neglect and scorn that Dickens had seen and reiterated, which aligns with the claim about Dickens's use of writing to highlight societal injustices.

Check for Relevance: Among the options, Option D is the most relevant to the claim.

Select the Best Option: Based on the analysis, Option D) "He had seen in his youth, and was never tired of reiterating what he had seen, of the suffering, the horrible and brutalizing suffering, caused by the world's neglect and scorn." is the best choice. It effectively illustrates how Dickens used his writing to highlight societal injustices.

▶ **QUESTION 9:**

Read the Claim Carefully: The claim is that in the story, Joyce delves into the complex psyche of a young boy, frequently contrasting the boy's naive worldview with the harsh realities of adult life.

Identify Key Points: The key points are "complex psyche of a young boy", "naive worldview" and "harsh realities of adult life".

Evaluate the Options: We now read the options, looking for a quote that contrasts the boy's naive worldview with the harsh realities of adult life.

Compare Options to Claim:

    A) This quote implies the boy's regret and dark stupor but doesn't effectively contrast the naive worldview with harsh realities.

    B) This quote states that the boy lived in his own world but doesn't contrast it with adult life.

    C) This quote reflects the boy's desire for adventures and his understanding that they happen abroad, not at home. It shows a contrast between his naive worldview and reality.

    D) This quote describes the boy witnessing a potentially serious scene, but doesn't explicitly contrast a naive worldview with adult life.

Check for Relevance: Among the options, Option C is the most relevant to the claim.

Select the Best Option: Based on the analysis, Option C) "I wanted real adventures to happen to myself. But real adventures, I reflected, do not happen to people who remain at home: they must be sought abroad." is the best choice. It effectively illustrates the contrast between the boy's naive worldview and the harsh realities of adult life.

▶ **QUESTION 10:**

Read the Claim Carefully: The claim is that in the poem, Whitman advocates the idea of self-love and self-acceptance.

Identify Key Points: The key points are "self-love" and "self-acceptance".

Evaluate the Options: We now read the options, looking for a quote that shows Whitman's advocacy for self-love and self-acceptance.

Compare Options to Claim:

    A) This quote expresses celebrating and singing oneself, which can be seen as expressions of self-love and self-acceptance.

    B) This quote encourages direct experience over secondhand knowledge, but it doesn't explicitly express self-love or self-acceptance.

    C) The assertion "I am large, I contain multitudes." indicates self-acceptance and understanding of the complexity within oneself.

    D) This quote signifies acceptance of self-contradiction, which is a form of self-acceptance.

Check for Relevance: Among the options, Option A and C are the most relevant to the claim.

Select the Best Option: Based on the analysis, Option A) "I celebrate myself, and sing myself, / And what I assume you shall assume, / For every atom belonging to me as good belongs to you." is the best choice. It effectively illustrates Whitman's idea of self-love and self-acceptance.

Read the Claim Carefully: The claim is that in the novel, Cather paints Antonia Shimerda as a character who is deeply connected and in tune with her natural surroundings.

Identify Key Points: The key points are "Antonia Shimerda" and "deeply connected and in tune with her natural surroundings".

Evaluate the Options: We now read the options, looking for a quote that illustrates Antonia's deep connection and attunement with her natural surroundings.

Compare Options to Claim:

A) This quote implies that natural things and creatures feel a kinship with Antonia, suggesting a deep connection with nature.

B) This quote talks about Antonia's love for cooking and housekeeping, not her connection with nature.

C) This quote speaks to Antonia's eyes and what they communicate, but not about her connection with nature.

D) This quote describes the impact of many years in the soil on the shape of Antonia's hands, indicating a deep connection with the earth.

Check for Relevance: Among the options, Option A and D are the most relevant to the claim.

Select the Best Option: Based on the analysis, Option D) "Antonia had not lost the fire of life. Her skin was brown and rugged; there was something in the shape of her hands, so many years in the soil had molded them into earthy forms." is the best choice. It effectively illustrates Antonia's deep connection with her natural surroundings.

► **QUESTION 12:**

Read the Claim Carefully: The claim is that in the essay, Woolf argues that the quality and depth of a society's literature have a profound impact on its collective psyche.

Identify Key Points: The key points are "quality and depth of a society's literature" and "profound impact on its collective psyche".

Evaluate the Options: We now read the options, looking for a quote that shows Woolf's argument.

Compare Options to Claim:

A) This quote talks about the importance of literacy, but does not directly connect the quality of literature to its impact on collective psyche.

B) This quote suggests the role of literature in providing self-reflection, but does not mention its impact on the collective psyche of a society.

C) This quote suggests that the vibrancy of a nation can be measured by its literature, but it doesn't clearly illustrate the profound impact on its collective psyche.

D) This quote suggests that the more cultivated a society is, the more important its literature becomes, implying its influence on societal values and principles, which can be linked to the collective psyche of a society.

Check for Relevance: Among the options, Option D is the most relevant to the claim.

Select the Best Option: Based on the analysis, Option D) "The more cultivated a society is, the more its literature matters. It helps shape societal values and principles." is the best choice. It effectively illustrates Woolf's argument about the profound impact of literature on a society's collective psyche.

► **QUESTION 13:**

Read the Claim Carefully: The claim is that in the story, Mansfield characterizes Miss Brill as a lonely woman whose cheerful appearance masks her deep-seated loneliness and desire for companionship.

Identify Key Points: The key points are "Miss Brill", "lonely woman", "cheerful appearance", and "deep-seated loneliness and desire for companionship".

Evaluate the Options: We now read the options, looking for a quote that illustrates Miss Brill's loneliness and desire for companionship beneath her cheerful demeanor.

Compare Options to Claim:

A) This quote suggests that Miss Brill sees herself as part of the performance, indicating her desire for companionship and recognition, but it doesn't clearly show her deep-seated loneliness.

B) This quote doesn't offer much information about Miss Brill's emotions or social situation.

C) This quote speaks more to Miss Brill's physical sensations rather than her emotional state or social desires.

D) The phrase "something light and sad—no, not sad, exactly—something gentle seemed to move in her bosom" could be interpreted as indicating hidden loneliness and desire.

Check for Relevance: Among the options, Option A and D seem more relevant to the claim.

Select the Best Option: Based on the analysis, Option A) "Even she had a part and came every Sunday. No doubt somebody would have noticed if she hadn't been there; she was part of the performance after all." is the best choice. While both options A and D are relevant, option A more directly illustrates her desire for companionship and her use of cheerful appearance to mask her loneliness.

▶ **QUESTION 14:**
Read the Claim Carefully: The claim is that Catherine Earnshaw is known to have a deep connection with the wild moors surrounding her home.
Identify Key Points: The key points are "Catherine Earnshaw" and "deep connection with the wild moors surrounding her home".
Evaluate the Options: We now read the options, looking for a quote that illustrates Catherine's deep connection with the moors.
Compare Options to Claim:
  A) This quote speaks directly to Catherine's love and deep connection with the moors.
  B) While this quote shows Catherine's knowledge about the environment, it doesn't clearly illustrate a deep connection with the moors.
  C) This quote illustrates Catherine's journey through the moors alone, which could indicate a deep connection with the wild moors.
  D) This quote shows Catherine's knowledge about the weather and nature, but it doesn't clearly suggest a deep connection with the moors.
Check for Relevance: Among the options, Option A and C are the most relevant to the claim.

Select the Best Option: Based on the analysis, Option A) "She had a love for the boundless moors. She found solace in the whispering wind and the sweeping heather. It was as though her spirit resided there, amidst the skylarks and the endless wild." is the best choice. It effectively illustrates Catherine's deep connection with the wild moors surrounding her home.

▶ **QUESTION 15:**
Read the Claim Carefully: The claim is that many popular diet plans emphasize short-term weight loss over sustainable, long-term health habits.
Identify Key Points: The key points are "short-term weight loss" and "sustainable, long-term health habits".
Evaluate the Options: We now read the options, looking for a quote that illustrates the emphasis on short-term weight loss.
Compare Options to Claim:
  A) This quote directly emphasizes rapid weight loss in a short period.
  B) This quote focuses on understanding nutrition and not just counting calories.
  C) This quote emphasizes a balanced lifestyle and not just weight loss.
  D) This quote acknowledges the diet's short-term nature.
Check for Relevance: Among the options, Option A and D are the most relevant to the claim.

Select the Best Option: Based on the analysis, Option A) "Lose 10 pounds in just 10 days with our rapid weight loss program!" is the best choice. It directly illustrates the emphasis on short-term weight loss, which the nutritionist criticizes.

▶ **QUESTION 16:**
Read the Claim Carefully: The claim is that many modern cities prioritize cars over pedestrians, leading to less walkable and more congested urban areas.
Identify Key Points: The key points are "prioritize cars" and "less walkable and more congested urban areas".
Evaluate the Options: We now read the options, looking for a quote that illustrates the prioritization of cars over pedestrians.
Compare Options to Claim:
  A) This quote directly emphasizes prioritizing traffic flow and parking for vehicles.
  B) This quote speaks about balancing pedestrian, bicycle, and vehicle spaces.
  C) This quote emphasizes creating spaces for people without vehicle interference.
  D) This quote focuses on expanding road networks for cars, sidelining public transportation.
Check for Relevance: Among the options, Option A and D are the most relevant to the claim.

Select the Best Option: Based on the analysis, Option A) "The primary goal of our urban development is to ensure smooth traffic flow and ample parking spaces for vehicles." is the best choice. It directly illustrates the prioritization of cars over pedestrians.

▶ **QUESTION 17:**
Read the Claim Carefully: The claim is that while fusion cuisine restaurants offer a blend of flavors, they sometimes risk overshadowing the rich traditions from which they draw.
Identify Key Points: The key points are "blend of flavors" and "risk overshadowing the rich traditions".
Evaluate the Options: We now read the options, looking for a quote that illustrates the risk of overshadowing traditional dishes.
Compare Options to Claim:
  A) This quote emphasizes the blend of flavors but doesn't mention overshadowing traditions.
  B) This quote directly addresses the risk of overshadowing the essence of a traditional dish.
  C) This quote focuses on blending culinary traditions harmoniously.
  D) This quote speaks about honoring the roots of each dish.
Check for Relevance: Among the options, Option B is the most relevant to the claim.

Select the Best Option: Based on the analysis, Option B) "While fusion allows us to innovate, there are times when the essence of a traditional dish might take a backseat to our experimental flair." is the best choice. It directly illustrates the critic's claim about the risk of overshadowing traditional dishes in fusion cuisine.

▶ **QUESTION 18:**

Read the Claim Carefully: The claim is that while many people romanticize the idea of a local bookstore, they often overlook the financial and logistical challenges these stores face in the modern era.

Identify Key Points: The key points are "romanticize the idea of a local bookstore" and "financial and logistical challenges".

Evaluate the Options: We now read the options, looking for a quote that illustrates the challenges faced by independent bookstores.

Compare Options to Claim:

A) This quote emphasizes the history of the bookstore and changing reading habits but doesn't address the challenges.

B) This quote directly addresses the challenges faced by independent bookstores due to online giants.

C) This quote focuses on the unique offerings of the bookstore but doesn't mention the challenges.

D) This quote emphasizes the community aspect of the bookstore but doesn't address the challenges.

Check for Relevance: Among the options, Option B is the most relevant to the claim.

Select the Best Option: Based on the analysis, Option B) "Despite the love we receive from our community, the reality is that online giants offer prices and convenience we simply can't match." is the best choice. It directly illustrates the journalist's claim about the challenges faced by independent bookstores.

▶ **QUESTION 19:**

Read the Claim Carefully: The claim is that in "Journey to the East," Hesse delves into the spiritual journey of its protagonist, Leo, suggesting that true enlightenment often comes from understanding one's own self and the world around them.

Identify Key Points: The key points are "spiritual journey," "true enlightenment," and "understanding one's own self and the world."

Evaluate the Options: We now read the options, looking for a quote that illustrates the spiritual journey and enlightenment.

Compare Options to Claim:

A) This quote touches on the limitations of words and the subjective nature of value and wisdom.

B) This quote hints at Leo's spiritual journey but doesn't directly address enlightenment or understanding.

C) This quote directly addresses the spiritual journey and the idea of enlightenment as understanding oneself and the world.

D) This quote touches on the idea of rebirth and transformation.

Check for Relevance: Among the options, Option C is the most relevant to the claim.

Select the Best Option: Based on the analysis, Option C) "For our goal was not only the East, or rather the East was not only a country and something geographical, but it was the home and youth of the soul, it was everywhere and nowhere, it was the union of all times." is the best choice. It effectively illustrates the claim about the spiritual journey and enlightenment in "Journey to the East."

▶ **QUESTION 20:**

Read the Claim Carefully: The claim is that in "The Dead," Joyce paints a vivid picture of a society trapped by its own traditions and the past, as seen through the protagonist, Gabriel Conroy.

Identify Key Points: The key points are "society trapped by its own traditions and the past" and "Gabriel Conroy."

Evaluate the Options: We now read the options, looking for a quote that illustrates the society's entrapment in traditions and the past.

Compare Options to Claim:

A) This quote is poetic and touches on the idea of the living and the dead, but it doesn't directly address the society's entrapment in traditions.

B) This quote directly addresses the idea of people becoming trapped by the past and traditions.

C) This quote focuses on a specific sentiment but doesn't address the society's entrapment in traditions.

D) This quote touches on Gabriel's personal feelings but doesn't directly address the society's entrapment in traditions.

Check for Relevance: Among the options, Option B is the most relevant to the claim.

Select the Best Option: Based on the analysis, Option B) "One by one, they were all becoming shades. Better pass boldly into that other world, in the full glory of some passion, than fade and wither dismally with age." is the best choice. It effectively illustrates the claim about society being trapped by its own traditions and the past in "The Dead."

8. Cross Text Answer

▶ **QUESTION 1:**

Read the Main Instruction: The main instruction is "Based on the texts, how would Dr. Emilia Harper (Text 2) most likely respond to the claims about consciousness presented in Text 1?" The keywords here are "Dr. Emilia Harper," "respond," and "claims about consciousness in Text 1."

Identify the Claims or Perspectives: In Text 1, the main claims are that the understanding of consciousness is still a challenge for modern science and it might not only be a human attribute, but could extend to other animals and even non-biological entities.

Analyze the Second Text: In Text 2, Dr. Emilia Harper is introduced, who is studying the potential for consciousness in AI systems. She posits that it might be possible for advanced AI to develop a form of consciousness, but this would be different from human consciousness. She also warns against anthropomorphizing AI systems.

Cross-Referencing: When comparing the two texts, Dr. Emilia Harper's viewpoints align with the idea presented in Text 1 that consciousness might not be exclusive to humans. She acknowledges the possibility of consciousness in non-biological entities (AI), but emphasizes its difference from human consciousness.

Review the Response Options: Each response option proposes a different reaction that Dr. Emilia Harper might have to the claims in Text 1.

Select the Best Response: The best response, based on the analysis, is: A) By agreeing with the possibility of non-human consciousness but highlighting the need for clarity on what consciousness means for AI systems

Justification: This answer best aligns with Dr. Harper's views as she doesn't refute the notion of consciousness in non-biological entities (option B), nor does she emphasize the need for more brain research before exploring non-human consciousness (option C), and she does not label the idea of non-human consciousness as speculative (option D). Instead, she agrees with the potential for non-human consciousness but stresses its difference from human consciousness and the need for caution in anthropomorphizing AI systems.

▶ **QUESTION 2:**

Read the Main Instruction: The main instruction is "Based on the texts, how would Dr. Alexander Norton (Text 2) most likely respond to the assertions about Bronze Age trade routes made in Text 1?" The keywords here are "Dr. Alexander Norton," "respond," and "assertions about Bronze Age trade routes in Text 1."

Identify the Claims or Perspectives: In Text 1, the main claims are that Bronze Age trade routes facilitated the acquisition of resources not available locally and might have enabled cultural exchange and the spread of technological advancements.

Analyze the Second Text: In Text 2, Dr. Alexander Norton studies Bronze Age trade routes. His findings support the fact that these networks facilitated resource acquisition, but he questions the extent of cultural and technological exchange. He emphasizes not to confuse trading goods with an exchange of ideas.

Cross-Referencing: When comparing the two texts, Dr. Norton agrees with the idea in Text 1 that trade routes helped in acquiring resources. However, he expresses skepticism about the extent of cultural and technological exchange.

Review the Response Options: Each response option proposes a different reaction that Dr. Norton might have to the claims in Text 1.

Select the Best Response: The best response, based on the analysis, is: A) By supporting the notion of resource acquisition but questioning the degree of cultural and technological exchange through these trade networks

Justification: This answer aligns best with Dr. Norton's views, as it reflects his agreement with the trade routes facilitating resource acquisition and his skepticism about the extent of cultural and technological diffusion. He does not refute the existence of extensive Bronze Age trade routes (option B), he does not emphasize the political nature of the trade routes (option C), and he does not argue against the archaeological evidence of long-distance trade routes in the Bronze Age (option D).

▶ **QUESTION 3:**

Read the Main Instruction: The main instruction is "Based on the texts, how would Dr. Leah Jensen (Text 2) most likely respond to the concerns about biodiversity outlined in Text 1?" The keywords here are "Dr. Leah Jensen," "respond," and "concerns about biodiversity in Text 1."

Identify the Claims or Perspectives: In Text 1, the main concern is that climate change significantly impacts global biodiversity, forcing some species to migrate and others to face extinction. This can disrupt ecosystems and lead to further environmental issues.

Analyze the Second Text: In Text 2, Dr. Leah Jensen agrees that climate change forces species to adapt or migrate, but also adds that it could lead to an unexpected increase in local biodiversity in some regions. However, she insists that this is not a positive effect of climate change and that the overall impact on global biodiversity is still harmful.

Cross-Referencing: When comparing the two texts, Dr. Jensen agrees with the concerns expressed in Text 1. She adds to it by mentioning possible increases in local biodiversity due to species migration, but clarifies that this doesn't diminish the overall negative effect on global biodiversity.

Review the Response Options: Each response option proposes a different reaction that Dr. Jensen might have to the concerns in Text 1.

Select the Best Response: The best response, based on the analysis, is: A) By affirming the concerns but adding the possibility of localized increases in biodiversity due to species migration

Justification: This answer aligns best with Dr. Jensen's views, as it reflects her agreement with the concerns outlined in Text 1 and her additional assertion of possible local biodiversity increase due to species migration. She does not reject the idea that climate change impacts biodiversity (option B), she does not claim that climate change only affects certain species (option C), and she does not argue that the effect of climate change on biodiversity is over-dramatized (option D).

▶ **QUESTION 4:**

Read the Main Instruction: The main instruction is "Based on the texts, how would Lena Simmons (Text 2) most likely respond to the claims about green spaces made in Text 1?" The keywords here are "Lena Simmons," "respond," and "claims about green spaces in Text 1."

Identify the Claims or Perspectives: In Text 1, the main claims are that green spaces in urban areas provide a number of benefits, including improving air quality, reducing heat, supporting urban wildlife, and enhancing the mental wellbeing and healthy lifestyle of city dwellers.

Analyze the Second Text: In Text 2, Lena Simmons and her team are proponents of 'blue spaces', which she suggests can provide many of the same benefits as green spaces and sometimes even more. For instance, blue spaces can help manage urban stormwater and support diverse aquatic ecosystems. However, she stresses that both green and blue spaces should be incorporated into urban planning.

Cross-Referencing: When comparing the two texts, Lena Simmons agrees with the claims made in Text 1 about the benefits of green spaces. In addition, she introduces the concept of blue spaces and their potential benefits, while advocating for a combination of both green and blue spaces in urban planning.

Review the Response Options: Each response option proposes a different way that Lena Simmons might react to the claims in Text 1.

Select the Best Response: The best response, based on the analysis, is: D) By acknowledging the benefits of green spaces but suggesting that blue spaces can provide additional advantages

Justification: This answer aligns best with Simmons's views, as it reflects her acknowledgment of the benefits of green spaces and her additional assertion that blue spaces can offer further advantages. She does not dismiss the advantages of green spaces (option A), she does not argue that blue spaces are superior in every aspect (option B), and she does not suggest that the focus on green spaces is outdated (option C).

▶ **QUESTION 5:**

Read the Main Instruction: The main instruction is "Based on the texts, how would Dr. Lisa Huang (Text 2) most likely respond to the theory presented in Text 1?" The keywords here are "Dr. Lisa Huang," "respond," and "theory presented in Text 1."

Identify the Claims or Perspectives: In Text 1, the main claim is that the extinction of dinosaurs was primarily caused by a massive asteroid hitting the Earth about 66 million years ago, which led to catastrophic changes in the Earth's climate.

Analyze the Second Text: In Text 2, Dr. Lisa Huang and her team agree that the asteroid impact played a significant role in the extinction event. However, they also suggest that significant volcanic activity around the same time could have contributed to the severe climate changes and thus to the extinction.

Cross-Referencing: When comparing the two texts, Dr. Lisa Huang agrees with the asteroid impact theory but introduces another potential contributing factor, significant volcanic activity, which could have jointly caused the mass extinction with the asteroid impact.

Review the Response Options: Each response option offers a different way Dr. Lisa Huang might react to the claims in Text 1.

Select the Best Response: The best response, based on the analysis, is: A) By acknowledging the impact of the asteroid collision but pointing out the potential role of volcanic activity in the K-Pg extinction

Justification: This answer aligns best with Dr. Huang's views, as it accurately reflects her acknowledgment of the asteroid impact theory and her suggestion that volcanic activity could have also played a significant role in the extinction. The other options either misrepresent or exaggerate her position.

▶ **QUESTION 6:**

Read the Main Instruction: The main instruction is "Based on the texts, how would Dr. Olivia Ross (Text 2) most likely respond to the discussion on remote work presented in Text 1?" The keywords here are "Dr. Olivia Ross," "respond," and "discussion on remote work in Text 1."

Identify the Claims or Perspectives: In Text 1, the main discussion is around the impacts of modern technology and remote work on work-life balance, job satisfaction, and mental health. The text mentions both positive aspects such as flexibility and improved work-life balance, and potential negative impacts such as an "always-on" culture which could increase stress.

Analyze the Second Text: In Text 2, Dr. Olivia Ross acknowledges the benefits of flexibility in remote work but also emphasizes the downside of blurred boundaries between work and personal life. She confirms the potential for the "always-on" culture to lead to burnout and advises the need for clear work-life boundaries in remote work.

Cross-Referencing: Comparing the two texts, it appears that Dr. Olivia Ross's views align with those in Text 1, both acknowledging the benefits of remote work but also raising concerns about its potential to lead to an "always-on" culture and burnout.

Review the Response Options: Each response option suggests a different way Dr. Ross might react to the discussion on remote work in Text 1.

Select the Best Response: The best response, based on the analysis, is: A) By supporting the notion of improved work-life balance but stressing the risks of an "always-on" culture and the importance of setting boundaries

Justification: This answer best aligns with Dr. Ross's views, as it correctly reflects her acknowledgment of the benefits of remote work and her concerns about the "always-on" culture. The other options either overstate or understate her position.

▶ **QUESTION 7:**

Read the Main Instruction: The main instruction is "Based on the texts, how would Dr. Karen Mitchell (Text 2) most likely respond to the points about AI presented in Text 1?" The keywords are "Dr. Karen Mitchell," "respond," and "points about AI in Text 1."

Identify the Claims or Perspectives: Text 1 discusses the transformative power of AI in various sectors and its ability to efficiently solve complex problems. However, it also mentions potential risks of relying heavily on AI, such as job displacement and ethical issues related to privacy and algorithmic bias.

Analyze the Second Text: Dr. Karen Mitchell acknowledges the benefits of AI in Text 2, but also warns about unchecked reliance on AI systems. She emphasizes the need for human oversight and robust ethical frameworks to minimize potential harm, including job displacement and algorithmic bias.

Cross-Referencing: Both texts present a balanced view of AI, acknowledging its benefits but also cautioning about its potential risks. Dr. Karen Mitchell's views align closely with those presented in Text 1, with an emphasis on human oversight and ethical considerations in AI use.

Review the Response Options: Each response option suggests a different way Dr. Mitchell could react to the points about AI in Text 1.

Select the Best Response: The best response, based on the analysis, is: A) By agreeing with the benefits of AI but emphasizing the need for human oversight and ethical considerations in AI deployment

Justification: This answer accurately reflects Dr. Mitchell's view as it acknowledges the benefits of AI but also highlights the importance of human oversight and ethical considerations, which are her primary concerns. The other options either downplay her concerns or don't fully reflect her stance on the issue.

▶ **QUESTION 8:**

Read the Main Instruction: The main instruction is "Based on the texts, how would Dr. Carlos Moreno (Text 2) most likely respond to the discussion on renewable energy presented in Text 1?" The keywords are "Dr. Carlos Moreno," "respond," and "discussion on renewable energy in Text 1."

Identify the Claims or Perspectives: Text 1 discusses the advancements and limitations of renewable energy technologies, noting their sustainability and environmental friendliness, but also highlighting their intermittent nature and dependence on specific geographical and weather conditions.

Analyze the Second Text: Dr. Carlos Moreno in Text 2 proposes energy storage systems as a potential solution to mitigate the limitations of renewable energy sources. He recognizes the challenge of intermittency in renewable energy and suggests storage systems as a way to overcome it. However, he also emphasizes the need for further research and innovation to improve the efficiency and cost-effectiveness of these systems.

Cross-Referencing: Dr. Moreno's views align with the issues raised in Text 1. He doesn't dispute the limitations but offers a potential solution—energy storage systems—to address one key limitation, i.e., the intermittent nature of renewable energy.

Review the Response Options: Each response option suggests a different way Dr. Moreno could react to the discussion on renewable energy in Text 1.

Select the Best Response: The best response, based on the analysis, is: A) By confirming the criticisms but suggesting that energy storage systems could address the intermittency of renewable energy sources

Justification: This answer correctly reflects Dr. Moreno's stance. He acknowledges the limitations of renewable energy (therefore confirming the criticisms) and suggests energy storage systems as a potential solution to the intermittency issue. The other options either downplay his proposed solution or don't accurately represent his perspective on the limitations of renewable energy.

▶ **QUESTION 1:**

Dr. Linda Evans hypothesized an inverse relationship between neighborhood density and responsiveness to emergency alerts. This means that as neighborhood density increases, responsiveness to alerts should decrease. To support this hypothesis, we are looking for evidence that high-density neighborhoods (like Oakwood) are less responsive to emergency alerts compared to low-density neighborhoods (like Brookside).

Analyze the Options:

A) TThis option discusses a lack of reaction from both neighborhoods but focuses on the community center staff's response, which is irrelevant to the hypothesis about density and neighborhood responsiveness.

B) This option mentions neighborhoods with similar density to Oakwood but claims Oakwood displayed high levels of emergency preparedness. This contradicts the hypothesis, as high-density Oakwood is supposed to be less responsive, not more.

C) This option compares responsiveness between Oakwood and Brookside, but it highlights that nearly all Oakwood residents acted on alerts, while only some Brookside residents did. This directly opposes the hypothesis, as it shows higher responsiveness in the high-density neighborhood.

D) This option directly supports the hypothesis. It shows that Brookside (low-density) had no reaction to the alerts, while Oakwood (high-density) showed high preparedness. This inverse relationship aligns with the idea that lower density leads to higher responsiveness.

Therefore, option D) "Brookside displayed no reaction when Dr. Evans and her team sent out emergency alerts, whereas Oakwood displayed high levels of emergency preparedness in response to the alerts." most directly supports Dr. Evans and her team's hypothesis by demonstrating an inverse relationship between density and responsiveness.

▶ **QUESTION 2:**

Dr. Turner and Dr. Fletcher argue for the preservation and rehabilitation of coral reefs to maintain marine biodiversity in the Pacific region, backing it up with their observation of declined species diversity in areas with degraded corals.

Analyze the Options:

A) This option points to another benefit of preserving coral reefs – protection against coastal erosion, which, while being a reason for preservation, does not directly support the argument concerning marine biodiversity. This finding directly supports the argument by showing a positive outcome (return of diverse fish species) as a result of implementing the suggested action (reef rehabilitation).

B) This option suggests water temperature as the primary influencer for fish species, thereby contradicting the central claim about the role of coral reefs in maintaining biodiversity.

C) This option talks about the decline in tourism activities in regions with degraded reefs, which is a negative outcome of coral degradation but does not directly address the biodiversity aspect that is central to the argument.

D) This finding directly supports the argument by showing a positive outcome (return of diverse fish species) as a result of implementing the suggested action (reef rehabilitation).

Therefore, option D) "Areas where coral reefs have been rehabilitated show a gradual return of diverse fish species over time." most directly supports Dr. Turner and Dr. Fletcher's argument.

▶ **QUESTION 3:**

The team of scientists hypothesized that megalodons migrated vast distances to follow their prey based on their analysis of trace elements in megalodon teeth.

Analyze the Options:

A) This option doesn't provide direct evidence supporting the migration pattern hypothesized for megalodons.

B) This option supports the hypothesis by indicating different living environments (warm and cold waters) for juvenile and adult megalodons, suggesting migratory behavior.

C) This option gives circumstantial evidence supporting the hypothesis by indicating that megalodon teeth have been found in cold regions, suggesting they visited these areas.

D) This option discusses the migration patterns of prey species and not directly about megalodons.

Therefore, option B) "Teeth from juvenile megalodons primarily show evidence of warm water temperatures, while adult teeth show a mix of warm and cold water markers." most directly supports the scientists' claim.

▶ **QUESTION 4:**

Dr. Farley argues that Australian Aboriginal art evolved primarily within Australia with minimal external influences. The focus here is on finding evidence to support Dr. Farley's claim regarding the independent evolution of Aboriginal art.

Analyze the Options:
- A) This option highlights similarities with Indonesian batik paintings, contradicting Dr. Farley's claim of minimal external influence.
- B) This option underscores a common theme in art pieces across different Australian regions, suggesting a unique and local evolution, supportive of Dr. Farley's argument.
- C) This option supports Dr. Farley's argument by presenting the art pieces as having unique types and themes not found in other cultures, indicating an independent evolution.
- D) This option supports Dr. Farley's claim by emphasizing the local-centric themes and unique techniques employed, indicating a lesser degree of external influence.

Thus, option C) "A large portion of the art pieces were of types and themes previously not seen in any other culture." provides the most direct support by highlighting the unique and unprecedented nature of the art pieces, implying a largely independent evolution.

▶ **QUESTION 5:**

Dr. Thompson hypothesized that the physical attributes of T. rex, including its bone structure and dental patterns, would align more with those of a predator than a scavenger. Therefore, to support her hypothesis, we need a finding that indicates that the T. rex had physical attributes that facilitated active hunting and predation, rather than scavenging.
Analyze the Options:
- A) This finding directly supports the hypothesis by indicating that the T. rex's teeth were adapted to biting through bone, a characteristic that is typically associated with predators who actively hunt and feed on large prey.
- B) This option talks about the location of the fossils rather than the physical attributes of T. rex. It suggests a possibility of scavenging behavior but does not directly support the hypothesis about being a predator.
- C) Suggesting that T. rex had a relatively slow walking speed doesn't directly support the hypothesis that it was more of a predator, as slower speed might indicate a scavenger behavior.
- D) While this finding suggests that there was a potential food source available, it doesn't provide direct evidence regarding the predatory nature of T. rex based on its physical attributes.

Therefore, option A) "The T. rex's teeth showed wear patterns consistent with biting through bone, suggesting active hunting and feeding on large prey." most directly supports Dr. Thompson's hypothesis.

▶ **QUESTION 6:**

Dr. Soo-Min Lee hypothesized that individuals who consume kimchi daily would have a more diverse and healthy gut microbiome compared to those who don't consume it regularly. Thus, we are looking for evidence that substantiates the positive impact of daily kimchi consumption on the gut microbiome.
Analyze the Options:
- A) This option indicates a positive effect of kimchi consumption on gut health by reducing harmful bacteria, which could indirectly support the hypothesis.
- B) This option directly supports Dr. Lee's hypothesis as it presents a case where daily kimchi consumption led to an increase in beneficial gut bacteria, pointing to a healthier gut microbiome.
- C) While it speaks to a potential benefit of kimchi, it doesn't necessarily show that kimchi consumption leads to a more diverse and healthy gut microbiome.
- D) This option does not provide evidence supporting the hypothesis about the benefits of daily kimchi consumption on gut microbiome health.

Thus, option B) "Individuals who consumed kimchi daily had a notable increase in beneficial gut bacteria such as Lactobacillus and Bifidobacterium, while those who didn't consume kimchi showed no such increase." most directly supports Dr. Lee's hypothesis.

▶ **QUESTION 7:**

Historian Julia Tan hypothesized that societies with progressive taxation systems during the late 18th century were more likely to avoid significant uprisings compared to those with proportional or regressive systems. To support this hypothesis, we are looking for evidence that directly connects the presence of a progressive taxation system to a lower likelihood or frequency of uprisings.
Analyze the Options:
- A) This option highlights that uprisings occurred even in areas with progressive taxation, which weakens rather than supports the hypothesis.
- B) This option directly supports the hypothesis by showing that regions with regressive taxation systems experienced more frequent peasant revolts, suggesting that progressive taxation was more effective in maintaining stability.
- C) This option states that regions with proportional and progressive systems had similar levels of unrest, which fails to differentiate the effectiveness of progressive taxation in reducing uprisings.
- D) This option discusses contributions of wealthier citizens under progressive taxation but does not connect this to uprisings, making it irrelevant to the hypothesis.

Therefore, option B) "A study of late 18th-century France found that regions with regressive taxation systems experienced more frequent peasant revolts than regions with progressive taxation systems." most directly supports Julia Tan's hypothesis by linking regressive systems to increased unrest and, by implication, progressive systems to greater stability.

▶ **QUESTION 8:**

Dr. Park hypothesized that active and coordinated fandom efforts have a significant influence on a K-pop song's position on global music charts. To support this hypothesis, we are looking for evidence that connects fandom activities directly with the international chart performance of K-pop songs.

Analyze the Options:

A) This finding directly supports Dr. Park's hypothesis as it correlates active fandom promotions on social media platforms with higher rankings on international music charts, demonstrating the significant impact fandom activities have on a song's global success.

B) While this option highlights the daily social media usage habits of K-pop fans, it doesn't specifically link these habits to the performance of K-pop songs on global music charts.

C) This option emphasizes the global popularity of K-pop but does not provide a direct link between fandom activities and a song's performance on the international charts.

D) This option discusses the marketing strategies employed by K-pop songs but does not focus on the fandom activities and their influence on the chart performance.

Therefore, option A) "K-pop songs that were actively promoted by fandoms on social media platforms consistently ranked higher on international music charts compared to those with less fandom engagement." most directly supports Dr. Park's hypothesis.

▶ **QUESTION 9:**

Dr. Srinivasan and her team hypothesized that the ability of octopuses to change their skin color and texture may serve as a form of communication among them, aside from being used for camouflage. To support this idea, we are looking for evidence that shows octopuses using their color-changing ability to communicate with other marine creatures or octopuses, and not just for camouflage.

Analyze the Options:

A) This option does suggest a difference in behavior based on the type of marine creatures present but does not clearly indicate communication among octopuses.

B) This option leans towards suggesting the use of the color-changing ability for camouflage, which does not support the hypothesis focused on communication.

C) This finding directly supports the hypothesis as it showcases the change in color and pattern in the presence of another octopus, indicating a potential for communication through color and pattern changes.

D) This option does show a change in color patterns around other marine creatures but does not clearly differentiate between communication and camouflage as the purpose behind the changes.

Therefore, option C) "The majority of octopuses showed no change in color or pattern when left alone in the observation tank but showed various colors and patterns when with another octopus." most directly supports the team's hypothesis.

▶ **QUESTION 10:**

Dr. Miller's team concluded that upbeat, rhythmic music energizes participants during exercise by increasing exercise duration, intensity, and heart rate. The critic argued that the music merely distracts from fatigue rather than increasing energy. To weaken this claim, we need evidence showing that elevated heart rates (a physiological indicator of energy) are linked to the upbeat music, as distraction alone would not cause this physiological effect.

Analyze the Options:

A) This option directly weakens the critic's claim. It shows that participants had consistently higher heart rates when listening to upbeat music, which suggests increased energy rather than mere distraction.

B) This option focuses on participants feeling more motivated, but motivation does not directly address the critic's claim about distraction versus energy.

C) This option suggests no difference in results between those who regularly listened to upbeat music and those who did not. This is irrelevant to the critic's argument about whether the music energizes or distracts.

D) This option discusses the practices of fitness trainers, which are anecdotal and do not provide direct evidence addressing the critic's claim.

Therefore, option A)"Participants listening to upbeat, rhythmic music had consistently higher heart rates during exercise compared to those listening to slow, relaxing music." most directly weakens the critic's claim by providing physiological evidence of increased energy, which distraction alone cannot explain.

9. Undermining a Claim Answer

▶ **QUESTION 1:**

The central hypothesis in this question is that expressing gratitude can enhance our sense of well-being and therefore encourage us to engage more positively with our community. In other words, the sociologists propose a cause-effect relationship, where expressing gratitude (cause) leads to enhanced well-being and positive community engagement (effect).

Analyze the Options:

    A) Participants who were asked to write a thank you note were no more likely to help pick up the dropped papers than those who were asked to write a grocery list.

        → This option undermines the hypothesis by showing a scenario where the proposed cause (expressing gratitude) is present, but the expected effect (engaging more positively with the community, represented by helping pick up papers) is not observed.

    B) Participants who were asked to write a thank you note reported feeling more positive emotions than those who wrote a grocery list.

        → This option does not undermine but rather supports the claim by suggesting a positive correlation between expressing gratitude and enhanced well-being.

    C) Participants who were asked to write a thank you note were significantly more likely to engage in a conversation with the research assistant after helping pick up the papers.

        → This option supports the hypothesis by suggesting that expressing gratitude can lead to more positive community engagement.

    D) Participants who were asked to write a thank you note felt more thankful and reported a higher sense of well-being than those who wrote a grocery list.

        → This statement also supports the hypothesis by affirming a positive effect of expressing gratitude.

Therefore, <u>option A</u> would most strongly weaken the researchers' claim.

▶ **QUESTION 2:**

Elena R. Vasquez and Liam P. O'Connor hypothesized that folk songs were effective tools for political resistance because they communicated subversive messages without drawing the attention of colonial authorities, thereby reducing reliance on more explicit and dangerous forms of written communication. To weaken this hypothesis, we need evidence that contradicts the claim that folk songs reduced the need for explicit written communication or that folk songs avoided detection by colonial authorities.

Analyze the Options:

    A) Folk songs used in political resistance during colonial occupations often contained coded messages understood only by members of specific communities.

        → This option emphasizes that folk songs contained coded messages understood only by specific communities, which supports the hypothesis rather than weakening it.

    B) Many folk songs created during colonial occupations were later adopted as anthems in post-colonial nation-building efforts.

        → This option discusses the later use of folk songs in post-colonial nation-building but does not address whether folk songs replaced explicit written communication or avoided detection during colonial resistance.

    C) Colonial authorities often banned certain folk songs, leading to the imprisonment of individuals caught singing them publicly.

        → This option shows that colonial authorities banned folk songs and imprisoned individuals for singing them, indicating that these songs did not avoid detection as the hypothesis claims. However, it does not address whether folk songs reduced reliance on written communication, so it partially weakens the hypothesis but not directly.

    D) Communities engaged in resistance during colonial occupations relied heavily on underground newspapers to organize protests and disseminate information.

        → This option directly weakens the hypothesis. It shows that communities still relied heavily on underground newspapers for communication and organization, suggesting that folk songs did not obviate the need for written communication as the researchers hypothesized.

Therefore, <u>option D)</u> most directly weakens the hypothesis by showing that explicit written communication remained necessary, contradicting the researchers' claim that folk songs replaced this need.

▶ **QUESTION 3:**

The claim to weaken is: The pottery style in Mesopotamia was likely influenced by trade with the Indus Valley. This hypothesis is based on evidence of similar pottery styles, documented trade routes between the Indus Valley and Mesopotamia, and the absence of evidence for connections with Central Asia. To weaken this claim, we need evidence suggesting alternative sources for the pottery influence or evidence undermining the link between Indus Valley pottery and Mesopotamian pottery.

Analyze the Options:
- A) This option directly weakens the claim by presenting an alternative origin for the pottery style. If similar pottery styles were produced in Central Asia earlier than in the Indus Valley, it suggests that Mesopotamian pottery could have been influenced by Central Asia rather than the Indus Valley.
- B) This option highlights a difference in the use of pottery but does not address the claim about stylistic influence. The purpose of pottery is irrelevant to determining its stylistic origin.
- C) This option weakens the claim somewhat by showing that Mesopotamian trade records do not mention pottery from the Indus Valley. However, absence of evidence is not necessarily evidence of absence, and pottery could have been exchanged without being recorded.
- D) This option points out a difference in the elaborateness of designs but does not challenge the possibility that Mesopotamian pottery was stylistically influenced by the Indus Valley. Differences in complexity do not preclude influence.

Therefore, option C would most directly weaken Gonzalez and her team's hypothesis by suggesting that vocal cord similarities exist between subspecies, indicating that the vocal difference may not be a driving factor for genetic and physical divergence.

▶ **QUESTION 4:**

The student's claim is that hierarchical spatial metaphors for political authority are universal across ancient civilizations. To weaken this claim, evidence must demonstrate that such metaphors were not universally employed in at least one ancient civilization.
Analyze the Options:
- A) While this shows an emphasis on moral principles, it does not specifically address the use of hierarchical spatial metaphors, so it is less directly relevant.
- B) This option directly challenges the universality of hierarchical spatial metaphors by providing evidence that some Egyptian inscriptions depict rulers at the same height as their subjects during public ceremonies.
- C) Describing rulers as protectors of balance and harmony does not necessarily contradict the use of hierarchical spatial metaphors; these concepts could coexist.
- D) While this highlights symbolic representations of rulers, it does not directly negate the use of hierarchical spatial metaphors, as alignment with divine principles might still involve spatial imagery.

Therefore, option B would most strongly weaken idea that rulers were always associated with elevation or height in their representations of authority.

▶ **QUESTION 5:**

To find the option that most strongly weakens the critic's hypothesis, we first need to identify what the critic is asserting. In this case, the critic believes that specialized coaching, which is tailored to the coaches' techniques and strategies, is unlikely to enhance an athlete's overall performance.
Analyze the Options:
- A) Athletes who received specialized coaching had a higher level of satisfaction and motivation compared to athletes who followed a generic, well-rounded training regimen.
  - → While this option shows a positive aspect of specialized coaching, it does not directly address the matter of "enhancing overall performance" as mentioned in the critic's hypothesis.
- B) Athletes who received specialized coaching tailored to their coaches' techniques and strategies consistently achieved better overall performance compared to athletes who followed a generic, well-rounded training regimen.
  - → This option directly opposes the critic's hypothesis by showing that specialized coaching leads to better overall performance compared to a well-rounded training regimen.
- C) Athletes who received specialized coaching reported fewer injuries and a lower rate of burnout compared to athletes who followed a generic, well-rounded training regimen.
  - → This option points to benefits of specialized coaching concerning health and wellbeing but does not necessarily imply enhanced "overall performance" in the sport.
- D) Athletes who received specialized coaching outperformed their peers in key performance metrics that are crucial for success in their chosen sport, such as speed, strength, or accuracy.
  - → This option indicates that specialized coaching helps in improving certain performance metrics, but it doesn't necessarily confirm better "overall performance."

Therefore, option B is the correct answer as it directly contradicts the critic's claim by showing that specialized coaching can lead to better overall performance compared to a more generic training approach.

▶ **QUESTION 6:**

To find the statement that weakens the argument, we must first identify what the argument is: The proponents believe that incorporating more online learning platforms into the school curriculum will cater to the diverse learning styles of all students, offering a personalized learning experience, which is better than a "one-size-fits-all" approach seen in traditional classrooms.
Analyze the Options:

A) Many online learning platforms require a stable internet connection, which some students may not have consistent access to at home.
  → This option presents a potential barrier to the success of online learning platforms, but it doesn't necessarily counter the argument regarding personalized learning experiences.
B) Traditional classroom teaching often incorporates various teaching methods to cater to different learning styles.
  → This option effectively counters the argument by suggesting that traditional classroom teaching can also cater to different learning styles, thus negating the supposed superiority of online learning platforms in this regard.
C) Online learning platforms often offer gamified experiences which can make learning more engaging for students.
  → This option supports the argument by highlighting a positive aspect of online learning platforms.
D) Schools that have incorporated online learning platforms have seen an increase in student participation.
  → This option also supports the argument by showing a benefit of incorporating online learning platforms into the school curriculum.

Hence, option B is the correct choice, as it weakens the argument by illustrating that traditional classroom teaching can also cater to the diverse learning styles of students, undermining the necessity to shift to online platforms for this purpose.

▶ **QUESTION 7:**
The argument is based on a survey that concludes high coffee consumption (more than three cups a day) directly leads to increased feelings of anxiety, and therefore reducing coffee intake can lessen anxiety. To weaken this argument, we need to find a statement that introduces an alternative explanation or undermines the direct cause-and-effect relationship established between high coffee consumption and increased anxiety.
Analyze the Options:
A) Many of the survey respondents who reported high coffee consumption also reported high levels of stress at work.
  → This option suggests that the reported anxiety might be caused by high levels of stress at work rather than coffee consumption, providing an alternative explanation for the correlation found in the survey.
B) The caffeine content in coffee can vary widely depending on the type and preparation of the coffee.
  → While this option talks about the variability in caffeine content, it does not specifically address the direct relationship between high coffee consumption and anxiety.
C) Some people drink coffee primarily in social settings, which can be relaxing and reduce feelings of anxiety.
  → This option implies that coffee consumption can sometimes reduce anxiety, thus contradicting the argument's claim that high coffee consumption directly leads to increased anxiety.
D) There are many other sources of caffeine, like tea and energy drinks, which lead to happiness.
  → This option indicates a limitation in the survey but does not specifically weaken the causal relationship established between high coffee consumption and anxiety.

So, the correct answer is A, as it introduces an alternative cause (high levels of stress at work) for the reported anxiety, undermining the direct cause-and-effect relationship established in the survey.

▶ **QUESTION 8:**
The argument posits that the surge in vehicles is the primary cause behind the deteriorating air quality and associated health issues in Lireo, based on data from a five-year study. To weaken this argument, we must find a statement that casts doubt on the claim that the increase in vehicles is the primary factor behind the worsening air quality and health issues.
Analyze the Options:
A) Lireo's rapidly growing industrial sector expanded significantly during the study, leading to increased emissions.
  → This option suggests an alternative significant source of increased emissions, challenging the conclusion that the surge in vehicles is the primary cause.
B) Lireo's public transport system is consistently ranked among the country's best.
  → While this speaks positively of Lireo's public transport, it does not directly weaken the argument regarding the source of increased pollutants and respiratory illnesses.
C) A notable portion of Lireo residents have transitioned to electric vehicles, which produce minimal emissions.
  → This option suggests a mitigating factor to the increase in vehicular emissions, but it doesn't fundamentally challenge the core of the argument regarding the primary cause of pollution.
D) The health department also observed a rise in non-respiratory illnesses during the same period.
  → The rise in non-respiratory illnesses does not directly challenge the argument's focus on air quality and respiratory illnesses.

Therefore, the correct answer is A, as it introduces another significant source of pollution, thereby weakening the argument that the surge in vehicles is the primary cause behind the deterioration in air quality and health issues.

▶ **QUESTION 9:**
Dr. Amelia Harper's theory is based on the discovery of distinct dental growth rings in Procoptodon, particularly in molars, as an alternative approach to studying Procoptodon's growth rates. This suggests that dental structures provide insights into growth rates, and this method is less affected by bone structural changes.

Analyze the Options:
A) As marsupials evolved into more advanced species, their growth rates increased.
    → This statement does not directly challenge Dr. Amelia Harper's theory but provides information about the broader context of marsupial evolution.
B) Growth rates for individual Procoptodon varied based on differences in dietary habits.
    → This statement does not directly challenge the use of dental growth rings for studying Procoptodon's growth rates. It introduces a factor (diet) that may affect individual growth rates.
C) Procoptodon had a significantly longer life span compared to other marsupials of its era.
    → This statement, while interesting, does not directly challenge the use of dental growth rings as an alternative approach to studying Procoptodon's growth rates. It provides information about life span.
D) Dental growth ring formation in Procoptodon is a random event.
    → This finding would most significantly challenge Dr. Amelia Harper's theory. If dental growth ring formation is random and not related to age or growth, it would render the use of dental growth rings as an alternative approach ineffective in determining growth rates.

Therefore, option D would most significantly challenge Dr. Amelia Harper's theory.

10. Completing a Text Answer

▶ **QUESTION 1:**
Read the text carefully: Residents of Brookfield tend to shop more frequently at large chain supermarkets because they offer more products, are numerous, and are conveniently located. Small, traditional shops struggle to compete.
Identify the clues: The primary clue is the dominance of large chain supermarkets over smaller shops in terms of consumer preference and growth potential.
Formulate a prediction: The missing text likely explains why large supermarkets experience higher growth compared to small shops.
Review all choices:
    A: "The overall growth rate of large chain supermarkets in Brookfield surpasses that of smaller, traditional shops." Matches the prediction.
    B: "Smaller shops offer fewer product choices." Unrelated to growth rates.
    C: "Large chain supermarkets modeled their strategies on small shops." Unsupported by the text.
    D: "Residents view both types of shops equally." Contradicts the focus on the preference for large chains.
Eliminate wrong choices: Eliminate B, C, and D.
Select the best fit: The best choice is A..

▶ **QUESTION 2:**
Read the text carefully: Illuminated manuscripts were rare and costly, requiring significant resources to produce. They were mainly found in monastic libraries and noble households.
Identify the clues: Illuminated manuscripts were more valuable than simple documents, indicating their rarity and the difficulty of production.
Formulate a prediction: The missing text will emphasize the rarity or exclusivity of illuminated manuscripts.
Review all choices:
    A: "Some monastic libraries contained primarily simple writings." Consistent with the text.
    B: "Most households possessed numerous illuminated manuscripts." Contradicts their rarity.
    C: "Illuminated manuscripts required fewer resources." Directly contradicts the text.
    D: "Local scribes frequently gave them away for free." Unrealistic and unsupported.
Eliminate wrong choices: Eliminate B, C, and D.
Select the best fit: The best choice is A.

▶ **QUESTION 3:**
Read the text carefully: The text discusses how viewers engage more frequently with well-known, mainstream creators than with niche, independent creators due to the larger volume of content available from the former.
Identify the clues:
Viewers engage with more videos from mainstream creators.
This is likely because there are more videos available from well-known creators.
Niche creators struggle to grow their audience.
Formulate a prediction: The missing text will likely emphasize the higher subscriber growth rate or visibility for mainstream creators compared to niche creators.

Review all choices:

    A: Aligns with the clues about higher engagement with mainstream creators.

    B: Unsupported by the text, which does not mention timing.

    C: Contradicts the struggle niche creators face in gaining visibility.

    D: Contradicts the text's emphasis on the advantage of mainstream creators.

Eliminate wrong choices: Eliminate B, C, and D as they either contradict or are unsupported by the text.

Select the best fit: The best choice is A.

▶ **QUESTION 4:**

Read the text carefully: The text discusses how storytelling has been used by various cultures to convey values and traditions.

Identify the clues: The main clue is that storytelling serves as more than a form of entertainment.

Formulate a prediction: The missing text might elaborate on the fact that storytelling serves various purposes beyond entertainment.

Review all choices: All the choices are read thoroughly.

Eliminate wrong choices: Options A and B are too general and do not directly follow the context of the passage. Option D is not supported by the information.

Select the best fit: The best choice is C as it correctly suggests that storytelling serves as more than a form of entertainment, encompassing various other functions.

▶ **QUESTION 5:**

Read the text carefully: Urban planners argue that traditional zoning no longer reflects modern urban development due to workplace dynamics, remote work, and demographic changes.

Identify the clues: Traditional zoning is described as outdated in capturing current urban complexities.

Formulate a prediction: The missing text will likely highlight the shortcomings of relying on outdated data for zoning decisions.

Review all choices:

    A: "Municipalities relying on old data may overlook new opportunities." Matches the argument.

    B: "Most cities have stable populations." Contradicts the focus on dynamic changes.

    C: "Zoning will remain unchanged." Contradicts the argument for rethinking zoning.

    D: "Urban planners should limit research to historical data." Opposite of the argument.

Eliminate wrong choices: Eliminate B, C, and D.

Select the best fit: The best choice is A.

▶ **QUESTION 6:**

Read the text carefully: The text talks about Scandinavian women being less likely to be entrepreneurs despite the region's high gender equality, and the researchers' hypothesis that this could be due to the family-friendly policies in the region.

Identify the clues: The hypothesis about family-friendly policies possibly contributing to fewer women entrepreneurs is the main clue.

Formulate a prediction: The missing text might suggest that these policies could inadvertently be discouraging entrepreneurship among women.

Review all choices: All the choices are read thoroughly.

Eliminate wrong choices: Options A and D make assumptions that aren't directly supported by the passage. Option C suggests a broader claim about gender equality that isn't directly tied to the entrepreneurship trend.

Select the best fit: The best option is B as it suggests that these family-friendly policies may unintentionally discourage women from pursuing entrepreneurship, which aligns with the prediction.

▶ **QUESTION 7:**

Read the text carefully: Catalyst Iron's activity increases in acidic conditions, while Catalyst Platinum's activity remains unchanged.

Identify the clues: The researchers' conclusion focuses on the difference in activity between the two catalysts under acidic conditions.

Formulate a prediction: The missing text will describe the relative effects of acidity on the two catalysts.

Review all choices:

    A: "Increase Catalyst Platinum's activity less likely than increasing Catalyst Iron's." Matches the conclusion.

    B: "Inhibit Iron's activity less likely than promoting Platinum's activity." Incorrect interpretation.

    C: "Yield any product less likely than affecting either catalyst." Irrelevant.

    D: "Maintain the current rate less likely than diminishing pH's importance." Contradicts the focus on activity.

Eliminate wrong choices: Eliminate B, C, and D.

Select the best fit: The best choice is A.

▶ **QUESTION 8:**

Read the text carefully: Reaction yields in industrial settings differed from those in tightly controlled lab conditions due to fluctuating variables.

Identify the clues: Real-world industrial processes introduce variability that affects outcomes.

Formulate a prediction: The missing text will highlight differences between lab and industrial results.

Review all choices:
    A: "Reaction yield significantly different in industrial settings." Matches the prediction.
    B: "Yield identical in both settings." Contradicts the variability mentioned.
    C: "Lowering temperature had no effect." Unsupported and speculative.
    D: "Changing solvent polarity irrelevant." Contradicts the focus on fluctuating conditions.
Eliminate wrong choices: Eliminate B, C, and D.
Select the best fit: The best choice is A.

▶ **QUESTION 9:**

Read the text carefully: Participants found evidence supporting widely accepted theories more credible than evidence for unconventional hypotheses, even when both were equally rigorous.
Identify the clues: Bias toward established theories is evident, even when the evidence is equally strong.
Formulate a prediction: The missing text will describe participants' tendency to favor established theories.
Review all choices:
    A: "Judged evidence for the established theory as more credible." Matches the findings.
    B: "Dismissed both sets of evidence as inconclusive." Contradicts the findings.
    C: "Perceived unconventional hypothesis evidence as stronger." Opposite of the findings.
    D: "Found the unconventional evidence more persuasive." Contradicts the findings.
Eliminate wrong choices: Eliminate B, C, and D.
Select the best fit: The best choice is A.

▶ **QUESTION 10:**

Read the text carefully: Communities using traditional farming methods reported satisfaction due to ancestral knowledge, while mechanized farming emphasized technology and efficiency.
Identify the clues: Both communities attributed their success to their respective methods.
Formulate a prediction: The missing text will describe each community's perception of its own approach.
Review all choices:
    A: "Perceived their approach as more effective." Matches the findings.
    B: "Questioned environmental conditions." Unsupported by the text.
    C: "Agreed mechanized farming offers better results." Contradicts the traditional community's views.
    D: "Shown preference for adopting other techniques." Unsupported.
Eliminate wrong choices: Eliminate B, C, and D.
Select the best fit: The best choice is A.

▶ **QUESTION 11:**

Read the text carefully: Informal trade and mutual aid were found in both urban and rural communities during economic instability.
Identify the clues: Urban centers also had informal networks, contradicting the assumption that these practices were exclusive to rural areas.
Formulate a prediction: The missing text will highlight the unexpected prevalence of informal networks in urban areas.
Review all choices:
    A: "Informal networks more common in urban areas than previously believed." Matches the findings.
    B: "Relied on informal networks primarily during instability." Partially correct but less focused.
    C: "Rural communities developed more robust systems." Contradicts the text.
    D: "Urban communities relied less on formal structures." Unsupported by the findings.
Eliminate wrong choices: Eliminate B, C, and D.
Select the best fit: The best choice is A.

▶

QUESTION 12:

Read the text carefully: The text discusses the adoption of smartphones and the challenges some users may face.
Identify the clues: The main clue is that some users may struggle to adapt to smartphones.
Formulate a prediction: The missing text might provide further information about the impact of these challenges.
Review all choices: All the choices are read thoroughly.
Eliminate wrong choices: Options A, B, and D provide information not directly relevant to the challenges users face with smartphones.
<u>Select the best fit:</u> The best choice is C as it acknowledges the transformative impact of smartphones despite the learning curve for some users.

▶ **QUESTION 13:**

Read the text carefully: The text discusses the Mayan civilization and a study comparing maize remains from the ancient city of Tikal to present-day maize in Veracruz.

Identify the clues: The main clue is the mention of similarities between the maize in Tikal and Veracruz that are not inherent to the maize cultivated at Tikal.

Formulate a prediction: The missing text might suggest a reason for these unexpected similarities.

Review all choices: All the choices are read thoroughly.

Eliminate wrong choices: Options A, C, and D do not logically connect to the provided clue.

Select the best fit: The best choice is B, as it offers a plausible explanation for the similarities between the maize in Tikal and Veracruz, suggesting a migration of Mayans to Veracruz that would have transferred their agricultural techniques.

▶ **QUESTION 14:**

Read the text carefully: The text discusses eco-friendly packaging solutions and the potential overcompensation by consumers.

Identify the clues: The main clue is that consumers may overcompensate for eco-friendly packaging.

Formulate a prediction: The missing text might explain the consequences of this overcompensation.

Review all choices: All the choices are read thoroughly.

Eliminate wrong choices: Option B and C provide information not directly related to the potential consequences of consumer behavior. Option D is too positive and does not address the issue of overcompensation.

Select the best fit: The best choice is A as it correctly suggests that consumers may offset the intended environmental benefits by using more of the product or generating additional waste, which is in line with the information provided in the passage.

▶ **QUESTION 15:**

Read the text carefully: The text discusses the influence of Socrates' teachings, despite his lack of written works, and raises a question about those who credit Socrates as the author of certain philosophical works.

Identify the clues: The main clue is that Socrates didn't write anything himself, and his student, Plato, recorded his teachings.

Formulate a prediction: The missing text should address the potential misconception or implications of crediting Socrates as the author of philosophical works.

Review all choices: All the choices are read thoroughly.

Eliminate wrong choices: Option B, while true, is not directly related to the issue of crediting Socrates for works he didn't write. Option C introduces an idea of misinterpretation, but this is not explicitly discussed in the passage. Option D is a factual statement about Socrates not writing anything, but it doesn't address the potential misconception.

Select the best fit: The best choice is A because it correctly suggests that those who credit Socrates as the author of certain philosophical works may inadvertently be attributing the works of Plato to Socrates, which aligns with the context of the passage. This choice highlights the potential misunderstanding that can arise when crediting Socrates for written works.

11. Infographics Answer

▶ **QUESTION 1:**

Understand the Question: The question is asking for a choice that effectively uses data from the table to complete the example regarding the unique pattern of brood care in Blue Rock Thrush. We need to find an option that aligns with the information presented in the table and reflects this unique behavior.

Study the Infographic: Examine the data table, which includes information about the mother of the brood, known sires of the brood, and males feeding the brood. This information represents the relationships among females and males involved in brood care.

Interpret the Data: To understand the unique pattern of brood care, observe how different males are feeding broods that are not necessarily their biological offspring. The data shows that multiple males are involved in feeding the broods, and not all of them are the known sires.

Link the Data to the Question: The researcher's claim is related to the unique pattern of brood care, where males involved in feeding aren't necessarily the biological fathers. We need to find an option that reflects this pattern in the data.

Answer the Question:

The most effective choice that uses the data to support this pattern is: C) Female G's brood was fed by males who weren't the known sires. This choice highlights that the brood care behavior observed in Female G's case aligns with the researcher's claim. It implies that the males feeding the brood are not the known biological fathers, thus supporting the unique pattern of brood care.

Check Your Answer: Reviewing this choice against the data in the table, you can see that it accurately reflects the pattern observed in Female G's case, where males other than the known sires are involved in feeding the brood, as indicated in the table.

▶ **QUESTION 2:**

Understand the Question: The question is asking for the choice that best describes data from the table that supports the researchers' suggestion regarding job openings and the percentage increase in jobs in the renewable energy sector.

Study the Infographic: Examine the data table, which includes information about different job types in the renewable energy sector, the number of job openings in 2018-2019, and the percentage increase in jobs from 2015 to 2019. It's essential to consider the job openings and the corresponding percentage increases.

Interpret the Data: The researchers suggest that certain sectors, despite having fewer job openings, have seen a higher percentage increase in jobs. To find data that supports this suggestion, you should identify sectors where the percentage increase is notably high relative to the number of job openings.

Link the Data to the Question: The researchers' claim is about the relationship between job openings and percentage increase in jobs. We need to find data in the table that reflects this relationship.

Answer the Question:
The choice that best describes data from the table that supports the researchers' suggestion is: B) The Bioenergy sector, despite having fewer job openings than Solar Power and Wind Energy, has the highest percentage increase in jobs. This choice highlights the Bioenergy sector, which has fewer job openings than Solar Power and Wind Energy but has the highest percentage increase in jobs. It directly supports the researchers' suggestion that some sectors with fewer job openings have seen a higher percentage increase in jobs.

Check Your Answer:
Reviewing this choice against the data in the table, you can see that it accurately reflects the relationship between job openings and the percentage increase in jobs, as observed in the Bioenergy sector.

▶ **QUESTION 3:**
Understand the Question: The question is asking for the choice that best supports the instructors' claim based on the data from the table regarding the impact of combined traditional and simulator training on reducing the average number of mistakes during a driving test.

Study the Infographic: Examine the data table, which includes information about two types of training methods (Traditional Training and Combined Traditional and Simulator Training) and the average number of mistakes made during a driving test for four different driving skills. Pay attention to the differences in the number of mistakes between the two training methods for each skill.

Interpret the Data: To support the instructors' claim that combined traditional and simulator training reduces the average number of mistakes, you need to find data in the table that demonstrates a decrease in mistakes when using the combined training method compared to traditional training alone.

Link the Data to the Question: The instructors' claim is about the effectiveness of the combined training method in reducing mistakes. You should identify data in the table that supports this claim.

Answer the Question:
The choice that best supports the instructors' claim based on the data from the table is: B) For each driving skill, the average number of mistakes made during the driving test is lower for those who underwent the combined traditional and simulator training compared to those who had only traditional training. This choice highlights that, for each driving skill, the average number of mistakes is lower when using the combined training method, which supports the instructors' claim of the combined method's effectiveness in reducing mistakes.

Check Your Answer: Reviewing this choice against the data in the table, you can see that it accurately reflects the trend of lower average mistakes in the combined training method, providing strong support for the instructors' claim.

▶ **QUESTION 4:**
Understand the Question: The question asks for the choice that uses the data from the table most effectively to observe the decline in memory performance with aging, given both the type of information (names vs places) and recall conditions (immediate vs delayed).

Study the Infographic: We have a data table showing percentages of immediate and delayed recall for names and places across various age groups.

Interpret the Data: Looking at the table, it's clear that as the age group increases, the percentages of both immediate and delayed recalls for both names and places decrease. The largest contrast in memory retention between immediate and delayed recalls across all age groups would offer the most effective observation of the memory decline pattern.

Link the Data to the Question: To find the most effective comparison, we should look at the age groups with the most significant decline in both categories - names and places, in both immediate and delayed recall.

Answer the Question:
The most significant differences in both immediate and delayed recall percentages for both names and places can be seen when comparing the youngest age group (20-29) with the oldest age group (80+). This gives a complete picture of how memory performance declines with aging. So, the answer would be: A) the age group 20-29 with the age group 80+.

Check Your Answer: Comparing the data for these groups, we see the substantial decline over time supports this choice, affirming the pattern of decline as age increases.

QUESTION 5:

Understand the Question: The question is asking to identify the statement that is most strongly supported by the data regarding the spending habits of local and visiting fans at music festivals.

Study the Infographic: We have a data table detailing the average spending of local fans, visiting fans, and combined spending in different categories.

Interpret the Data: Looking at the table, it can be noted that visiting fans spend more in every category compared to local fans.

Link the Data to the Question: To find the statement most strongly supported by the data, we need to focus on clear, unequivocal data trends that back up one of the options.

Answer the Question:

Observing each statement against the data, it is clear that option B accurately represents the data as visiting fans have a higher average spending in each category mentioned in the table compared to local fans. So, the answer would be: B) Visiting fans spend more on every category of expenses than local fans.

Check Your Answer: Rechecking the data, it's evident that this choice is consistently supported across all the spending categories presented, making it the most strongly supported statement by the data in the table.

QUESTION 6:

Understand the Question: The question is asking to complete the statement with the most appropriate factor that portfolio managers take into consideration, following "investor's risk tolerance (3.15)" in the list of factors in the investment decision-making process. The option needs to not only accurately represent the data from the table but also suitably fit in the context of the sentence, emphasizing the "multi-faceted expertise" of portfolio managers.

Study the Infographic: We need to analyze the table which lists different factors that influence investment decisions according to a survey of portfolio managers. The ratings of different factors are given on a scale of 1 to 4.

Interpret the Data: Looking at the data, we can see that after "investor's risk tolerance (3.15)" the next highest rated factor is "government policy" with a rating of 3.20.

Link the Data to the Question: The data shows that "government policy" was rated quite high, being the next highest rating after "investor's risk tolerance". This indicates it is a significant factor considered by portfolio managers, fitting into the sentence structure and narrative described in the question about the multi-faceted approach of portfolio managers.

Answer the Question:

Given that the highest rating following "investor's risk tolerance" is "government policy" with a rating of 3.20, option A most effectively uses data from the graph to complete the sentence. So, the correct answer is: A) government policy (3.20) quite high, demonstrating that they must pay attention to both individual investor profiles and broader economic policy.

Check Your Answer: Checking the answer, we see that it correctly follows the rating order from the table and logically fits in the context described in the question, illustrating the complex and multifaceted considerations of portfolio managers.

QUESTION 7:

Understand the Question: The question is asking for the answer choice that most weakens the argument that Michael was influenced by Sheila's grandma's recipes due to the similarity and uniqueness of the recipes in both books.

Study the Infographic: The data provides information about Sheila's grandma's 2020 recipe book and Michael's 2022 recipe book, including the number of unique recipes introduced and the number of shared recipes.

Interpret the Data: Sheila's grandma introduced 150 unique recipes, and Michael introduced 200 unique recipes in his book. Both authors have 37 shared recipes, implying some similarity in their recipes.

Link the Data to the Question: The argument is based on the similarity of recipes between Sheila's grandma and Michael's books, suggesting that Michael might have been influenced by Sheila's grandma. We need to find an answer that weakens this argument by providing an alternative explanation.

Answer the Question:

Among the answer choices, A) provides an alternative explanation by suggesting that there is a family recipe collection known to both Sheila's grandma and Michael. This common source of recipes weakens the argument that Michael was directly influenced by Sheila's grandma's book.

Check Your Answer: Answer choice (A) is indeed the correct choice as it weakens the argument by offering an alternative explanation. If both authors had access to a common family recipe collection, it diminishes the likelihood of direct influence.

▶ **QUESTION 8:**

Understand the Question: The question is asking for the choice that effectively highlights an exception to the researchers' suggestion that higher melatonin production is associated with survival mechanisms in areas of high predator exposure.

Study the Infographic: The data table provides information on melatonin production levels for different mammal species and their exposure to predators.

Interpret the Data: Nocturnal mammals generally have higher melatonin production compared to diurnal mammals. The table includes data on specific melatonin production levels for various mammal species, along with their eating location/exposure to predators.

Link the Data to the Question: The researchers suggest a link between melatonin production and survival mechanisms in areas with higher predator exposure. To challenge this suggestion, we need to find a case that doesn't fit this pattern.

Answer the Question:
Among the answer choices, A) is the most effective choice. It presents the Virginia Opossum, a nocturnal mammal with the highest melatonin production, but it lives in an area with low exposure to predators. This contradicts the researchers' suggestion that higher melatonin production is associated with survival mechanisms in areas with high predator exposure.

Check Your Answer: Answer choice (A) is indeed the correct choice as it effectively illustrates an exception to the researchers' suggestion. The Virginia Opossum's high melatonin production and low predator exposure challenge the pattern proposed by the researchers.

▶ **QUESTION 9:**

Understand the Question: The question asks which choice best showcases data from the table that aligns with the researchers' hypothesis that direct, personalized customer service interactions result in significantly higher customer satisfaction compared to indirect or no interactions.

Study the Infographic: Examine the table presenting the customer satisfaction percentage corresponding to different types of customer service, including direct methods (online live chat support, phone call support, email support) and indirect methods (self-service support) and no interaction.

Interpret the Data: Analyzing the data, we can see a trend where direct customer service methods (online live chat support and phone call support) have higher customer satisfaction percentages compared to indirect methods or no interaction, with online live chat having the highest at 72.90%, followed by phone call support at 68.20%.

Link the Data to the Question: Now, linking this data interpretation to the researcher's hypothesis, we see that it supports the idea that direct methods yield higher customer satisfaction, with the highest satisfaction being associated with the most direct, personalized service method: online live chat support.

Answer the Question:
Given this, we can select option A) "The highest customer satisfaction rate was reported for online live chat support, a direct method of customer service." as the choice that best describes data from the table that supports the researchers' hypothesis.

Check Your Answer: Looking back at the table, we can affirm that choice A) correctly mirrors the data presented in the table and backs the researchers' hypothesis that direct, personalized customer service interactions bring about higher customer satisfaction compared to indirect methods or no interaction, by highlighting that the most direct method had the highest satisfaction rate.